The Wrongs of Tort

Law and Social Theory

Series editors:
PETER FITZPATRICK
Professor of Law, Queen Mary and Westfield College
University of London
COLIN PERRIN
Faculty of Law, The University of New South Wales

Also available

THE WRONGS OF TORT
Second Edition

JOANNE CONAGHAN AND WADE MANSELL

Pluto Press

LONDON • STERLING, VIRGINIA

First published 1999 by Pluto Press
345 Archway Road, London N6 5AA
and 22883 Quicksilver Drive
Sterling, VA 20166–2012, USA

British Library Cataloguing in Publication Data
A catalogue record for this book is available from the British Library

ISBN 0 7453 1298 5 hbk
ISBN 0 7453 1293 4 pbk

Library of Congress Cataloging in Publication Data
Conaghan, Joanne.
   The wrongs of tort/Joanne Conaghan and Wade Mansell. – 2nd ed.
      p.   cm. — (Law and social theroy)
   Includes bibliographical references and index.
   ISBN 0–7453–1298–5 (hc.)
   1. Torts—Great Britain. 2. Negligence—Great Britain.
I. Mansell, Wade. II. Title. III. Series.
KD1949.C66   1999
346.4103—dc21   98–44294
                                                          CIP

10   9   8   7   6   5   4   3   2

Designed and produced for Pluto Press by
Chase Publishing Services
Typeset from disk by Stanford DTP Services, Towcester
Printed in the European Union by
Antony Rowe, Chippenham and Eastbourne, England

To our Parents

Billy and Marie Conaghan and Halsey and Lois Mansell

Contents

Table of Statutes

EC LEGISLATION

OVERSEAS LEGISLATION

Table of Cases

Acknowledgements

The first edition of this book appeared without acknowledgements. A felicitous explanation for the omission might well have been an unwillingness to implicate the innocent. Unfortunately, the true explanation is more mundane and reflects less well upon us. By the time we had drafted our thanks the book had proceeded inexorably to an irrevocable stage. These acknowledgements, therefore, begin with a sincere apology to the many who provided so much help for so little recognition in 1993. Remarkably, and nothing better illustrates the qualities of our friends and colleagues (the terms are not mutually exclusive), those of help in the first edition who might reasonably have been offended by this omission were helpful again. In particular, those with whom we have taught at Kent Law School have been generous both with time and comments. We are especially aware of the debt we owe to Paddy Ireland, John Wightman and Alan Thomson. Joanne Scott and Paul Conaghan have also contributed an invaluable amount of time and assistance to the project. Other colleagues, past and present, have helped both directly and indirectly. In this category we would record our thanks to Donald McGillivray, Nick Jackson, Belinda Meteyard, Peter Fitzpatrick, William Howarth, Richard de Friend, Steve Uglow, John Fitzpatrick, Graham Horgan and Ian Grigg-Spall. We continue to appreciate the ambience and collegiality of the Kent Law School and remain convinced that it makes a distinctive contribution to legal education in which politics are not allowed to remain secreted in the interstices of procedure – or indeed anywhere else.

The central intention of this book is to provide an accessible and stimulating introduction to a critique of the doctrines of tort law. Without the constant stimulus provided by our students this would not have been possible. We are grateful to almost all of them. Others who have assisted in the production of this book include Liz Cable and the Kent Law School office, Karen Toseland, Rory Mates, Sally Sheldon, Karen Scott and Sarah Harman.

The reviewers who (with one exception) provided critically enthusiastic comments about the book are also to be thanked. Their comments have been of immense help to us and we hope that we have encompassed at least some of their perceptions. Student comments have also been welcome, appreciated and useful. We remain receptive to comments about this edition. The omission of acknowledgements in the first edition did have the advantage of obviating the need for a tedious acceptance that all errors are the responsibility of the authors. While we do so accept, we each think that any errors that may be discovered are the responsibility of the other. This is just one of the many advantages of joint authorship.

Finally, on a personal note, we express our heartfelt gratitude to our partners, Paddy Ireland and Sara Mansell. They have been privileged with more child and house care than they might have thought they wished. The children and the book are the beneficiaries.

1
Introducing a Critical Perspective[1]

The subject of tort is one of the most beguiling to students whose conception of legal study is about discrete subjects apparently clearly defined and governed by a satisfying intermingling of statute and case law. If the textbooks are to be believed, tort appears to consist of a number of general principles (in most cases strongly corresponding with common sense) exemplified by case application which seem, if the premises of tort are accepted, logical, coherent and essentially just. Additionally the cases themselves are often memorable because of the bizarre and commonly tragic facts with which they deal. Tragedy is only barely concealed by the application of legal principles and the cases bear out well the view that humour is intimately connected with misfortune. Individuals being struck on the head by cricket balls, suffering dermatitis through impure underpants, trapped in a toilet with a defective door, vomiting because of decomposed snails in opaque ginger-beer bottles are the very stuff of tort.

It seems then that tort is a morbidly attractive subject to study and at times an exhilarating subject to teach – rigorous, principled and even entertaining. Yet despite these manifest attractions, the lure of tort is greatly diminished by closer critical examination. While the popular image of tort remains both coercive and appealing, it is very two-dimensional: the object of this book is to present a view of the law of tort which is multi-dimensioned and at the same time radical, both in its evaluation of the existing system and in its prescription for change. The book will focus primarily on the tort of negligence not just because of its significance in conventional tort texts and syllabuses but also because much of its reasoning and its ethos have permeated other areas of tort, particularly through the concept of 'reasonableness'. We will, however, direct some attention to other torts which assume a considerable role in tort courses including nuisance (Chapter 6), and the 'intentional' torts (Chapter 7). Inevitably there are gaps in coverage. Much could be said, for example, about the judicial creation and development of the 'economic torts', or about the values and assumptions implicit in the law of libel. But space precludes anything resembling an exhaustive critical analysis of the subject of tort. We hope, however, that the coverage that we do offer will furnish the

1

critical student with the will and (some of) the way to pursue the critical project into more offbeat tortious terrain.

THE NATURE OF CRITIQUE

One object of this text is to introduce students to a number of different techniques by which they may critique the materials they are studying. There is of course no hard and fast method of 'critique' and indeed much depends on the particular perspective of the critic. But clearly a primary object of any critique is to evaluate and to seek to understand. Of course, many might differ as to the standard of evaluation employed and the criteria by which the subject of critique is measured. Likewise there may be considerable controversy over how a thing is understood and about what perspective is brought to bear on the interpretation of the subject-matter. There is no 'correct' method of critique and no one true critical conclusion towards which all should be drawn. Having said that, this book openly concedes to preferring some critical approaches over others and therefore promoting some critical conclusions over others. Acknowledging that the whole process of critique is a value-laden enterprise (as indeed is the pursuit of scholarship generally), we take here particular values, such as equality and social responsibility and *critically* apply them to the formidable edifice of the tort system, to evaluate the system in the light of them. Of course, during this exercise we will encounter and explore some competing values which lay claim to tort (such as individual responsibility or economic efficiency), but it must be emphasised that the enterprise of critique, like tort itself, is neither impartial nor objective. It is our contention that an evaluative exercise cannot be otherwise because it depends entirely on the standard of evaluation, the unit of measurement which is adopted.

There is, however, another dimension to the idea of critique. To see it solely as the process of evaluation is to divest it of its radical content and character. To present it simply as a technical concept which takes its content, quite arbitrarily, from the unit of measurement selected by the critic is to deny its liberating potential. To critique is partly to excavate. But the critical lawyer cannot approach her subject like the disinterested scientist examining the finds of an archaeological dig. (Indeed, were she disinterested, she would not be digging in the first place.) To acquire a critical understanding of law involves the acceptance of the impossibility of a neutral, disinterested point of view. And this in turn produces a strange and paradoxical result: on the one hand, the rejection of neutrality undermines the legitimacy of those positions which posit themselves as neutral by showing that they are in fact partial rather than universal points of view; on the other hand, it confers legitimacy on those points of view generally regarded as partial and political on the grounds that neutrality is no longer a criterion for legitimacy. In other words, it shifts the terms of the debate. The issue is no longer what is the correct (that is, objective, verifiable) legal position but rather what is the *preferred* legal and political solution. Articulating the politics of law is thus a crucial step in the process of securing a good society through open discourse and participatory decision-making. It is in this sense that the critical project is a radical one. Additionally, by perceiving that law, in this case tort law, expresses a partial and contingent rather than a general and universal point of view, one is free to imagine the possibility of alternative arrangements and ultimately, to pursue them.

THE POLITICS OF TORT LAW

Conventional texts such as *Winfield & Jolowicz on Tort* proceed on the basis that tort law consists of a basically uncontentious and apolitical body of principles (Rogers, 1994). This encourages a view of tort law as 'largely common sense' and often corresponds closely with many students' perception of what is just and fair. This tendency to take the common sense of tort for granted impedes the development of a reflective and critical approach to the subject. Tort law appears apolitical because it is experienced as largely uncontentious and because it is uncontentious we do not tend to question its politics. But the politics are there. It is vital to understand that tort, its texts and its syllabuses, are inherently political and this is no less true because the politics are hidden. The foundation of tort law reflects a particular ideological and philosophical perspective (essentially captured by the principle of individual rather than societal responsibility for the misfortune of others) which is, in our view, highly contentious. Indeed, if the basic subject-matter of tort is concerned with how the law responds, or fails to respond, to the misfortunes which afflict individuals in our society, it can be strongly argued that the tort system represents a political solution which is undesirable both because of the arbitrariness of its results and because of the underlying callousness of its ideology. Additionally, it can be contended that the legal form which tort doctrine assumes, as a body of knowledge which is coherent, principled and neutral as to outcomes, operates in fact as a major impediment to political change.

Of course this criticism is also political and its underlying premises should be made explicit: it is that society should assume considerable responsibility for the misfortune of its citizens and that political and legal energy should be redirected towards the consideration and possible construction of alternative loss distribution mechanisms based on the acceptance of *social* responsibility for individual misfortune. In part, this text seeks to support this position by focusing upon the woeful inadequacy of the tort system as a compensation and loss-distribution mechanism and, moreover, its demonstrable inability to satisfactorily perform any of the tasks it defines as desirable. But more importantly, we seek to stress, by the systematic unravelling of a political content in tort doctrines which is not highlighted or even acknowledged in the conventional text, that the popular presentation of the law of tort as 'largely common sense' not only inhibits an understanding of harm as socially and legally constructed but also prevents most of the most fundamental questions which the law of tort addresses from ever being considered.

It is appropriate at this point to explain the idea of the 'conventional text' as used in this book. A common misgiving about the critical enterprise is its alleged tendency to set up 'straw men' which are then quite easily knocked down. It might be contended that our idea of the 'conventional text' is an 'ideal-type' which does not capture the rich variation in tort textbooks currently available. It might be argued further that our notion of the 'traditional syllabus' takes little account of the change in tort courses brought about by the emergence of a more 'contextual' approach to tort in the 1970s (Chapter 5). In other words it could be said that the subject of our critique is a 'straw man/person' which we ourselves have created and demolished. While acknowledging the force of this general concern, we do not think it applies in this particular case. 'Conventional' texts do abound and hold sway in the teaching and learning of tort law. Apart from the ancient and venerable texts such as *Winfield & Jolowicz* (Rogers, 1994), *Street on Torts* (Brazier, 1993) and *Salmond and Heuston* (Heuston and Buckley, 1996), all of which continue to present tort in an essentially formalistic fashion, the number of 'nutshells' and crammers (which, after all, have as their very objective the simplistic presentation of complex issues) seems continually to increase. Having said this, we freely acknowledge the existence of a more recent variety of tort texts which seek to challenge the prevailing formalism by offering a more dynamic, less rule-based presentation of legal doctrine (Howarth, 1995; Markesinis and Deakin, 1994) or by engaging in innovative reconceptualisations of tort categories (Stanton, 1994; Cane, 1997). Such developments are to be welcomed not least because competing presentations of the content of tort further expose its contingent and partial nature. Yet we would contend that, the emergence of new and less conventional texts notwithstanding, legal formalism still continues to permeate most students' understanding of tort not least because it is the discourse which dominates their experience of legal education as a whole. Thus, even where tort syllabuses are presented in a broadly contextual or critical fashion, students too often find their way to the traditional text whose respectability is assured. We are not then tilting at windmills. The presentation of law in a rigidly formalistic manner is still sufficiently prevalent and commonplace to warrant serious concern and attention.

CRITICAL APPROACHES

It seems appropriate, at this point, to consider, in a general sense, some of the questions this book seeks to raise. How might a critical analysis of, for example, the law of negligence proceed and develop?

Such an analysis could take a number of different forms: first, one might exhume and examine the political and moral underpinnings of various doctrines (historically and currently) within negligence; second, one could focus on the *form* of negligence as an allegedly coherent and rational body of rules and consider to what extent this form corresponds to content; finally it might be useful to look at a number of different theoretical perspectives on negligence as a way of unravelling the complex political and moral norms which compete for recognition and realisation in the courtroom and the classroom.

Law and Values

It is clear that negligence law is imbued with political and moral values which, while never far from the surface, are rarely articulated and even more rarely questioned or challenged. Why, for example, should 'omissions' be treated as often incurring less liability than 'acts'; why should the intervention of a third party operate as a brake on liability when the damage is done and the defendant is a negligent cause of it; why should mental distress and economic loss be treated differently from physical damage? These questions conjure up generally accepted rules and principles which permeate the tort of negligence (though neither their boundaries nor their doctrinal status is very clear) and which are often defended in moral terms. Thus it is contended that moral responsibility for 'omissions' is somehow less than for 'acts' and therefore they should not attract the same liability even where the damage is identical. This assumption is in turn based on ideas about limiting individual responsibility particularly in relation to obligations imposed by the state. It is often argued that the imposition of positive obligations on people discourages action and inventiveness and consequently economic growth and wealth creation. Hence, the legal tendency to treat 'omissions' differently from 'acts' reflects a particular economic and political perspective closely associated with nineteenth-century capitalism with its accompanying aversion to collectivism. Again, careless actors are somehow viewed as less responsible if, in the arbitrary scheme of things, some third party comes between them and subsequent harm. The old and venerated concept of the *novus actus interveniens* (a new intervening act) operates here to shift our attention away from the negligent behaviour of the defendant towards the more immediate wrong inflicted by the intervening actor and posits the strange conclusion that the original negligent actor is no longer at fault because he is no longer a 'legal cause' of the injury. Such an authoritative pronunciation of causation acts as a smokescreen which clouds the presence of a policy operating to limit the responsibility of individuals for their acts (Chapter 3). This is further illustrated in the tendency to eschew mental distress and economic loss liability on the grounds that they place too heavy a burden of liability on the defendant, an assumption which does of course presuppose that there should be some correlation between the harm done and the penalty imposed, and that the harm done in such cases is self-evidently less serious than where a plaintiff suffers personal injury. It is likewise assumed in such cases that somehow economic loss and mental distress open up 'floodgates' which are better left closed (Chapter 2).

Of course alternative rationales based upon economic efficiency, deterrence, insurance, risk distribution and compensation can also be offered in defence of or in opposition to any of these doctrines. But the presence of such competing alternatives simply serves to reinforce their strongly political content. The point remains that tort law does not operate in a 'value-free zone' but takes its content, shape and direction from norms which should rightly be a primary focus of any study of the subject.

Such a consideration of the underlying assumptions behind tort doctrine (and their controversial nature) opens up for discussion a host of issues which are rarely addressed and certainly never adequately explored in the traditional text. Critical of course are the problems arising from the centrality of the concept of fault in the tort of negligence. Essentially negligence embodies the principle that where harm to someone is caused through the fault of another party, that party will be liable to compensate for the injury and loss caused. This statement is of course unacceptably broad as the qualifications relating to duty, breach and damage, exhaustively discussed in every text on tort indicate (see Chapters 2 and 3). But the basic idea that it is just that those who injure through carelessness should compensate and that those who suffer through carelessness should be compensated by the perpetrators of the careless act remains crucial to our understanding of negligence doctrine. This focus upon the cause of the injury or loss in determining whether compensation is payable results in the unequal distribution of compensation to those who have suffered identical harm but not by identical means. Fault dictates full compensation but in the absence of fault losses must lie where they fall, subject of course to the meagre and uncertain benefits of the current welfare system.

The merits of the 'fault principle' are not in our view so self-evident as to require such inattention to its demerits. While the maxim 'no liability without fault' may make a certain sense, its corollary – 'no compensation without fault' – is much more questionable because identical needs are met with different responses on the basis of a difference which is irrelevant to the need itself. Why *should* fault determine who gets what? Equally importantly, *does* fault determine who gets what (the inflictor of economic loss or nervous shock is, it seems, strangely immune from liability), and when it does not, why not? Furthermore, if fault determines liability, why should it not also determine the 'price' to be paid? At present there is no correlation between the magnitude of the carelessness and the size of compensation payable, thus creating an illogical and unsatisfactory ideological conflict between the principle of liability which is fault-based and the principle of compensation which assesses according to need.

More fundamentally, what is fault? How is it recognised? The traditional answer, namely that fault involves unreasonable behaviour, merely restates the question in a different form (Chapter 3). These sorts of questions about the moral content of negligence doctrine are at the centre of a critical approach to legal education and are not set aside and marginalised as they are by the black-letter focus of the conventional text.

The Form of Law

A common impression of the form of negligence is as an essentially black-letter discipline with perhaps more 'furry edges' than most and a more explicit if nevertheless limited role for 'policy considerations' in the determination of results.[2] This is certainly the impression created for students by classical tort texts such as *Winfield & Jolowicz* and *Street* (Rogers, 1994; Brazier, 1993). Students are encouraged to see negligence law as rule-based. The task for the student is to discover the 'rules' and also to determine which of them are uncertain or unresolved. They are provided with a framework within which the rules fit and the implication is that rules which do not readily fit the framework are the 'hard cases' of particular interest (at least to examiners). Underlying such a presentation of negligence is a belief that it is, to some extent at least, coherent, logical, rational and deducible from previous cases and fundamental principles.

Yet it is arguable that, in fact, negligence abounds with demonstrable incoherence, evidenced in almost all aspects of doctrine. It is because this fact is seldom observed, or is observed only to be ignored, that we explore the tort of negligence in Chapters 2 and 3 in an attempt to exemplify its incoherence (see also Chapter 6 for a similar approach to the tort of nuisance). Here, instead of attempting to impose order on the cases in the usual textbook manner, we refuse to make or readily accept the fine and often contingent distinctions necessary to 'reconcile' cases, arguing rather that the doctrine is, at best, inconsistent and, at worst, indeterminate.

Despite such manifest uncertainty within particular doctrines, the traditional textbook writers together with 'learned' commentators in 'scholarly' journals continue to perpetrate the myth of doctrinal coherence subject to 'room for argument' or 'areas of uncertainty' (Brazier, 1993, p. 253). Furthermore, judges and commentators alike continue to cling to the organising concept of fault as the 'universal principle' underlying the edifice of negligence. It does not seem to matter that negligence law is riddled with situations when the fault principle is mysteriously and inexorably suspended as in the cases concerning nervous shock or economic loss recovery.

Nor does it seem to matter that in practice fault has little to do with tort recovery but is in fact hostage to the availability of insurance. It is extraordinary how little attention is paid to this significant disparity between negligence as an academic and legal category, and negligence as an operational reality. For law students, negligence consists of appellate cases which reach the pages of *Winfield & Jolowicz* while negligence, the system, is presented as something quite different and less important. While Atiyah's *Accidents, Compensation and the Law* (now in its fifth edition, Cane, 1993) remains the authoritative text addressing the disparity between negligence in books and negligence in practice, its trenchant criticism of the system seems to have had only a marginal effect upon academic courses in negligence (Chapter 5). Yet the problems Atiyah's work continues to address concerning the operation of negligence actions (see also Atiyah, 1997) such as delay, cost, quantification, settlement and uncertainty of result are far from marginal. Indeed, in recent years they have been the subject of considerable political and legislative scrutiny presaging a series of significant reforms in the civil justice system (see further Chapter 5). Yet, despite recent and anticipated changes, it is likely that the administrative expenses of the negligence system will remain far too high relative to the total amount of compensation paid out. In 1978 it was estimated that administrative costs equalled about 85 per cent of the value of the sums paid out as compensation (or 45 per cent of the total of compensation and operating costs), indicating that the system is certainly not as practically satisfactory as it might be theoretically (Pearson, 1978, Vol. 1, para. 83). To enter the arcane realms of 'calculating' injury and loss, both present and future, in money terms is also revelatory in terms of the practical and highly technical difficulties which riddle judicial methods of calculation (Chapter 3). The form of negligence as a 'black-letter' discipline quickly loses much of its alleged coherence when viewed through the lens of 'what really happens'.

Theoretical Perspectives

This book clearly adopts a particular perspective, namely one which challenges the central conception of fault and individual responsibility in the allocation of compensation. It also maintains that, in operation, negligence is an irrational system for redistributing loss arising from particular circumstances. It *is* a system only in that some things it does consistently, but it is a system so remarkable for its overall inconsistency that as a system of compensation it has few defenders beyond those who profit from its operation. The criticism of negligence then is both from within and from without. We maintain that it fails, first, on its own terms as a rational, self-perpetuating, self-evaluating system of neutral rules; and second, as a social response to particular goals – those of compensation and loss redistribution. Of course, such an assertion opens up for debate the whole question of what goals or objectives tort law is or should be pursuing. This is a question about which there is divergent theoretical opinion. In our view such divergence must be an important focus of critique because, clearly, different approaches to evaluating the system (for example in terms of economic efficiency, deterrence, compensation or fault and individual responsibility) generate different assessments of the system's worth and different prescriptions as to its cure (where deemed appropriate). Even tensions within cases, between judgments and different judicial styles, can often be understood in terms of conflicts about goals (or even about whether the law of torts is goal-oriented at all rather than simply a mechanism to facilitate the pursuit of a variety of individual goals). It is essential to examine the law of negligence in the wider context of arguments about its political and social role. Such a focus serves a dual purpose: first, in providing a forum within which the political content of torts can be properly aired and explored; and second, in giving students a framework which aids their understanding of the evolutionary and dynamic aspects of tort doctrine and at the same time renders it impossible to present the subject as a static black-letter discipline more likely to blur rather than illuminate the student's grasp of the subject. Such an approach encourages the student to regard negligence not as a set of rules but rather as a series of arguments which compete for persuasiveness drawing upon institutional resources ('precedent'), the ascendancy of a particular moral tradition ('principle') and political acceptability ('policy'). Through such an approach students not only experience law as political and controversial (which it is), but also acquire the sorts of skills and insights which inform and direct legal practice.

CONCLUSION

Of course this book has an agenda. We are presenting (*inter alia*) a particular political argument about the need for a humane and adequate compensation system and exploring the law of negligence in the light of that concern (for a parallel argument about the need for an adequate and informed environmental policy, see Chapter 6). But if we have an agenda, so do all writers and commentators on tort; so do the judges who develop the doctrine; so do the litigators who formulate arguments in terms of their particular clients' demands. To view the law of tort as anything other than an armoury of conflicting 'agendas' is to be both naive and myopic. To teach the law of tort without addressing this insight is to fail to teach at all. It is rather to mislead.

The critical student should arm herself with a scepticism of what passes as 'received' knowledge in the texts, in lectures and in classes. She should refuse to take for granted as wisdom that which is written by the learned of the law. She should proceed on the basis that law is intimately connected with politics and finally she should not allow the authority of the text, the teacher or the institution to invalidate her understanding and assessment of the issues which she confronts.

2
The Duty of Care in Negligence

As I have tried to navigate my fragile craft to judgment, I have become aware that it is a tidal sea which flows as causes of action are extended and then ebbs as limitations are placed upon them. I can only console myself that if I am cast up among the flotsam and jetsam at the high water mark on the beach, I shall lie, I hope unnoticed but among such battered treasures as *Anns* v. *Merton London Borough Council (per* Ward J. in *Ravenscroft* v. *Rederiaktiebolaget Transatlantic* (1991) at 76).

DUTY, FAULT AND CULPABILITY

The concept of a duty of care in negligence is an essential factor in determining whether it is proper to redistribute the plaintiff's loss to the defendant.[1] This is, in turn, informed by the assumption that individuals should, in general, bear their misfortunes alone unless there is some good reason for shifting the loss on to someone else. As Oliver Wendell Holmes observes, 'the general principle of our law is that loss from accident must lie where it falls' (Holmes, 1881, p. 94). From this assertion it follows that there is no injustice in allowing an innocent victim of life's vicissitudes to shoulder the burden alone, while there is a considerable risk of injustice, in the absence of good reason, in shifting such a burden on to someone else.

The traditionally accepted reason for shifting a loss from one person to another is captured by the fault principle according to which

> ... it is just that a person who causes loss or damage to another by his fault should be required to compensate that other; and ... it is just that a person who causes loss or damage to another without fault should *not* be required to compensate that other. (Cane, 1987, p. 413).

Fault, for these purposes, is usually understood as synonymous with carelessness. But, in fact, carelessness by itself does not provide grounds for liability in negligence, which requires not just carelessness but also a relationship where carelessness carries legal consequences. Duty defines the necessary relationship in this context and, in its absence, carelessness gives rise to no cause of action regardless of the harm it inflicts.

In this sense, the common perception that negligence is a reflection of accepted moral standards of culpability is somewhat misleading. Culpability is a legal not a moral concept. Morally reprehensible behaviour (for example, failing to rescue a small child drowning in a shallow pool of water) can often generate no legal culpability because of the absence of a duty of care. At the same time the imposition of a duty (for example, between road users), when followed by carelessness causing harm, can occasion legal culpability of extraordinary magnitude although the moral failing may involve little more than a momentary lapse of concentration (Cane, 1993, p. 150). This undermines the moral tone which negligence law exudes.

Moreover, in practice, even legal culpability rarely results in the loss in fact being shifted from the plaintiff to the defendant. Because few defendants have the resources to meet a substantial claim (including legal costs), the loss will almost always fall upon someone other than the perpetrator of the negligent act – sometimes upon employers (through the doctrine of vicarious liability) – but more often upon insurance companies (under an insurance policy held by the defendant). Indeed, it is seldom worth suing an uninsured negligent defendant. Because of the operation of insurance, the plaintiff's loss is distributed, not to the careless defendant but, through insurance premiums, to all those who were not careless but who had insured against the possibility of being so. By the back door, the presence of insurance goes some way towards the destruction of the central fault principle itself. More importantly, it fundamentally undermines the traditional assertion that negligence is *just* in delineating the range of circumstances in which a loss should be shifted from one person to another, because it is clear that, in practice, through liability insurance, negligence operates as a mechanism whereby losses are *spread* not shifted, often among a very wide range of people.

Thus, one of the problems with the traditional perception of negligence is that it is predicated on the idea of *loss-shifting* rather than *loss-spreading*. To shift a loss generated by the vicissitudes of life from one poor unfortunate to another hardly seems consonant with justice, whereas to *spread* it so widely that it is scarcely noticed by the multitude of people who absorb it is an entirely different matter – and, indeed, forms the basis of the philosophy behind the welfare state. Yet the notion of culpability implicit in the concept of fault ensures that loss-shifting not loss-spreading remains the primary rhetorical focus of negligence. Ironically, while individual responsibility continues to be the perspective which informs most cases, collective responsibility and loss-spreading through the mechanism of liability insurance tends to be the incidental by-product.

Thus, from the very outset, negligence proves paradoxical. The goal to which it claims to aspire (loss-shifting on grounds of fault), it rarely attains and the idea against which it stands in opposition (loss-spreading among those who are not at fault), is its most commonplace effect. It is against this background, in which all is not what it seems, that the concept of duty in negligence should be considered.

CONCEPTUALISING THE DUTY OF CARE

The effect of requiring a duty of care is to circumscribe those situations where carelessness resulting in harm leads to a legal obligation to compensate. Unless it can be shown that the defendant owed a duty of care to the plaintiff, no matter how gross the carelessness or how great the loss which results, the plaintiff will be unable to recover. Duty of care is a *sine qua non* of negligence.

At its broadest and least explicit, the criterion for determining the existence of a duty of care can be found in Lord Atkins's 'neighbour principle' in *Donoghue* v. *Stevenson* (1932):

> You must take reasonable care to avoid acts or omissions which you can reasonably foresee would be likely to injure your neighbour. Who then, in law is my neighbour? The answer seems to be persons who are so closely and directly affected by my act that I ought reasonably to have them in contemplation as being affected when I am directing my mind to the acts or omissions which are called into question. (580)

Broad though this is, as a criterion it leaves much to be desired. The phrases 'reasonably foresee' and 'ought reasonably' do not limit necessary relationships with clarity. What is considered reasonably foreseeable by one judge might be considered quite unforeseeable by another. Moreover, even if reasonable foreseeability *could* be ascertained with some precision, it would require a very peculiar piece of reasoning, since it compels a judge to decide in retrospect what she could reasonably have expected a defendant to have reasonably foreseen would be the result of her contemplated act upon people who might be affected, had the defendant foreseen the accident itself – which, in most cases, she almost certainly did not or a different course of action would probably have been pursued! In other words, the judge places herself, with the advantage of hindsight, in the position of a reasonable defendant who would have considered, or perhaps should have considered, the very possibility which the actual defendant failed to consider. The *Donoghue* v. *Stevenson* expression of principle that a neighbour in law is one who is so closely and directly affected by the defendant's acts that the defendant ought reasonably to have them in contemplation, simply begs the critical question and does not in fact tell us anything.

Despite its extraordinary emptiness, the neighbour principle for many years occupied an unassailable position in the doctrinal exposition of negligence. Its high-water mark is usually identified with *Anns* v. *Merton London Borough Council* (1978) where Lord Wilberforce was of the opinion that the neighbour principle should apply to create a duty of care unless there were 'other considerations' which made the imposition of such a duty inappropriate.[2]

> ... the question (of duty) has to be approached in two stages. First one has to ask whether, as between the alleged wrongdoer and the person who has suffered damage there is a sufficient relationship of proximity or neighbourhood such that, in the reasonable contemplation of the former, carelessness on his part may be likely to cause damage to the latter – in which case a *prima facie* duty of care arises. Secondly ... it is necessary to consider whether there are any considerations which ought to negative, or to reduce or limit the scope of the duty or the class of person to whom it is owed or the damages to which a breach of it may give rise. (751–752)

Williams and Hepple considered the effect of this statement to be the creation of a rule whereby anyone who was at fault could be found to be in breach of a duty of care unless there were conflicting considerations of policy for finding otherwise (Williams and Hepple, 1984, p. 102; see also Howarth, 1995, p. 164). In *Leigh & Sillivan* v. *Aliakmon Shipping Co Ltd* (1986), Robert Goff LJ went so far as to suggest that Lord Wilberforce's speech dictated a reconsideration of past judicial attitudes to the duty question, especially in cases of pure economic loss (discussed below).

Perhaps it was precisely such a threat to existing principles which led to the eventual rejection of the *Anns* 'two-stage test' (as it was known) in *Yuen Kun-yeu* v. *Attorney General of Hong Kong* (1987). Disillusionment with the *Anns* formula began some years before *Yuen*, after the decision in *Junior Books* v. *Veitchi* (1982) expanded recovery for 'pure economic loss' in negligence to a hitherto unprecedented extent. Because Lord Roskill, delivering the leading judgment in *Junior Books*, relied heavily on Lord Wilberforce's dictum in *Anns* and because the extension of liability in *Junior Books* was generally received disapprovingly as a departure from tradition, the *Anns* formula, by association, fell into judicial disrepute culminating in an outright assault upon it by Lord Keith in *Yuen Kun-yeu*.[3]

The defendant in this case was the Commissioner for Banking in Hong Kong. One of his duties, derived from a statutory ordinance, was to compile a register of licensed deposit-taking companies. The plaintiffs had deposited large sums of money with a company on the Commissioner's register. The company subsequently went into liquidation and the plaintiffs lost their money. It emerged that the company had been conducting their affairs fraudulently and speculatively and were in breach of a number of obligations and restrictions which their registration with the Commissioner created. The plaintiffs sued the Commissioner arguing that he had failed to take reasonable care in carrying out his duties in relation to registering and licensing the company. The question arose as to whether the Commissioner owed the plaintiffs a duty of care. In the course of finding that no duty arose, the Privy Council closely examined Lord Wilberforce's judgment in *Anns* in which context Lord Keith emphasised that mere foreseeability of harm (which he regarded as a common but misguided understanding of the first stage in the *Anns* formulation) did not by itself create a duty in the absence of a relationship of 'proximity'. Proximity was not, for these purposes, synonymous with foreseeability (as some may wrongly have assumed) but was rather a composite concept which embraced a number of factors relevant to the determination of whether or not a relationship was sufficiently close and direct to give rise to a duty of care.[4]

It might be suggested that Lord Keith's objections to *Anns* derived more from a disagreement about the meaning of words than from any substantive concern. After all, the *Anns* test recognised the relevance of 'other considerations' besides foreseeability in the determination of the duty question. But Lord Keith did not like the two-tier presentation of the issue, perceiving that it gave too great a weight to foreseeability as the determinative criterion.[5] To de-emphasise its importance, Lord Keith widened the meaning of proximity to include factors which might ordinarily be considered under the second limb of Lord Wilberforce's formulation.[6]

In the aftermath of *Yuen*, the courts engaged in the formulation of a new concept of duty to replace the approach identified with *Anns*. In a series of cases[7] culminating in the judgment of the Court of Appeal in *Caparo* v. *Dickman* (1989) (which proceeded to the House of Lords in 1990, see below), the courts developed a 'three-stage' approach to the determination of duty. First, was the harm reasonably foreseeable? Second, was the relationship between the plaintiff and the defendant sufficiently proximate? And third, was it 'just and reasonable' to recognise a duty of care in these circumstances? The third enquiry, in allowing the court to consider the fairness or equity of imposing or failing to impose a duty of care, was also regarded by some courts as embracing considerations of policy (*Pacific Associates Inc* v. *Baxter* (1989). Subsequent decisions have confirmed this view of the role of policy as an aspect of considerations of justice and reasonableness; see, for example, *Osman* v. *Ferguson* (1993); X v. *Bedfordshire CC* (1995)).

Did the shift from a two-tier to a 'three-tier' formulation produce anything other than a cosmetic change in the judicial approach to the duty question? It is arguable that the *Caparo* approach tells us little and, indeed, seldom dictates a particular result. Any of the leading cases which were so critical of Lord Wilberforce's approach could perfectly easily have been decided as they were by using his formulation. For example, in *Yuen Kun-yeu* v. *Attorney General of Hong Kong* (1987), the first part of Lord Wilberforce's test was clearly satisfied: the Commissioner could reasonably have foreseen that if an uncredit-worthy company were placed on or allowed to remain on the register, persons who might in the future deposit money with it would be at risk of losing that money. But having decided that a *prima facie* duty of care arose, the court could have held further that there existed here those 'other considerations' mentioned by Lord Wilberforce which ought to negative or reduce or limit the scope of the duty or the class of persons to whom it is owed. In particular, the factors which led Lord Keith to decide that no relationship of proximity existed between the parties (note 4 above) might also have been regarded as sufficient under *Anns* to negative any *prima facie* duty of care owed. Similarly, the decision in *Caparo* v. *Dickman* (1990) could have been reached by a path consistent with Lord Wilberforce's formulation.[8] The House of Lords might have argued just as cogently that the relationship between shareholders and auditors was, indeed, one of proximity or neighbourhood since it must be obvious even to the meanest auditory intelligence that shareholders may well rely upon a company's audited accounts in taking investment decisions, but that notwithstanding, there were good reasons for not transferring the plaintiffs' loss to the defendant. The central point is that had such an approach been deployed, the result would not have been dictated by Lord Wilberforce just as it was not dictated by any 'new' formulation.

What, then, is behind the judicial change of rhetoric? If the same results could have been achieved by Lord Wilberforce's formulation, why were the courts, and the House of Lords in particular, at such pains to limit its significance? The answer to this question is of much greater interest and significance than the debate about what the correct formulation of duty should be, although the latter issue has received a lot more legal 'airtime' than the former. Nor is the answer to be found by looking at the cases alone for it requires a reconsideration of the function and purpose of the concept of duty. As we have said, the object of such a concept is apparently to circumscribe those situations where carelessness leading to harm generates a redistribution of loss from the plaintiff to the defendant. The problem facing the courts, however, is how to justify such decisions in a way that appears rational, consistent and fair. Although the decision is essentially a policy one (as is clearly illustrated by Howarth's recent 'summary of duty arguments' in

Howarth, 1995, pp. 165–7), many judges are unwilling to invoke reasons of policy to justify a decision, not least because such an approach indicates that a political choice is being made. In this context, the move away from Lord Wilberforce's formulation might be understood as an attempt to play down the role of policy in judicial decision-making by using a broadened notion of proximity or neighbourhood to narrow the 'formal' role assigned to policy by the *Anns* approach.

Policy then, is not a legitimation with which the courts feel comfortable, not least because it undermines the 'black-letter' separation of law and politics. 'Proximity' and 'neighbourhood', 'just and reasonable', 'common sense' and 'practical' are phrases with which the courts are much more comfortable, although their use is nearly always pre-emptive and obfuscatory. The point is that whether the courts deny the existence of a duty for reasons of policy, or whether they justify the refusal on the grounds that it would not be 'just and reasonable' to impose a duty, they are essentially engaged in the same subjective exercise. But they find the rhetoric of fairness much more appealing than the language of policy-based choice.

Perhaps, then, what has changed is less the *criteria* by which duty is determined than the means used to *legitimate* such determinations – the latter remaining subjective decisions made with policy considerations primarily in mind.[9] Indeed, cases subsequent to *Caparo* bear this out; while policy is, increasingly, the factor which is most likely to inform judicial determinations of duty (particularly where they involve public bodies), the couching of such decisions within the neat framework of the *Caparo* criteria confers a legitimacy which renders them more acceptable despite their controversial content.[10]

However, while a judicial desire to avoid the appearance of openly playing the role of policy-maker may in part explain the change in approach to the formulation of duty questions, it is not the whole story. It might also be speculated that the *Anns* formulation was regarded with judicial suspicion because of its alleged liability expansive tendencies, particularly in the aftermath of *Junior Books* v. *Veitchi* (1982) (although, as we have pointed out, Lord Wilberforce's formulation does not necessarily *compel* a liability expansive interpretation). In the years after *Junior Books*, expressions of concern about the expansion of negligence-based liability increased with rising insurance premiums. The widening net of tort liability became perceived by some as a threat to those principles of individual freedom and responsibility which tort law was supposed to reflect. The imposition of negligence liability for structural defects in real property (*Anns* v. *Merton LBC* (1978)), the expansion of liability for nervous shock (particularly in *McLoughlin* v. *O'Brian* (1982)) and the recognition of a duty of care in relation to the acts of others (*Home Office* v. *Dorset Yacht Co* (1970) all appeared to manifest a general tendency to impose weighty obligations on individuals or bodies in relation to the well-being of others, obligations which both encroached upon individual freedom and, at the same time, fettered the pursuit of self-interest. So viewed, *Anns* and its legacy appeared to express a gradual legal encroachment on individual liberty and the operation of the free market (for a flavour of this kind of critique, see Smith and Burns, 1983; for a 1990s version, see Atiyah's attack on the 'blame culture', discussed in Chapter 8).

For some, the slippery slope toward social responsibility, which the liability expansive tendency was perceived to reflect, began with the decision in *Donoghue* v. *Stevenson* (1932), extending a positive invitation to widen liability (Smith and Burns, 1983).[11] *Donoghue* purported to offer a general rationale for negligence liability which could, subject to necessary modification to meet particular facts, apply in all circumstances to establish whether a duty of care was owed and if so what its scope was. The search for such a generalising principle can be traced back to the nineteenth century, in particular to the judgment of Lord Esher in *Heaven* v. *Pender* (1883) (see Chapter 4). Reflecting particular intellectual trends of the time, the approach in *Donoghue* quickly began to replace the previous pragmatic, case-by-case recognition or denial of 'duty situations' according to 'the wisdom of our ancestors' (Landon, 1941, p. 183).

Anns v. *Merton LBC* (1978) emerged as the modern expression of the principle-based approach of *Donoghue* v *Stevenson* (1932). But, as has been pointed out, the principle thus expressed, if it has any meaning at all, is capable of being understood very widely. Arguably, it is the width of the principle, combined with its rhetorical power *as a principle*, which produced the liability expansive tendency of *Anns*. Thus, the judicial approach to duty in the 1980s sought to eschew not only the principle itself but, to a considerable extent, the principled approach. This is particularly evident in the judgments of Lords Oliver and Bridge in *Caparo* which manifest an unwillingness to be bound by any strict formulation of the duty concept, whether composed of two tiers or three:

> ... it is difficult to resist a conclusion that what has been treated as three separate requirements are ... merely facets of the same theory ... Proximity is no doubt a convenient expression so long as it is realised that it is no more than a label which embraces not a definable concept but merely a description of circumstances from which pragmatically the courts conclude that a duty of care exists. (*per* Lord Oliver at 633)

> ... the concepts of proximity and fairness embodied in these additional ingredients are not susceptible of any such precise

definition as would be necessary to give them utility as practical tests, but amount ... to little more than convenient labels to attach to the features of particular specific situations ... which ... the law recognises pragmatically as giving rise to a duty of care ... I think the law has now moved in the direction of attaching greater significance to the more traditional categorisation of distinct and recognisable situations as guides to the existence ... of the varied duties of care. (*per* Lord Bridge at 574)

The approach to duty pioneered in *Yuen Kun-yeu* was refined in *Caparo* to operate not as a 'practical test' but as a 'guide' to decision-making. The concept of duty was to be captured not by a single principle or principles but was acknowledged to be 'varied', composed of 'distinct and recognisable situations'. The task of the court was identified as that of proceeding 'pragmatically' and 'incrementally by analogy', paying particular attention to the configuration of facts in individual cases. Moreover, the three considerations which the House of Lords proffered in *Caparo* as a guide to determining the duty question were not to be regarded as three necessary and separate requirements (in contrast to the approach of the Court of Appeal in the same case) with fixed and mutually exclusive meanings. There was a noticeable shift away from a 'blueprint' which captures the essential meaning of duty towards a case-by-case approach, sensitive to specific situations.

So viewed, while the case law from *Donoghue* v. *Stevenson* (1932) to *Anns* v. *Merton LBC* (1978) witnessed a change in direction *away* from a case-by-case approach towards the application of a universal principle of liability, cases from *Junior Books* through to *Caparo* appeared to evidence a reversal of this trend; the judicial period of liability expansion ground to a halt, if only temporarily. Even the decision in *Anns* itself (imposing a duty of care on a local authority in relation to the negligent inspection of inadequate foundations resulting in structural damage to real property) was dramatically overruled by the House of Lords in *Murphy* v. *Brentwood District Council* (1990),[12] by which time the leading cases of the day seemed almost always to indicate circumstances where a duty of care would *not* arise rather than pointing to situations where one would.

The interrelation between liability restriction and the rejection of a universal principle seems clear. Close attention to the particular facts facilitates the drawing of fine and distinct lines in deciding in what circumstances a duty will arise. The court is not so easily bound by a precedent which places particular weight on the facts at hand. The overall effect is to free the courts from any constraint which a principled approach might impose and allow for a much wider range of reasons for finding or denying liability. At the same time, the invocation of concepts of proximity, foreseeability and justness and reasonableness, furnish, where appropriate, sufficient continuity of language and form to provide the necessary legitimation for decisions in terms of abstract rules of conduct whose content varies in accordance with the context in which they arise.

This approach is strangely resonant with the work of Friedrich Hayek, a well-known right-wing philosopher and economist whose thinking influenced the Conservative government in the 1980s. From a Hayekian perspective, the retreat from *Anns* can be understood as signifying a judicial rejection of instrumental, goal-oriented uses of tort law in favour of an approach which views the common law as purposeless, as having no goal beyond that of articulating general and abstract rules of just conduct in accordance with which individuals can plan and pursue their own particular ends. (Hayek, 1982, Vol. 1, pp. 94–123). The emphasis in *Anns* on 'other considerations' was, arguably, too much of an invitation to judges to play the role of legislator (Lord Keith in *Murphy* v. *Brentwood DC* (1990) disparagingly described *Anns* as 'a remarkable piece of judicial legislation' (923)). It asked them to look beyond the facts of the case to the broader implications of the decision, to imbue the law of negligence with a purpose rather than to see it as 'the articulation as rules of practices that have proved their worth' (Thomson, 1991, p. 85). By contrast, Lord Keith and his colleagues in *Yuen* and subsequent cases sought to divest the duty concept of its reliance upon policy and purpose in favour of a very general framework of rules (duty, breach, damage) which operated to guide rather than command human conduct and, at the same time, by virtue of that very generality, facilitated attention to detail in the resolution of individual disputes.[13]

It is more than coincidence that the change in judicial rhetoric in 1980s tort cases echoed the political philosophy of Hayek. It is, surely, not accidental that the courts eschewed liability expansion, and the (admittedly limited) concept of social responsibility which it reflected at a time when the government of the day was ideologically committed to reducing the state and promoting individual responsibility (see Chapter 5). The correlation between legal and political rhetoric underlines the fact that the doctrinal debate carried on in the decade of cases running from *Anns* through to *Caparo* did not take place in a vacuum (although the texts would have us believe so), but took place against a political background in which the very issues which resounded and reverberated so strongly in the cases were being openly and widely debated.

What, then, of judicial trends in the 1990s? David Howarth suggests that we may be witnessing a return to principles: 'just as *Anns* ... marked the highpoint of the last upswing of the general principles approach, *Caparo* may mark the high point of the swing in the opposite direction' (Howarth, 1995, p. 165). It is certainly true that in the area of economic loss in particular, the courts appear to be in the midst of constructing principles of liability which allow recovery in some cases (see further below). On the other hand, despite Lord Keith's apparent turning away from policy arguments in *Yuen*, the 1990s have seen their continued deployment to deny liability, so much so that it is probably accurate to say that policy arguments feature *more* in judicial considerations of the duty question now than they did in the period immediately after *Anns* (see, for example, *X* v. *Bedfordshire CC* (1995); *Osman* v. *Ferguson* (1993); *Stovin* v. *Wise* (1996); *Hill* v. *Chief Constable of West Yorkshire* (1989)). Moreover, all this must be viewed against a background of rising litigiousness (Atiyah, 1997). Despite the concern of the courts in the 1980s to end the trend of liability expansion, litigants have continued to challenge the boundaries of existing doctrine with a view to carving out new areas of liability, a process scornfully described by Atiyah as 'stretching'. Ironically, it is probably this very triumph of individual over social responsibility, a legacy of the 1980s, which has produced the revitalised and infinitely contestable tort law of the 1990s. In the absence of adequate state provision for injury and disability, individuals are increasingly compelled to utilise 'private' mechanisms of redress against those whom they perceive (rightly or wrongly) to be 'responsible' for their loss. At the same time, the pervasiveness of market values legitimises the 'have a go' mentality which views tort not as an expression of justice but rather as yet another game to be played and won.

PARTICULAR APPLICATIONS OF DUTY

We will now consider three areas of contemporary legal debate which clearly illustrate the fundamental shortcomings in the concept of duty expounded above. We will begin with the difficulties negligence law has had in rationalising the extensive but not complete ban on recovery for pure economic loss. The most recent decisions have undoubtedly partially clarified the law, but the doctrinal rationale remains questionable. Similarly, the law relating to psychiatric damage remains contentious and the rhetorical shift from 'nervous shock' to 'psychiatric damage' is not insignificant. Finally, we will consider the doctrinal consistency of recent cases considering the liability of public emergency services such as the police, the fire service and the coastguard with a view to further highlighting the ideological, political and doctrinal tensions which inform judicial decision-making in this area.

Pure Economic Loss

In recent years, there has been extensive litigation on the question of 'pure economic loss' recovery in negligence, only a proportion of which has been successful. According to traditional assumptions, such loss is not recoverable in negligence except and unless it arises directly from physical damage (*Weller* v. *Foot & Mouth Disease Research Institute* (1966)). Quite why this should be so is not immediately obvious, but it is historically well established (*Cattle* v. *Stockton Waterworks Co* (1875)) and, although it clearly seems inconsistent with common justifications for negligence, namely that where foreseeable loss is caused to another through carelessness that loss should be transferred to the tortfeasor, the bar on economic loss recovery (in the absence of physical damage) reflects a widely held assumption that the careless infliction of economic harm raises for consideration issues which do not generally arise in the context of claims for physical damage.

Many reasons have been offered in defence of this position, including the view that economic losses are more appropriately distributed through the mechanism of contract, that they are accepted risks in the use of capital, or that they are more easily insured against by the victim than by the tortfeasor (Cane, 1987, p. 74). Concern has also frequently been expressed about the 'floodgates' aspects of economic loss recovery, creating 'liability in an indeterminate amount for an indeterminate term to an indiscriminate class', and the danger too that wealth-creating activity will be deterred by the 'crushing weight of liability' (Stanton, 1994, pp. 332–3; Deakin and Markesinis, 1994, p. 85).

It might be questioned whether such justifications properly distinguish claims of economic loss from those of physical damage. While the arguments might hold good when comparing the infliction of widespread economic loss through careless activity with a run-of-the-mill traffic accident, the distinction does not seem so clear in the context, for example, of mass drug litigation involving thousands of potential claimants. It might be more consistent and less irrational for the courts directly to address the policy reasons for denying liability in the case at hand rather than distinguishing claims on the basis of different types of damage (and thereby presumptively placing all claims of pure economic loss into the same category of presumed immunity). However, it would make their decisions infinitely more contestable; it is much easier to deny liability by invoking a rule than by proffering an opinion as to whether or not, in the circumstances, liability *ought* to be recognised.

Yet, it is precisely the judicial sense that all cases of economic loss in negligence do *not* demand the same treatment which has given rise to difficulties. To some extent, the crests and troughs of liability for economic loss correspond to the patterns of liability expansion and restriction which characterise the conceptualisation of duty of care in general. Indeed, although addressing the question of duty more widely, many of the leading duty cases concern economic loss (for example, *Yuen*, *Caparo* and, more contentiously, *Anns*). But the case law is also complicated by judicial efforts to carve out pockets of liability in some contexts while denying them in others as the courts sway between incremental advances in favour of plaintiffs and retreats from the gains they themselves have conferred. The result is inconsistency and doctrinal uncertainty.[14]

In exploring the kinds of arguments which have figured in judicial considerations of economic loss recovery, one detects a persistent if rather frayed distinction between liability arising from negligent acts (or omissions) and liability arising from negligent misstatements, particularly where they take the form of advice to the injured party. It is probably accurate to say that there is more authority for recovery in the context of the latter than in the former. However, as we shall see, the distinction between negligent words and negligent acts is not the only device to which the courts appeal in their quest to draw fine but non-arbitrary lines. In particular, recent cases evidence a definite trend towards the articulation of *general principles* of liability in the context of economic loss recovery.

The otherwise moribund distinction in tort between words and acts,[15] commonly attributed to *Derry* v. *Peek* (1889) and *Donoghue* v. *Stevenson* (1932), was given a new lease of life in the case of *Hedley Byrne & Co Ltd* v. *Heller & Partners Ltd* (1964) when it was held that a negligent misstatement causing purely economic loss might be actionable at a time when received wisdom was to deny such a claim where the negligence alleged took the form of an act. A precondition of liability under *Hedley Byrne* was the existence of a 'special relationship' between the parties, generally captured by the twin notions of assumption of responsibility by the giver of the statement and reliance on the statement by the recipient (see, in particular, the judgments of Lords Morris and Devlin at 502–503 and 528–530, respectively). Thus, the legacy of *Hedley Byrne* was to appear to create a distinct category of cases governed by a 'sub-rule' (the 'special relationship' requirement) for the determination of duty in the context of economic loss. During the 1970s and early 1980s, the judicial tendency was towards collapsing questions of negligent misstatement and economic loss into the broader question of when a duty of care should be recognised (*Ross* v. *Caunters* (1980); *Junior Books* v. *Veitchi* (1982)), but *Caparo* signalled a reversal of this trend in favour of 'the categorisation of distinct and recognisable situations' giving rise to 'varied duties of care' (*per* Lord Bridge in *Caparo* v. *Dickman* (1990)), suggesting that 'negligent misstatement' would remain a discrete category to which special considerations apply. In articulating such considerations, their Lordships adopted a very restrictive approach to the scope of liability in this context, so much so that commentators after *Caparo* questioned whether *Hedley Byrne* itself would pass the strict criteria their Lordships laid down (Martin, 1990). Thus, a duty of care would only arise in relation to a negligent misstatement where the person making the statement was fully aware of the transaction the plaintiff had in mind, knew that the statement would be communicated to the plaintiff directly or indirectly and knew that it was very likely that the plaintiff would rely on that statement; and where the statement was, in fact, relied upon by the plaintiff to her detriment. Even these conditions, however, were not to be regarded as either conclusive or exclusive, and decisions immediately following *Caparo* (for example, *James McNaughten Paper Groups Ltd* v. *Hicks Anderson & Co* (1991); *Morgan Crucible Co plc* v. *Hill Samuel Bank Ltd* (1991)) confirmed that their Lordships' wisdom had brought little in the way of either clarity or certainty to this area of law.

Nevertheless, it remained the case that after *Caparo*, and despite the restrictive nature of the judgments therein, negligent misstatements appeared to be almost the only category in which pure economic loss recovery would be contemplated by the courts: 'English law, with the exception of negligent misstatements, operates a strong presumption against awarding compensation for negligently caused pure economic loss' (Howarth, 1995, p. 273). Such a view was reinforced by their Lordships' dramatic reversal of *Anns* in *Murphy* v. *Brentwood DC* (1990) in which the characterisation of the harm at issue was considered determinative of the question of whether or not a duty of care should arise (for a summary of the facts, see note 12 above). It may seem intuitively strange to characterise structural damage to real property as 'pure economic loss' and, indeed, judges have not always endorsed this view. In *Dutton* v. *Bognor Regis United Building Co Ltd* (1972), for example, Lord Denning analysed a similar claim (in relation to defective premises) in terms which perhaps correspond more closely to common sense perceptions of the nature of the harm done and the responsibility of those who caused it to occur:

> ... Mrs Dutton has suffered a grievous loss. The house fell down without any fault of hers. She is in no position herself to bear the loss. Who might in justice bear it? I should think those who were responsible. Who are they? In the first place the builder was responsible. It was he who laid the foundation so badly that the house fell down. In the second place, the council's inspector was responsible. It was his job to examine the foundations to see if they would take the load of the house. He failed to do it properly. In the third place, the council should answer for his failure. They were entrusted by Parliament with the task of seeing that houses were properly built. They received public funds for the purpose. The very object was to protect purchasers and occupiers of houses. Yet they failed to protect them. Their shoulders are broad enough to bear the loss. (475)

Similarly, their Lordships in *Anns* struggled to avoid a characterisation of the harm suffered by the plaintiffs as 'purely economic' by emphasising the potential danger to health and safety created by the structural damage in question. Both approaches were rejected by the House of Lords in *Murphy* who held that *Donoghue* v. *Stevenson* (1932) did *not* generally apply to structural defects in real property because although it covered cases 'where latent defects *result* in physical injury to anyone, whether owner occupier, visitor or passer-by or to the property of any such person' (Lord Keith at 917), it could not cover situations where the only property damaged was the building itself. There was, they argued, a clear distinction between damage to person or property caused by a latent defect in a carelessly manufactured article and liability for the cost of rectifying a discovered defect (obviously no longer latent) which had caused no damage to person or property other than to the defective property itself. In the latter case, the loss was purely economic and there was no considered precedent in negligence which allowed such recovery. There was, further, no good reason for distinguishing, for these purposes, between a latent defect in a building and a latent defect in a chattel. As both were economic loss, principle demanded that they be treated by law in the same way, in which case no cause of action in tort should arise.

It is worth paying some attention to the language the judges used to make their point of principle. They refer to a defective product as something which is 'valueless', which can be 'discarded' and 'scrapped', implying that the same can be said about defective buildings. But to suggest that the occupier of a defective building can casually 'scrap' her investment and her home, to imply that the law should look at the problems of the homeowner, faced with some terrible structural defect in the same light as the problems of the purchaser of a flat bottle of ginger beer, is absurd. Indeed, to offer 'reason' and 'principle' for such a proposition is bizarre. (It is interesting that the House of Lords placed such an emphasis on principle having apparently eschewed it in favour of 'pragmatism' in *Yuen* and *Caparo* (1990).)[16] By deciding that a structural defect in real property is 'merely' economic loss, the House of Lords appeared confident that they had restored doctrinal coherence to a hitherto confused area. What is startling is that they saw anything rational and coherent in what they were doing. Their confusion was evident in their unwillingness to completely rule out the possibility of a claim in circumstances whose distinguishing features are not clearly apparent to the casual observer (see note 12 above and Giles and Szyszczak, 1991).

It is important to realise just what the House of Lords accomplished here. If they are to be believed, their decision followed inexorably from precedent, although if this is so, it is worth wondering why the Court of Appeal in *Murphy* and, more particularly, the House of Lords in *Anns*

v. *Merton London Borough Council* (1978) could have so misinterpreted this area of law. Moreover, when Lord Bridge observed (at 931; Lord Oliver makes similar observations at 938) that while there might be cogent reasons of social policy for imposing liability on the authority, it was pre-eminently for the legislature to decide whether these policy reasons should be accepted as sufficient for imposing on the public the burden of providing compensation for private financial losses, the implication is that the House of Lords was not taking a policy decision. Obviously, it was. Indeed, their Lordships' invocation of judicial constraint in relation to matters more properly left to Parliament seems somewhat disingenuous given that the effect of *Murphy* was to disrupt liability rules which had governed this area for the previous twelve years. The House's acknowledgement that there might be good policy reasons for imposing a duty on local authorities but that it was not their place to do so, is a legitimation which judges commonly invoke to justify denying a remedy where common sense and justice demand one. To leave an occupier with no effective remedy where, clearly, the carelessness and irresponsibility of others have made her home uninhabitable is demonstrably unfair; but to deny such a remedy where one has existed, whatever the appeal to principle and however much it is denied that a choice is being made, is to take a decision which is inevitably informed by judicial considerations of who should more appropriately bear the loss.

Why, then, did the House of Lords decide that the local authority should *not* bear the loss? In *Smith* v. *Eric Bush* (1989), they did not seem unduly troubled about imposing liability on building societies in relation to economic loss suffered by house purchasers following negligently carried out surveys commissioned by those societies, even in the face of an exclusion clause. Why the different approaches in *Smith* and *Murphy*? How relevant to the decision was it that the defendant in *Murphy* was a local authority? *Murphy* was decided at a time when the dreaded phrase 'poll tax' was on everybody's lips. Was that of any relevance? In 1972, Lord Denning described local authorities as having 'broad shoulders', a view which had radically changed by 1991. Was it purely coincidental that, at a time when local authority financing was the political controversy of the day, the House of Lords decided to change the law, reverse its own decision and remove the burden of legal liability from the now considerably narrower shoulders of public bodies?[17]

Whatever lay behind their Lordships' volte-face in *Murphy*, there is no doubt that in the period immediately following it, the prospects of those seeking damages for pure economic loss sustained as a result of another's negligence looked bleak. Remarkably, however, the obituaries for economic loss recovery have proved to be distinctly premature. Rather, in a series of cases including *Henderson* v. *Merrett* (1994), *Spring*

v. *Guardian Assurance plc* (1994), *White* v. *Jones* (1995) and, most recently, *Williams* v. *Natural Life Health Foods and Mistlin* (1998), the House of Lords have once again joined the fray, not only rationalising and extending *Hedley Byrne* beyond its original ambit, but, according to some, perhaps even restoring *Junior Books* to something like respectability (Howarth, 1995, pp. 293–4).

The facts of *Spring* v. *Guardian Assurance plc* (1994) are not complicated, and if a cynical reader might, on the facts as reported, have judged the plaintiff less generously than did the trial judge, that is of course irrelevant. In essence, Mr Spring, having been dismissed without explanation from a company for whom he sold insurance policies and which had been taken over shortly before his dismissal, applied to sell the policies of another company. Before that company could employ Mr Spring, it had to request a reference from Guardian Assurance, under rules made pursuant to the Financial Services Act 1986. The request having been received, Guardian Assurance was bound to provide the reference which it did, relating, as required, to Spring's character, aptitude and competence. The reference can be described as 'crackingly dreadful'. Counsel and judge agreed that it was truly the 'kiss of death' to an insurance sales person's career (*per* Lord Woolf at 168). The judge further found that the allegations in the reference could not be sustained, and that, but for them, Spring might have gained employment. The reference had been prepared carelessly and Spring sought damages for pure economic loss arising from the defendant's negligent misstatement.

Two immediate difficulties faced Mr Spring. First, there was the issue of whether or not relief should be provided in negligence in circumstances where a defamation claim would meet a defence of qualified privilege.[18] Second, did the principle in *Hedley Byrne* extend to cover these facts? In particular, could it be said that the plaintiff *relied* upon the defendant's statement in the sense of acting upon it? In relation to the first point, although the reference was defamatory, defamation could not aid the plaintiff (indeed, it was not pleaded) because, in the absence of malice (of which the trial judge held there was no evidence), the reference was covered by a qualified privilege protecting the writer from a civil claim. Did the same reasons which supported the application of a qualified privilege to defamatory statements in such circumstances also compel denial of a claim in negligence? Lord Keith, dissenting, explored in some depth the public policy reasons for the defence of qualified privilege in the law of defamation and thought them equally coercive when the claim is based on negligence:

> If liability in negligence were to follow from a reference prepared without reasonable care, the same adverse consequences would

flow as those sought to be guarded against by the defence of qualified privilege. Those asked to give a reference would be inhibited from speaking frankly lest it should be found that they were liable in damages through not taking sufficient care in its preparation. They might well prefer, if under no legal duty to give a reference, to refrain from doing so at all. Any reference given might be bland and unhelpful and information which it would be in the interest of those seeking the references to receive might be withheld. (at 137)

However, the majority of the House of Lords felt otherwise and did not share Lord Keith's apprehension about the inhibiting effects of liability in such circumstances. Lord Goff was particularly adamant on this point stating that he could see no good reason why the employer's duty to exercise due care and skill should be negatived because if the plaintiff were instead to bring an action for damage to his reputation, he would be met by the defence of qualified privilege (at 151). He went on to observe: 'it is not to be forgotten that the *Hedley Byrne* duty arises where there is a relationship which is, broadly speaking, *either contractual or equivalent to contract*' (our emphasis) as if this somehow explained why Lord Keith's public policy concerns were not applicable. Yet applied to the facts, this argument is highly problematic. *Hedley Byrne* involved a relationship between the person to whom the advice was given and the giver of the advice, not, as here, between the *subject* of the advice and its giver. The quasi-contractual nature of the relationship in *Hedley Byrne* was important because it is generally only where the relationship is close to contractual (but lacking consideration) that the giver of the advice will be in a position to make clear that the gratuitous advice is given without the acceptance of liability in the event of an error. Indeed, as in *Hedley Byrne* itself, it was the relationship between the giver and the receiver of advice which allowed the bank to say, in effect, that advice which is free (that is, non-contractual) was given without any voluntary assumption of liability. In *Spring*, the reference was requested from the defendant by a third party in circumstances where they were precluded from refusing to provide it (because of the code of conduct to which they subscribed) and where the lack of a present relationship with the plaintiff effectively prevented them from refusing to accept liability to him for work performed without consideration. Certainly, this seems less obviously the sort of quasi-contractual relationship which the facts of *Hedley Byrne* typify.

This point obviously relates to the second difficulty – the applicability of the *Hedley Byrne* principle itself. It was the view of Lord Keith that the plaintiff could not be said to have relied upon the defendant's statement. Therefore, although his primary reasons for denying liability related to public policy concerns, he did not think the necessary ingredients of *Hedley Byrne* liability had been made out (at 136). Lord

Goff, on the other hand, was not only of the view that *Hedley Byrne* liability *had* been made out on the facts (although, it is probably fair to say he assumed, rather than established, reliance), but also that, were this not the case, no liability should arise (at 143–144). The rest of the House, while agreeing with Lord Goff as to the outcome, preferred to rest their decision upon the *Caparo* criteria: as the harm was clearly foreseeable, as the relationship was sufficiently proximate and as, in their view, it was just and reasonable to recognise a duty of care in the circumstances, liability should arise.

It is worth emphasising two particular points of importance emerging from *Spring*. First, there is some ambivalence in the decision as to how best to approach the resolution of economic loss claims. Three of their Lordships expressed a preference for general duty criteria, particularly as they were not convinced that *Hedley Byrne* was sufficient to dictate a result. By so doing they reinforced a view evident in other decisions, for example, *Marc Rich & Co* v. *Bishop Rock Marine Co* (1995), that the type of loss sustained was not of direct relevance to a determination of the duty question. Lord Goff, on the other hand, was fairly committed to a '*Hedley Byrne* or nothing' approach, at least on these facts. However, his Lordship did go on to state that the principle in *Hedley Byrne* extended beyond negligent misstatements and applied to the provision of 'other services' (at 145). This suggests a broader role for the *Hedley Byrne* principle than had been the case hitherto, a suggestion which has since been reinforced by subsequent decisions.

White v. *Jones*, for example, further evidences a willingness by the courts to provide a remedy in cases of negligently inflicted economic loss, even to the extent of circumventing well-established rules in contract. *White* involved a firm of solicitors who, having received instructions from a testator to prepare a new will, carelessly failed to do so before the testator's death, with the result that the testator's intended beneficiaries (his hitherto disinherited daughters) each missed out on a bequest of £9000 while those under the old will profited in a way which was clearly contrary to the deceased's wishes. The testator's daughters sued the solicitors for damages in negligence and the case turned upon whether the solicitors owed them, as intended beneficiaries, any duty of care. The judge at first instance held that they did not but both the Court of Appeal and the House of Lords (with Lords Keith and Mustill dissenting) held a duty to have existed and been broken. Although not involving a negligent misstatement as such (indeed, problematically, the alleged negligence took the form of an omission to act), the House of Lords once again relied on *Hedley Byrne* in concluding that a duty of care arose, notwithstanding significant doctrinal obstacles in the way of a such a conclusion. One of these was, of course, the doctrine of privity in contract which generally precludes suits upon a contract by third parties. Their Lordships' self-conscious effort to circumvent this basic principle by permitting the plaintiffs to obtain a remedy through tort on the basis of a contract made between other parties for their benefit may seem an attractive outcome for reasons relating to 'the strong impulse to do practical justice' (*per* Lord Goff at 703), but its potential for doctrinal disruption should not be underestimated. Another difficulty arose from the fact that what the intended beneficiaries had suffered was a loss of *expectation*, rather than damage to an existing right or interest. This, it could be argued, was more properly remediable through contract, particularly as the effect of damages in tort was to increase the value of the deceased's estate (the technical beneficiaries remaining entitled to inherit under the unamended will). Most problematically, however, the crucial ingredients of *Hedley Byrne* appeared to be missing, certainly in relation to the plaintiffs. While the defendant solicitor had clearly assumed a responsibility to the testator, the weight of authority suggested that no such responsibility was thereby assumed towards intended beneficiaries. Similarly, it could not comfortably be said that intended beneficiaries *relied* upon a solicitor in such circumstances, particularly when they might have no idea of the testator's intentions, as would often be the case, for example, in relation to bequests to charities.

Given these difficulties, and whatever one's sympathy for disappointed beneficiaries, it is difficult to dismiss as unreasonable Lord Keith's statement that: 'I am unable to reconcile the allowance of the plaintiffs' claim with principle, or to accept that to do so would represent an appropriate advance on an incremental basis from decided cases' (at 694). How, then, *was* a remedy justified? In essence, it seems that, to the majority, the facts themselves so clearly called out for redress, they were unable to accept that the common law could not respond. Lord Goff, whilst bravely grappling with the doctrinal difficulties posed by the case, nevertheless observed: 'it seems to me that it is open to your Lordships' House to fashion a remedy to fill a lacuna in the law and so prevent the injustice which would otherwise occur on the facts of cases such as the present' (at 710). Likewise, Lord Browne-Wilkinson argued that it would be unacceptable if, because of some technical rules of law, the wishes and expectations of testators and beneficiaries generally could be defeated by the negligent actions of solicitors without there being any redress. Overwhelmed by the impulse to do practical justice, their Lordships ran the gamut of doctrinal obstacles circumventing not just the privity rule but also the rules against economic loss recovery, the presumption against liability for omissions and the conceptual difficulty posed by the nature of the plaintiff's 'loss'. This was achieved by 'extending' the *Hedley Byrne* remedy owed to the testator to the intended beneficiaries, Lord Goff reasoning that as the remedy was of little use to the testator himself (not just because he was dead but also because he could not in law be said to have suffered any harm), it might as well be applied to the benefit of those who needed it, in this case, the intended beneficiaries. This was not so much a dilution of *Hedley Byrne* as a strategic redeployment (albeit one legitimised by reference to the German doctrinal notion of 'transferred loss'), which relied upon distinguishing the criteria generating liability from entitlement to sue.

It might be argued that *White* v. *Jones* is best understood as a decision on its facts which seeks to protect the small time, one-off 'consumer' of bequests from injustice. Indeed, Lord Goff emphasises that it is where both the bequest and the firm of solicitors charged with responsibility for executing it are relatively small, that mistakes such as arose in *White* are most likely to occur. He thus concludes that 'it tends to be people of modest means who suffer' (at 702), a concern which for him further compels a remedy. Yet, there is little doubt that *White* is expressive of a broader concern to free the categories of contract and tort from the consequences of doctrinal rigidity by carving out a principle of liability which cuts across traditional boundaries. This becomes even more evident in *Henderson* v. *Merrett* (1994) and *Williams* v. *Natural Life Health Foods and Mistlin* (1998), a recent House of Lords decision which relies heavily on *Henderson*.

Tony Weir's description of the facts in *Henderson* is succinct and droll:

> The facts of *Henderson* were that individuals rich enough to provide a certificate of wealth and become 'names' at Lloyds agreed to being placed, either by their own agents or by names selected by those agents, on syndicates which issued policies rendering the names personally liable to the full extent of their estate should an insured event occur. After several profitable years the names discovered to their dismay that insurance involved risks as well as profits, the risks being due to the exuberant law of tort and the dismal weather in the United States. Reacting after the manner of investors with burnt fingers, they sued both their own agents and the sub-agents whom their agents had retained. (Weir, 1996, pp. 67–8)

Whether or not the agents were in breach of contract (it was accepted by all sides that they were obliged to carry out their contractual duties with reasonable care and skill), the plaintiffs were precluded from bringing a contractual claim as they were out of time, time running from the breach of contract not from the occurrence of harm. The question as to whether either they or the sub-agents owed the plaintiffs a duty of care in tort was answered in the affirmative by all the courts who considered it and the plaintiffs recovered for their loss.

A cynic might remark that the willingness of the courts to find a remedy for the economic loss sustained by Lloyds' Names had more to do with a judicial affinity with the class affected than the merits of the claim itself. Certainly, there is something intuitively troubling about granting relief to investors who, while happy to reap the benefits of their investment for years, are not willing to accept responsibility in the event of loss. Nor can it be said in this instance that those affected 'are likely to be of modest means'. Such misgivings aside, *Henderson* represented another important step forward in the revitalisation of *Hedley Byrne* as a 'superprinciple'. The leading judgment was given yet again by Lord Goff who reinforced the view he first expounded in *Spring* that *Hedley Byrne* extended beyond negligent misstatement, offering a general principle of liability for negligently inflicted economic loss. The necessary ingredients for the application of this principle were an assumption of responsibility by the defendant for the plaintiff's economic welfare followed by the plaintiff's reliance on the defendant's undertaking; these features remained the conditions determining the imposition of liability. Lord Goff emphasised that whether or not a responsibility had been assumed was to be assessed objectively on the facts; it did not depend upon the defendant's subjective understanding of the situation. He also stated that the presence of *Hedley Byrne* conditions of liability dispensed with any need to consider the *Caparo* criteria, particularly the third limb requiring a consideration of whether it is fair, just and reasonable to impose liability – 'a point which is, I consider, of some importance in the present case' (at 521).

A further important dimension to the *Henderson* decision was the relevance of the contractual framework governing relations between the parties. It was strongly contended by the defendants that the contracts were definitive of their contractual obligations and that no liability in tort should arise outside their ambit. This contention was supported by considerable authority (see especially *Tai Hing Cotton Mill* v. *Liu Chong Hing Bank Ltd* (1986); *Pacific Associates Inc* v. *Baxter* (1989)) including, it was argued, *Hedley Byrne* itself, which the defendants said applied to relationships 'equivalent to contract' and *not* to relationships which were themselves contractually defined. This line of argument was rejected by Lord Goff who emphasised that the principle of liability in *Hedley Byrne* cut across the boundaries of contract and tort except in so far as the parties were free to exclude such liability in their contractual arrangements if they so chose (a further application of the *White* principle of 'transferred loss'). While acknowledging that this could not be *expressly* derived from the judgments in *Hedley Byrne*, Lord Goff believed that '[their] internal logic ... led inexorably to [that] conclusion' (at 532).

In *Williams* v. *Mistlin* (1998), the House of Lords has recently reaffirmed the approach outlined by Lord Goff in *Henderson*. Although the leading judgment is given by Lord Steyn and although, on the facts, liability for negligently inflicted economic loss was denied, the case confers an unquestionable seal of approval on Lord Goff's elevation of the extended *Hedley Byrne* principle: it is, in the words of Lord Steyn 'the *rationalisation or technique* (our emphasis) adopted by English law to provide a remedy for the recovery of damages in respect of economic loss caused by the negligent performance of services' (at 581). Moreover, it operates without the need to consider whether or not it is 'fair, just or reasonable' to impose liability (*ibid*).

Lord Steyn also seeks to counter criticisms of the principle of voluntary assumption of risk which forms the linchpin of *Hedley Byrne* liability. This principle has been widely criticised, mainly by academics, on the grounds that it is merely a fictional device facilitating the imposition of liability, rather than a fact to be determined by the court. Commentators have emphasised the lack of any real evidence of an assumption of legal responsibility to the plaintiffs in any of the leading cases; indeed, even in *Henderson*, the agents' assumption of responsibility is asserted rather than proved. Lord Steyn reiterates the need for finding an assumption of risk on the facts. It is its very absence on the facts in *Williams* which leads him to deny the plaintiff a remedy. However, once again following Lord Goff's lead in *Henderson*, Lord Steyn also states that the determination of whether or not a risk has been assumed is to be objectively not subjectively assessed: 'The touchstone of liability is not the state of mind of the defendant. An objective test means that the primary focus must be on things said or done by the defendant or on his behalf in dealings with the plaintiff' (at 582). His Lordship acknowledges that, even on an 'objective' assessment, it is virtually impossible to identify an assumption of responsibility in all of the existing authorities, but *White*, he emphasises, was decided 'on special facts' (likewise *Smith* v. *Eric Bush* (1989) which, rather problematically, recognised liability even in the context of an express disclaimer) and, in any case, 'coherence must sometimes yield to practical justice' (at 584).

It is this particular observation which reveals Lord Steyn's hand: in the name of justice he is engaged not just in the fine-tuning of a principle of liability for economic loss, but also in the wholesale recon-struction of the doctrinal boundaries between contract and tort. *Hedley Byrne* provides 'an essential gap-filling role' to counter the deficiencies of the contractual doctrines of privity and consideration, particularly their failure to provide a remedy against conduct which, perhaps, can best be captured by the notion of 'letting others down' (McBride and Hughes, 1995). This, in turn, relates to the displacement of the *Caparo* criteria in economic loss cases despite the fact that it is in precisely such a context that they first appeared. The shift from pragmatism back to principle which the rejection of *Caparo* expresses requires explanation. It seems too simple merely to observe that the courts tend to invoke arguments of policy and pragmatism to deny liability, and arguments of principle to extend it, although this is not a claim entirely without foundation. More pertinently, the judicial concern to articulate a principle of liability may signify a more general dissatisfaction with the doctrinal boundaries as traditionally drawn. It is arguable that the courts in cases such as *Henderson* and *White* are not 'doing tort' at all but creatively addressing perceived deficiencies in current contract law and engaging in a task which clearly compels a principled engagement because that is the main discursive framework within which contract doctrine operates.

All this does not mean we should be deluded into thinking that the courts have finally 'sorted out' economic loss. It is worth reminding ourselves that despite the doctrinal and, indeed, moral appeal of the *Hedley Byrne* principle, it is rarely, if ever, comfortable in the context of the facts to which it has been applied. Moreover, it continues to sit uneasily alongside the *Caparo* criteria. Could, for example, a court still engage in the three-pronged enquiry in *Caparo* to find liability where the *Hedley Byrne* criteria have not been met? Could the impulse to do practical justice result in liability where neither *Hedley Byrne* nor the *Caparo* criteria have been met? Is the decision in *Anns* implicitly restored on the grounds that responsibility was voluntarily assumed by the council and relied upon by the plaintiffs? It is certainly a more convincing example of *Hedley Byrne* liability than some which have succeeded it. Finally, what is the role of policy in all of this? Will it again raise its ugly head to muddy the clear blue water of *Hedley Byrne* liability? Or is it, even now, lurking unseen but ready to pounce? Time will tell. In the meantime, what we can most readily conclude from recent case law is that the identification and demarcation of those situations where a duty of care arises remains both contingent and elusive.

Psychiatric Harm

Earlier, we suggested that the retreat from *Anns* v. *Merton LBC* (1978) reflected, in part, a judicial discomfort with the kind of legitimations implied in the *Anns* test. Similarly, it might be argued that judicial disenchantment with the *Caparo* criteria, at least in the context of pure economic loss, arose from a gradual realisation that, far from escaping the speculative and policy-oriented character of the *Anns* formula, *Caparo* pragmatism entailed an equally speculative and highly policy-oriented enquiry into considerations of fairness, justice and reasonableness. In this context, the return to principle in economic loss cases is, perhaps, less than surprising. Nor should it come as a (nervous) shock to discover that the courts have endeavoured to bring similar order to the case law determining when a duty of care should arise in relation to the negligent infliction of psychiatric harm. More doubtful is whether such efforts at rationalisation have achieved the twin aims of certainty and fairness.

As with economic loss, there is a traditional understanding in tort that the infliction of psychiatric harm not consequent upon physical injury generally attracts no liability in negligence. According to Tony Weir, this corresponds with the intuitive, if medically indefensible, sense of justice of the common man:

> There is no doubt that it is *harm* to be rendered unfit to cope with the daily exigencies of life, to have one's merriment turned to misery, to feel one's peace of mind shattered by a shocking occurrence. So, too, it is harm to lose a limb and have to hobble about. But there is equally no doubt that the public – crass and ignorant as it may be – draws a distinction between the neurotic and the cripple, between the man who loses his concentration and the man who loses his leg. It is widely felt that being frightened is less than being struck, that trauma to the mind is less than lesion to the body. Many people would consequently say that the duty to avoid injuring strangers is greater than the duty not to upset them. The law has reflected this distinction as one would expect, not only by refusing damages for grief altogether, but by granting recovery for other psychical harm only late and grudgingly and then only in very clear cases. In tort, clear means close – close to the victim, close to the accident, close to the defendant. (Weir, 1992, p. 88)

Of course, such a position is highly problematic for a number of reasons, not least of which is the difficulty in drawing a workable distinction between physical and psychiatric harm. Physical injury is often accompanied by emotional distress while psychiatric harm is regularly exhibited through an array of physical symptoms (such as vomiting, insomnia, weight loss and other 'stress-related' illnesses). This difficulty is compounded by advances in medical knowledge which further confirm the close and symbiotic relationship between mental and physical health. However, changes in medical perceptions of psychiatric harm are slow to penetrate the doctrinal assumptions which underpin the law of negligence and, as a consequence, the doctrinal obstacles to recovery are more rooted in medical ignorance than in rational thought. Although efforts have been made of late to ensure a closer correlation between legal and medical categories (Sprince, 1998), it is still fair to say, as Windeyer J observed in 1970, that law's attempts to keep up with medical knowledge have left it 'in the rear and limping a little' (*Mount Isa Mines Ltd* v. *Pusey* (1970) at 395).

Regardless, then, of whether the distinction between physical and mental harm properly withstands close medical scrutiny, it remains deeply embedded in the doctrinal substance of negligence law. However, while the derivation of specific controls on recovery in this context predominantly relate to judicial perceptions of the nature of the harm, the modern justification of such controls is undoubtedly rooted in policy considerations. In *McLoughlin* v. *O'Brian* (1982), these were articulated by Lord Wilberforce to include the alleged danger, if liability is extended, of a proliferation of claims, the increased risk of fraudulent claims, the potential unfairness to the defendant of imposing damages out of all proportion to the negligent conduct (including the increased burden of insurance which would impact eventually on all policy holders) and, finally, the anticipated increase in evidentiary difficulties and time-consuming litigation which a generous approach to recovery would engender.[19] These arguments, which have recently been considered by the Law Commission in its report on *Liability for Psychiatric Illness* (Law Commission No 249, 1998, paras 6.5–6.9), do not, however, survive close scrutiny. Indeed, the Commission expresses considerable scepticism in relation to most of the policy arguments invoked, pointing out, quite rightly, that many of them apply equally well to claims for physical injury. For example, fraudulent or exaggerated claims are at least as likely where physical harm has occurred – medicine can determine that an injury has occurred but it cannot ascertain with any great precision the degree of pain and suffering it has generated. Similarly, the absence of proportionality between culpability and consequences is as prominent and problematic in physical injury claims (consider, for example, the momentarily careless driver) as where the harm sustained is psychiatric. Finally, uncertainty, evidentiary difficulties and prolonged litigation are no more likely in cases of psychiatric harm than in an averagely complicated medical malpractice case. The Law Commission acknowledges, however, that some weight must be accorded to floodgates concerns, that is, to the fear that the removal of restrictions on recovery for psychiatric harm will lead to a proliferation of claims. For that reason, it remains of the view that some controls on the scope of recovery should remain, while considering the controls which currently operate to be unduly restrictive (see further below).

Arguably, then, the convoluted and often contradictory set of rules which govern recovery for negligently inflicted psychiatric harm rest on extraordinarily shallow and inadequate foundations. Not only is the legal conceptualisation of a distinct category of psychiatric harm at odds with a far more nuanced and complex medical understanding, but the reasons for different standards of liability come down, at bottom, to a speculative fear of increased litigation, an inevitably troubling reason for denying a right to recovery where justice would otherwise compel it. Ultimately, however, the greatest difficulty with the regime of rules which governs recovery in this area is the arbitrariness of results it produces. Why should the traumatised police officers involved in the Hillsborough tragedy recover (*Frost* v. *Chief Constable of the South Yorkshire Police* (1997)) yet many of the bereaved relatives be denied redress (*Alcock* v. *CC of South Yorkshire* (1991))? Why should an overworked and highly stressed social worker succeed in suing his employer for psychiatric harm (*Walker* v. *Northumberland CC* (1995)) but not a traumatised worker on a support vessel, going to the aid of those trapped on the Piper Alpha oil rig in which 164 men died (*McFarlane* v. *EE Caledonia Ltd* (1994))? Why should a mother recover damages after seeing her family in hospital a few hours after a tragic road accident (*McLoughlin* v. *O'Brian* (1982)) but not a father, who sat at his son's bedside for 14 days and watched him slowly die as a result of medical negligence (*Sion* v. *Hampstead Health Authority* (1994))? It may be that all of these outcomes can be explained in terms of the web of rules which have been spun round cases of psychiatric harm but that does not make them any more defensible when placed side by side and considered in terms of justice and basic common sense. In any case, the relevant rules possess none of the elegance or definition of a spider's web. While it is possible to *present* them in an orderly and rational fashion, such a presentation belies their fundamental incoherence.

In order to recover for psychiatric harm not consequent upon physical injury, the following preconditions generally need to be met: (1) the harm must amount to a 'recognised psychiatric illness' (*Hinz* v. *Berry* (1970)); and (2) the harm must be reasonably foreseeable in the sense that a person of ordinary courage and fortitude would, in the circumstances, be likely to sustain it (*Brice* v. *Brown* (1984)). It may also be necessary that the harm is sustained as a result of the sudden appreciation of a shocking or horrifying event rather than involvement in a gradual but distressing occurrence, but it is quite unclear to what extent this requirement applies beyond the category of secondary victims, understood as those who witness but are not directly involved in accidental injury to another (see further below).[20]

Assuming the prerequisites have been met, further determination of the plaintiff's claim is reliant upon her status as a primary or secondary victim. This distinction, which is usually attributed to the House of Lords decision in *Page* v. *Smith* (1995), is, in fact, derived from comments of Lord Oliver in *Alcock* (at 922–923) and operates not just as a framework within which such cases should now be decided but also as a reinterpretation or rationalisation of past decisions. Primary victims are those 'directly involved' in the accident concerned. Such plaintiffs can recover for negligently inflicted psychiatric harm if they can show either (a) that they are within the range of foreseeable physical injury (*Page*); or (b) that they have a reasonable fear of physical injury (*McFarlane*); or (c) that they are rescuers (*Frost*); or (4) that they are 'involuntary participants' in the sense of being placed by the defendant's negligent act in the position of believing that they are responsible for the actual or anticipated injury to another (as in *Dooley*

v. *Cammell Laird & Co Ltd* (1951)). The category may also include employees who sustain reasonably foreseeable psychiatric harm as a result of their employer's breach of her duty to maintain a safe system of work, although it is probably more accurate to see such claimants as occupying a category of their own (see, in this context, the discussion of Henry LJ in *Frost* at 557–568).

Secondary victims, those who are *not* directly involved in the negligent event but are witnesses or mere bystanders in relation to it, will only recover if they can demonstrate a relationship of proximity with the defendant. Proximity is defined in terms of the presence of close ties of love and affection between the primary and secondary victim, temporal and spatial proximity to the accident and sensual perception of the trauma-causing event or its immediate aftermath (*Alcock*). As long as these requirements can be met, recovery will be allowed, subject, of course, to the fulfilment of other general conditions of liability, including breach of duty and causation.

Close scrutiny of this apparently seamless framework of rules reveals deep flaws and irreconcilable contradictions. For example, the requirement that the plaintiff must suffer a 'recognised psychiatric illness' not only denies the existence of duty where reasonably foreseeable grief or distress *not* amounting to a 'recognised psychiatric illness' is the direct result of the defendant's negligence (as in *Reilly* v. *Merseyside AHA* (1995) where a severely distressed couple were denied compensation after being trapped in a lift) but is reliant on precise definitions of what is or is not a psychiatric illness in circumstances where, in fact, such definitions are constantly evolving and subject to change. Indeed, as the Law Commission has observed, it may be more accurate to see the distinction as one of degree rather than kind (para. 6.8), in which case the need to establish an 'illness' is really just a means of ensuring that the medical rather than the legal profession draws the line as to who qualifies for recovery.[21]

The requirement that psychiatric harm be reasonably foreseeable in a person of ordinary courage and fortitude is equally fraught with difficulties. In the first place, it might be observed that such harm is a reasonably foreseeable consequence of almost any tragic or traumatic occurrence. The difficulty lies in the fact that, unlike physical harm, only some individuals will suffer psychiatric consequences from identical incidents. The very peculiar notion of 'reasonable phlegm' (*Bourhill* v. *Young* (1943)) has been used to qualify the usual negligence principle that a tortfeasor takes her victim as she finds him, but this merely perpetuates the entirely false notion that there is a reasonable response to the occurrence of tragedy from which the plaintiff may or may not have deviated. There is also an implicit and rather troubling judgmentalism in the assertion that some emotional reactions to personal tragedy are less deserving of legal compassion than others particularly when, having accepted in *Attia* v. *British Gas plc* (1987) that a person of reasonable phlegm might suffer nervous shock as a result of seeing her house and property destroyed through negligence, the courts, in a peculiar perversion of values, appear to have held in the context of the Hillsborough tragedy that nervous shock sufferers outside the parent/spouse relationship or its equivalent may generally be expected to suffer only grief if they possess reasonable phlegm! Such a position is also strangely and paradoxically at odds with the thin-skull rule which, once it comes into play (namely, after it has been judicially determined that a person of normal courage and fortitude *would* have been psychologically affected by the trauma-causing event), allows for full recovery regardless of how far the plaintiff's reaction departs from the standard of 'reasonable phlegm' (*Brice* v. *Brown* (1984)). Moreover, in *Page* v. *Smith* (1995) the House of Lords ruled (by a 3:2 majority) that where the plaintiff is a primary victim, his reaction does *not* have to correspond to that of the reasonably courageous person at all. So long as she is within the range of foreseeable physical injury (in this case the plaintiff was involved in a car crash but was physically uninjured), a duty is owed in relation to any psychiatric harm which results, whether or not reasonably foreseeable in a person of ordinary courage and fortitude. One is left wondering on what moral basis can the distinction between those from whom a reasonable psychological reaction is required and those from whom it is not, be defended. It might be suggested that the distinction derives its legitimacy not from the fairness of result it produces but rather from the degree of legal certainty it promotes, but this is hardly persuasive, for it is not at all certain after *Page* when the test of reasonable phlegm applies and when it is suspended. In particular, are all categories of 'primary' victim included in the *Page* v. *Smith* exemption? After *Frost*, this seems unlikely: the judgments of both Rose LJ and Henry LJ suggest that where the claimants are outside the range of foreseeable physical injury, they must continue to demonstrate the reasonable foreseeability of psychiatric harm.[22]

Uncertainty as to when psychiatric harm must be foreseeable is closely linked to a more fundamental lack of judicial precision as to the boundaries of the primary/secondary victim distinction. According to *Page*, a primary victim is someone who is within the range of foreseeable physical danger, in which context a duty of care is owed in relation to psychiatric harm on the same basis as it is owed in relation to physical injury. It follows that, regardless of whether or not physical injury occurs, liability will lie for psychiatric harm because 'once it is established that the defendant is under a duty of care to avoid causing personal injury to the plaintiff, it matters not whether the injury in fact sustained was physical, psychiatric or both' (*per* Lord Lloyd at 761). In describing such a plaintiff as a 'primary victim', Lord Lloyd was invoking a terminology earlier deployed by Lord Oliver in *Alcock*: 'Broadly [nervous shock cases] divide into two categories, that is to say those cases in which the injured plaintiff was involved, either mediately or immediately, as a participant, and those in which the plaintiff was no more than the passive and unwilling witness of injury caused to others' (at 923). However, difficulty arises from the fact that, although both judges invoke the primary/secondary distinction, it is far from clear that they mean the same thing. Although Lord Lloyd does characterise the primary victim as 'a participant' and someone who is 'directly involved' in the event (at 755), the whole thrust of his judgment is to confine the category of primary victim to one who is at risk of physical injury. Lord Oliver, on the other hand, quite obviously envisages a broader range of plaintiffs to include rescuers and 'unwilling participants' of the *Dooley* variety (above). These difficulties are further compounded by the application of the primary/secondary dichotomy, explicitly or implicitly, in subsequent decisions. In *McFarlane*, for example, Stuart Smith LJ concluded that Lord Oliver's notion of 'participant' embraced not only a person in actual physical danger but also someone who reasonably believed that they were and suffered psychiatric harm as a result of that belief (at 10). In *Frost* v. *Chief Constable of the South Yorkshire Police* (1997), the Court of Appeal devoted much energy to delineating the boundaries of the primary/secondary dichotomy with regard to the status of rescuers and employees, but the decision, as a whole, offers little in terms of clarity or coherence except to further reveal the lack of a judicial consensus as to precisely where those boundaries lie. In part, the difficulties in *Frost* arise from the judicially perceived need to convincingly justify awarding compensation to traumatised police officers while denying it to many bereaved relatives in the context of the same tragic event, an outcome which is all the more unpalatable given that responsibility for the Hillsborough tragedy lies with those whose officers were the successful litigants in *Frost*. What is abundantly clear is that the efforts, both of the House of Lords in *Alcock* and the Court of Appeal in *Frost*, illustrate with terrible poignancy not only the very real difficulties which the courts confront in seeking to distinguish between those who are and those who are not 'deserving' of compensation in relation to the undisputed wrongdoing of another, but also the genuine doctrinal muddle in which they now find themselves as a result of those efforts.

The Hillsborough disaster in 1989 presented the courts with the most spectacular opportunity to test the principles governing recovery for nervous shock to date. The tragedy arose from a football match in Hillsborough stadium in which, as a direct result of police negligence (they allowed too many spectators into an enclosed area), 95 spectators were crushed to death and over 400 injured. The event generated claims for 'nervous shock' both from the bereaved and from police officers who participated in events that day. While the House of Lords in *Alcock* articulated a fairly strict set of principles governing recovery in the former category, *Frost* relaxed those criteria in the context of the claims by police officers, essentially by invoking the primary/secondary dichotomy to distinguish the claims.

In *Alcock*, 16 plaintiffs who suffered psychiatric illness in the aftermath of Hillsborough sued the Chief Constable of South Yorkshire, alleging that their nervous shock was a foreseeable result of police negligence (*Alcock v. CC of South Yorkshire* (1991)). The plaintiffs' cases were test cases to determine liability in 150 other cases. The chosen plaintiffs covered a full spectrum of possible claimants, ranging from those who had witnessed the events on television, to those who had been present at the ground, to one who heard the events described on the radio, to one who learned of the tragedy in conversation and then saw a subsequent news broadcast. The plaintiffs all had friends or relatives at the match, 13 of whom were among those killed, two of whom were injured and one unharmed. The relationship of the plaintiffs to those who were killed or injured included a wife, parents, sisters, brothers, uncles, a grandfather, a brother-in-law, a fiancée and a friend of various victims.

The trial court (*per* Hidden J) found in favour of ten of the plaintiffs and rejected the claims of the other six. The Court of Appeal rejected all the claims as, eventually, did the House of Lords on the ground that in no case was the requisite proximity between the plaintiffs and the defendants established. In articulating guidelines as to what was required to establish proximity in such instances, the House of Lords held that proximity could be established (1) where the plaintiff's relationship with the accident (primary) victim was sufficiently close to make it reasonably foreseeable that she might suffer psychiatric harm; (2) the plaintiff was proximate to the accident in terms of time and space; and (3) a recognised psychiatric injury resulted. The House of Lords rejected the approach suggested by the lower courts which sought to control the scope of recovery by drawing a strict line at certain classes of relationships. So long as the relationship was demonstrably close enough in terms of ties of love and affection to give rise to the reasonable expectation that physical harm to one party would occasion psychiatric harm in the other, that relationship was sufficient. Although some relationships would come almost automatically into this category (for example, parents and/or spouses), the closeness of the relationship, rather than its formal status, would, ultimately, be determinative.[23] On the question of recovery for psychiatric harm induced by radio or TV transmission, their Lordships (by a majority) decided that this was not sufficiently close in time and space to satisfy the proximity requirement, although Lords Ackner and Oliver thought that it might be sufficient if the transmission was simultaneous and very graphic and/or harrowing.

Alcock signalled an abrupt end to the trend towards liability expansion in nervous shock cases resulting from the application of the 'immediate aftermath' concept in *McLoughlin* v. *O'Brian* (1982).[24] For subsequent victims of nervous shock, the tragedy of Hillsborough continues to have reverberations. Because Hillsborough led to a plethora of claims which might be seen to support the worst fears of those concerned with the 'floodgates' possibility, a decision was taken which might well have been different had the case involved but a single tragedy of the kind in *Hevican* v. *Ruane* (1991) or *Ravenscroft* v. *Rederi-aktiebolaget Transatlantic* (1991) (above, note 24). Yet, despite the cautious tone of the *Alcock* decision and its implications, not least for those 16 plaintiffs who were denied compensation, litigation in the context of negligently inflicted psychiatric harm has continued undeterred, in circumstances where the courts are frequently unwilling to deny recovery. Indeed, it is these circumstances which presaged Lord Lloyd's invocation of the primary/secondary dichotomy in *Page*. It was precisely his concern to find *in favour* of the plaintiff which led him to distinguish the claim before him from that of the claimants in *Alcock*, while, at the same time, relying upon Lord Oliver's language in *Alcock* to do so. Yet, as the Law Commission has recently pointed out, part of the reason why Lord Lloyd in *Page* and Lord Oliver in *Alcock* draw a different line demarcating the primary/secondary boundary is because the purpose of line-drawing in each case is different (Law Commission, No 249, 1998, para. 2.55). Unlike Lord Lloyd, Lord Oliver was seeking not to extend recovery but to restrict it; moreover, his object in articulating the primary/secondary distinction was to delimit the area of proximity with a sufficient degree of precision to facilitate future decision-making. Lord Lloyd, on the other hand, was concerned primarily to ensure that, as far as possible, the law should not arbitrarily distinguish between physical and psychiatric harm: in this context, Lord Oliver's concept of 'secondary victim' allowed him to limit the reach of the *Alcock* criteria.[25]

It seems, then, that the courts are not only failing to apply the primary/secondary dichotomy with any consistency but are invoking it to serve different and even conflicting purposes. No wonder it is of so little guidance where it is most needed, as in cases such as *Frost*.

When the six representative police officers sued their Chief Constable for damages for post-traumatic stress disorder suffered as a result of their experiences at Hillsborough (*Frost* v. *Chief Constable of the South Yorkshire Police* (1997)), they claimed to be distinguishable from the *Alcock* plaintiffs either because they became involved in the tragedy in the course of their employment or because they were rescuers.[26] The Court of Appeal, which, by a majority decision, allowed the appeal of five of the plaintiffs against a trial court decision dismissing their claims, was, nevertheless, far from certain as to the basis upon which they succeeded. According to Rose LJ, three of the police officers qualified as rescuers by virtue of their involvement in the events of the day. The other two, being within the range of foreseeable danger, physical or psychiatric, resulting from their employer's negligence were owed a duty of care as employees while the sixth (unsuccessful) officer was deemed neither a rescuer nor within the scope of her employer's duty of care and failed to recover. Henry LJ leaned towards a finding of liability based upon the claimants' status as employees, in which context both judges considered foreseeability of psychiatric harm as sufficient to create the necessary proximity. Both judges also considered the successful plaintiffs to be primary victims, although Henry LJ acknowledged that Lord Lloyd and Lord Oliver's definition of primary victim diverged and concluded by observing that 'I am not sure that the labelling of each plaintiff as a primary or a secondary victim really matters' (at 561).

Judge LJ dissented from the majority findings, pointing out, with the aid of some heart-rending examples, that many of the bereaved claimants in *Alcock* had been as involved as the police officers in *Frost* in the events of the day, yet had been denied recovery. Judge LJ also emphasised that nothing in *Page* justified the broad assumption operating in *Frost* that rescuers should automatically recover observing that, had this been the case in *Alcock*, the number of successful claimants would have been much greater. He therefore concluded that the plaintiffs' argument 'places too much weight on the categorisation of the plaintiffs ... as rescuers and thus avoids the necessary analysis of the precise activity and involvement of each individual at the scene' (at 573). Applying Lord Lloyd's narrow definition of primary victim in *Page*, Judge LJ held that all of the claimants, not being within the range of foreseeable physical danger at any point, were secondary victims and, therefore, could only recover if the necessary relationship of proximity was established. This, in turn, depended upon satisfaction of the *Alcock* criteria, which all of the officers failed to do.

It seems, then, that of the three appeal court judges in *Frost*, two reached diametrically opposed conclusions as to the status of the claimants as primary or secondary victims, while one acknowledged that he really wasn't sure but he didn't think it mattered in any case. The Law Commission has similarly concluded that 'the courts ... be encouraged (to abandon) attaching practical consequences to whether the plaintiff may be described as a primary or secondary victim' (Law Commission, No 249, 1998, para. 5.58). Seeking to avoid reliance upon a conceptual framework which they have concluded to be useless, the Law Commission itemises a range of situations in which different conditions trigger access to recovery for negligently inflicted psychiatric loss, eventually coming up with around nine different categories of claimants. This is hardly a satisfactory situation. The Commission's extremely commendable exposition of the principles governing recovery in this area only serves further to underline their inadequacy as claimants rush to ensure that their own particular situations can be manipulated into one or more of the categories on offer. At the same time, the Commission's proposals in favour of limited legislative reform (including a 'fixed list' of secondary victims to replace the current *Alcock* criteria), while on the whole eminently sensible, are troubling in their failure to recognise the fundamental source of the problems the judiciary face – the focus on cause rather than need, particularly in situations where the need is so compelling.

Thus, the problems evident in the Hillsborough case go to the heart of the wrongs of tort. The social facts of the tragedy of Hillsborough – the pain and suffering of those killed and injured, the psychiatric disorders of those affected by what happened, the needs of all those who were adversely affected economically and emotionally by such an appalling tragedy – are clear. To some extent, those needs are even quantifiable, although the difficulties associated with trying to compensate injury and trauma with money remain (Chapter 3). But the needs of the victims are, in the first instance, irrelevant to a court of law. By translating the social facts into legal questions, we focus not on the need of the sufferer but on what could reasonably have been foreseen, on what consequences should be regarded as sufficiently proximate to the act of negligence and, most recently, on whether or not the sufferer qualifies as a primary or a secondary victim. Even then, it seems clear that answers are dictated neither by precedent nor reason but by imperfectly articulated policy concerns of questionable validity.

Strangely, however, while policy considerations remain crucial, even the Law Commission is loathe to scrutinise them *too* closely. Yet it cannot be said that policy decisions are not being made. Indeed, the choices which are being made are deeply political, reflecting a continuing ideology of personal responsibility, individual freedom and limited connection with others. Of even greater concern than the choices themselves, however, is the courts' refusal to recognise that they make these political choices, for it means that the factors which ultimately shape decisions are rarely openly addressed.

Extending the Scope of Immunity for Negligence: Omissions, Third Party Acts and the Liability of Public Bodies

Unfortunately for those seeking compensation for accidental injury, the courts appear more and more willing to deny a duty of care in circumstances where serious personal injury is a consequence of a tortfeasor's carelessness. For example, in recent years a local authority has been held to owe no duty of care for the careless failure to prevent the long-term neglect and abuse of five young children by their parents (*X* v. *Bedfordshire County Council* (1995)); the police owe no duty to a boy and his father who were stalked and injured by a deranged schoolteacher (the father, in fact, was killed), even though the police were fully aware of the teacher's dangerous proclivities and were called upon by the family on a number of occasions to intervene (*Osman* v. *Ferguson* (1993)); and a highway authority owes no duty of care to road users in relation to its failure to render safe an accident black spot despite the fact that it recognised the risk posed and failed to act out of sheer administrative incompetence (*Stovin* v. *Wise* (1996)).

The delineation of a wide range of circumstances where liability does not arise despite the occurrence of foreseeable physical harm belies the suggestion made by Stanton and others that: 'it must now be accepted that ... the test of reasonable foreseeability provides a workable general criterion for the imposition of liability in personal injury cases' (Stanton, 1994, p. 332). Cases such as those listed above are indicative of the unwillingness of the courts to allow free rein to reasonable foreseeability as the determining test of duty, even where personal injury is the primary or sole result. Regardless of the degree of carelessness, the courts are pursuing a course whereby particular defendants (largely, but not exclusively, public bodies) are in many circumstances rendered immune from the civil consequences of their wrongful acts. Of course, it might be argued that some of the cases in which a duty has recently been denied arise from facts which have not hitherto been the subject of negligence litigation; that, for example, suits against local authorities on the basis of their alleged failure to prevent the homicidal acts of deranged lunatics are instances of the modern trend towards civil litigation in contexts in which the affected parties would not previously have contemplated it (see, for example, *Clunis* v. *Camden & Islington Health Authority* (1998) and *Palmer* v. *Tees Health Authority* (1998);[27] in short, that the courts are not so much closing doors as failing to open them. However, while *Clunis* and *Palmer* may be viewed as distinctly modern in their conversion of horrifying acts of violence into questions of duty of care, decisions such as *Stovin* and many of those involving claims against emergency rescue services (see below) do not seem so far removed from standard tort fare, and their outcomes – denying liability on grounds of an absence of duty – are strikingly anti-intuitive. It is certainly troubling that if a fire engine, on its way to a fire scene, deviates for no good reason, it will attract no liability in negligence whatsoever. In the words of Stuart Smith LJ, if the fire service 'fail to turn up or fail to turn up in time because they have carelessly misunderstood the message, got lost on the way or run into a tree, they are not liable' (*Capital and Counties plc* v. *Hampshire County Council* (1997), p. 878). It is equally perplexing that a highway authority should be free to ignore warnings about potential sources of danger affecting the highway,[28] while the momentarily careless driver, who falls into the trap effectively set by the authority's dereliction, is left to shoulder full responsibility for any accident which results. What compels such apparently absurd outcomes? Can they rationally be defended?

A perusal of the relevant case law reveals recurrent themes which have traditionally presented difficulties in the context of determining duty. So, for example, many of the cases where liability has been denied have involved omissions rather than acts (*Stovin* v. *Wise* (1996); *X* v. *Bedfordshire CC* (1995)).[29] Simultaneously, these and other cases raise the spectre of imposing liability on one party for the careless, wilful or criminal acts of another (*Osman* v. *Ferguson* (1993); *Topp* v. *London Country Bus Ltd* (1993); see also *Palmer* and *Clunis* above, note 27), an outcome with which the courts have always felt uncomfortable because it conflicts with traditional notions of individual responsibility.[30] Finally, many of the recent cases where a duty of care has been denied despite the occurrence of personal injury involve action or inaction by public bodies, bringing into play a range of policy reasons for denying a duty (usually discussed under the *Caparo* rubric in terms of fairness and reasonableness), including (1) express consideration of the resource implications of imposing liability (*Hill* v. *Chief Constable of West Yorkshire* (1989), *Stovin* v. *Wise* (1996)); (2) a concern that liability will encourage defensive practices (*Hill*, *Stovin*, *X* v. *Bedfordshire CC* (1995)); and (3) a concern that the statutory functions of public bodies will be undermined by the imposition of civil liability (*Hill*, *Bedfordshire*; see also *Hughes* v. *NUM* (1991) and *Mulcahy* v. *MOD* (1996)) or that public bodies will be constrained in the determination of policy matters within the ambit of their discretion (see, in particular, *Hill* and *Bedfordshire*). This judicial fear of financially burdening or fettering the discretion of public bodies has led to the elaboration of a complex web of rules identifying the limited range of circumstances in which the exercise of statutory powers may give rise to common law liability (see the judgment of Lord Brown-Wilkinson in *Bedfordshire*, discussed in Conaghan, 1998, pp. 153–5).

Thus, a potent doctrinal cocktail comprising rules about omissions, third party acts and the liability of public defendants has generated a series of civil immunities which, while not impenetrable – see, for example, the successful breach of the police 'immunity' in *Swinney* v. *CC of Northumbria* (1996) and the more recent piercing of the *Bedfordshire* immunity in *W* v. *Essex CC* (1998) – are powerfully dissuasive of any recognition of a duty of care where these circumstances combine. In this context, the question of the liability of emergency service providers is a prominent point of convergence. Whether or not services such as the police, fire authorities, coastguard or even ambulances have a duty to respond to emergency calls immediately raises for consideration the question of liability for omissions: are professional rescuers under a *duty* to rescue? Their conduct in the course of rescue similarly raises the spectre of liability for the acts of a third party – to what extent should emergency services be responsible for damage which is not, initially, of their making (a fire, a road accident, an accident at sea)? Finally, the often public character of emergency service providers and the duties they perform raises to prominence the issue of correspondence between public and private duties – does the existence of a *public* duty to rescue create a private common law duty of care giving rise to a right to sue?

Perhaps not surprisingly, given the presence of so many factors problematising the issue of duty, the courts have been very reluctant to impose a duty of care on emergency care providers. As a series of recent cases reveals, the current legal position appears to limit the potential liability of emergency services to those situations in which their involvement actually operates to make matters worse than would have been the case had they not intervened at all. To this extent, the legal position corresponds closely to traditional doctrine relating to omissions for which, in the absence of an affirmative duty to act, no liability generally arises. Moreover, where, in such circumstances, a defendant does act, her liability will be confined to a duty not to increase the harm to the plaintiff as a result of her intervention (*East Suffolk Rivers Catchment Board* v. *Kent* (1941)).

With respect to emergency service providers, this position can be gleaned mostly from recent decisions concerning the scope of liability of fire services, although suits against the police (for example, *Alexandrou* v. *Oxford* (1993)) and coastguard (*OLL Ltd* v. *Secretary of State for Transport* (1997)) also lend support. In the 'fire services' cases, a series of claims against fire authorities were jointly considered by the Court of Appeal (*Capital and Counties plc* v. *Hampshire CC; Digital Equipment Ltd* v. *Hampshire CC; John Munroe (Acrylic) Ltd* v. *London Fire and Civil Defence Authority; Church of Jesus Christ of Latter Day Saints* v. *West Yorkshire Fire and Civil Defence Authority* (1997); for a thorough discussion of the issues raised by these cases, see Bagshaw, forthcoming). The *Capital and Counties* and *Digital* cases involved claims arising from a decision by a fire officer to turn off the sprinkler system as a consequence of which the fire spread more rapidly and eventually consumed the whole building. *John Munroe* involved the negligent inspection of a fire scene by firefighters during which they failed to detect a fire which later caused severe damage. *Church of the Latter Day Saints* considered the liability of a fire authority which failed to provide a proper water supply, contrary to a statutory duty under s. 13 of the Fire Service Act 1947, as a consequence of which the firefighters arriving on the scene were unable to fight the fire for some time. Although in each of the cases the firefighters actually attended the fire scene, the Court of Appeal began by considering whether or not they were under a common law duty to do so. Did the existence of a statutory *power* to act, in this case conferred by the 1947 Act, create a common law duty to do so? Relying *inter alia*, on the decision in *Stovin* v. *Wise* (1996), the Court concluded that a fire authority was under no duty of care at common law to respond to an emergency call-out. Their failure to do so could not, therefore, be actionable. The next question was whether or not, having turned up, fire authorities were under a duty of care to fight the fire competently. Did their presence at the scene create the necessary proximity giving rise to a duty of care? Again, the Court of Appeal ruled that no duty to take care arose, despite the existence of some authority to the contrary. As Stuart-Smith LJ made clear, where the emergency services created the danger which caused the plaintiff's injury, a cause of action would lie but, where, as in most cases, the relevant rescue or protection service merely responded to a danger created by a third party or an Act of God, then no duty of care arose, however negligent the rescue service's performance. The only exception to this general position lay where the acts of the rescue service increased the risk of danger to the plaintiff, and the defendant could not show that the danger would have occurred in any event. The Court concluded that the decision to turn off the sprinkler system in the *Hampshire* case fell into this category and the fire service should, therefore, be liable for the additional damage which resulted (on difficulties with the concept of 'additional damage', see Bagshaw, forthcoming). Interestingly, the Court of Appeal did not look sympathetically upon the range of policy reasons offered as grounds for denying liability (these included a concern that liability will lead to 'defensive firefighting' and related resource and insurance implications). Indeed, they expressed scepticism about the wisdom of creating blanket immunities on public policy grounds, preferring to rest their decision on the presence or absence of proximity.

The implications of the 'fire services' decision are portentous. Presumably, an ambulance service has no duty to respond promptly to a 999 call, nor do the police have an obligation to respond to a cry for help. In *OLL* v. *SS for Transport* (1997), which involved litigation arising from the Lyme Regis canoeing disaster in which four schoolchildren died, a court applied the fire services decision to hold that the coastguard owe no duty of care in relation to the carrying out of rescue operations at sea, other than a duty not to cause greater injury than would have occurred if they had not intervened at all. In fact, the plaintiffs argued that the coastguard, by misdirecting other rescue services involved in the search (a lifeboat and a Royal Navy helicopter) *had*, thereby, aggravated the harm. However, the parallel between this and turning off sprinklers was rejected by May J on the strange ground that misdirecting other rescuers did not amount to the infliction of direct physical injury on those in peril and did not, therefore, fall into the category of additional harm.

These decisions are troubling because of a sense we have that rescue services *ought* to be responsible if they do not do their job properly. Can it really be that an ambulance driver who stops on the way to an accident scene to get a hamburger is under no duty of care? Don't rescue services assume a responsibility (along *Hedley Byrne* lines) for the safety and well-being of those under their protection? Is this not a situation where a defendant has undertaken a task which he holds himself out as having a special skill and competence to undertake, a skill and competence upon which the plaintiff is dependent? In *Barrett* v. *MOD* (1995), a naval officer was held to have assumed a responsibility for a drunk and comatose airman and, therefore, to owe him a duty of care to ensure that he received adequate medical attention. Might it not be argued that once the fire or ambulance services intervene, they also assume responsibility for those whom they attend?

The sharp lawyer might respond by asserting the need for some evidence of detrimental reliance to create the necessary relationship of proximity. Surely, this is addressed by the requirement that liability will attach to the infliction of additional damage? But isn't there a more *general* sense in which we rely upon emergency services? If we could not rely upon the police to respond to a 999 call, we might act quite differently in relation to our personal safety in certain situations. If we were not sure the fire service would turn up, we might make arrangements for private contractors to fight our fires. Maybe, if we didn't rely upon the coastguard, we wouldn't go canoeing at sea. Such considerations of 'general reliance', which have some basis in authority (see, in particular, the Australian decision of *Sutherland Shire Council* v. *Heyman* (1985) in which Mason J expressly includes firefighters in his list of examples of those whose duties could be founded on such a concept), were in fact considered by the Court of Appeal in the 'fire services' decision but were dismissed as unsupported by English authorities. General reliance was also considered by Lord Hoffmann in *Stovin* v. *Wise*, but he was similarly unpersuaded of its relevance to the liability of highway authorities. It is probably fair to say that in neither decision did the concept get much of an airing, although, even in Australia, it seems to have lost its judicial appeal (see *Pyrenees Shire Council* v. *Day* (1998) which casts doubt on the utility of the general reliance concept).

The point is that there may be good doctrinal arguments for recognising a duty of care, at least in some of these instances. Practical reasons, such as the presence of insurance, might also inform a decision on liability. For example, in the fire services decision and in the suit against the police in *Alexandrou* v. *Oxford* (1993), the damage was merely to property and the practical concern of the litigants was whether or not the loss should be borne by the plaintiffs' insurance companies or whether it should be shifted to a public body, supposedly doing a difficult job with limited resources. As Mullis and Nolan (1997) astutely observe:

> Since most of these claims will ultimately fail, it all seems rather pointless, especially when one remembers that these actions are very rarely by the real victims of the defendants' negligence but are initiated by insurance companies and (as in *OLL*) primary tortfeasors seeking to offload their own liabilities onto the taxpayer. There in a nutshell lies the case for public policy immunity.

Nevertheless, while this makes some sense in the context of damage to property (certainly most real property will be insured), it makes much less sense where personal injury occurs. While insurance considerations clearly justify a denial of liability in *Alexandrou* v. *Oxford* (involving a negligent police inspection of recently burgled premises), they are of no assistance in defending the outcome in *Osman* v. *Ferguson*. While there are undoubtedly good reasons for protecting the integrity, viability and solvency of those public services charged with responsibility for the safety and well-being of the community, a legal regime where life is needlessly lost or impaired with no opportunity to secure proper redress, is, too, a far from desirable situation. It may be that these difficulties raised by considerations of equity and, in some circumstances, basic human rights may eventually generate overwhelming pressure for some public form of accountability in circumstances where tortious liability is denied. In particular, the imminent incorporation of the European Convention of Human Rights into English law by means of the Human Rights Bill may create a range of arguments for compensation in the event of public wrongdoing which are independent both of the doctrinal constraints of tort law and the particular concept of harm which it traditionally embodies.[31]

CONCLUSION

One object of this discussion of the duty of care in negligence has been to suggest that for all the myriad of precedents, the concept lacks not only objectivity but coherence and clarity. Rather than developing a coherent policy determining which classes of victims and which types of loss should be fully or partially compensated and by whom, the tort of negligence has developed an internal pseudo-logic of its own which has led to manifestly inconsistent and incompatible decisions. Furthermore, the resulting irrationality is not apolitical. When judges decide to whom a duty of care is owed in relation to emotional distress, when they determine that investors (and for some purposes even shareholders) have no right to rely upon audited company accounts, and when they determine that pure economic loss cannot be recovered in tort except in extraordinary cases, they are determining matters of policy. They are deciding that in some cases the losses of the unfortunate victim, though attributable to the carelessness of others, need not be compensated. 'Pragmatically', this may be because it is thought that recognition of claims could open floodgates, or because tortfeasors could be called upon to pay excessive compensation, or because the victim was better able to insure against the risk. But, a *choice* is being made – one which allows the loss to fall upon an innocent victim even when there is, arguably, someone to blame. Surely, the decision that a blameless victim should receive no compensation from a blameworthy party who could have been expected to foresee such a loss undermines the very foundation of the rationale of negligence?

The implications of this are immense. Because of the decisions of the courts in reinforcing individual responsibility for at least some of the vicissitudes of life, while failing to find logical distinctions to exclude others, even within its own terms negligence lacks the coherence that it claims. When this is recognised, it becomes appropriate to demand properly articulated and debated *political* answers to the problems of loss redistribution – answers in which the self-proclaimed 'pragmatism' and disingenuous avowals of 'principle' of negligence have no part to play.

3
Carelessness, Cause and Consequence

In Chapter 2 we argued that the concept of duty operates to legitimate policy decisions by the courts about when loss is to be redistributed. However, it would be a mistake to see this as the only variable open to judicial manipulation. In fact, all the central questions which require answers before liability will be established in negligence carry with them inherent problems without the possibility of objective resolution. It would be excessive to detail these problems similarly but it may be useful to briefly outline how such arguments might be made. We shall begin by considering some aspects of how a breach of duty is established and then go on to explore questions of causation, the criteria which determine the extent of damage for which a tortfeasor may be held responsible, and matters relating to the characterisation and assessment of damages. All these areas are obviously interrelated and to some extent overlap, both with each other and with questions concerning duty. Indeed, the traditional exposition of the law of negligence in terms of three component parts – duty, breach and damage – is arguably both artificial and misleading, artificial because it bears little relationship to how negligence issues are viewed and framed in the practical world of negotiation and settlement, and misleading in implying that the three components constitute three separate enquiries. This should become more evident as we proceed.

BREACHING THE DUTY OF CARE

The question of whether or not a duty of care has been breached is a question of standards. According to what (or whose) standards does one determine whether or not a person's behaviour amounts to a breach? The law's traditional answer to this question conjures up the presence of the ubiquitous 'reasonable man', a personage described by Atiyah as 'an odious and insufferable creature who never makes a mistake' (Cane, 1987, p. 37). Traditionally, the reasonable man has been invoked to represent an objective standard of care against which all are measured. He is thus devoid of all characteristics which make him human. By so denuding him of those 'idiosyncrasies of the particular person whose conduct is in question' (*Glasgow Corporation* v. *Muir*

(1943), *per* Lord MacMillan at 457), the reasonable man poses as the average man, thereby providing a single and universal standard purporting to correspond with reasonable behaviour.[1]

However, despite such pretensions, the objective character of the reasonable man has long been called into question (Cane, 1987, pp. 35–9). As Hepple and Matthews observe:

> The standard of care which is formulated is that of the 'reasonable man', but it is important to realise that he is a fictional character, the reference to whom is a thin disguise for the value judgement which is made by the judge. (Hepple and Matthews, 1991, p. 247)

Thus, despite his distinguished pedigree, the reasonable man represents little more than the subjective viewpoint of a particular judge. This, of course, begs the question as to exactly what that viewpoint is and how it is arrived at. In this context, it is frequently asserted that a judge's class, race, gender or other facets of his or her personal experience are likely to influence the decision reached. Given the still prevailing practice of recruiting the judiciary from an extremely narrow slice of human experience – English public school and Oxbridge (Griffiths, 1997) – any consistency in the standard which emerges is likely to belie its partial and subjective content.

One of the most sustained critiques of the reasonable man standard has come from feminist legal scholars who have argued that it embodies a male point of view, thereby holding women to a standard which was devised without them in mind (Bender, 1988; Martyn, 1994; Conaghan, 1997). This charge of 'maleness' goes well beyond a dislike of the gender-specificity of the standard as traditionally expressed. It is rather a critique of the *approach* which the reasonableness standard represents, an approach which assumes that behaviour can be fairly and objectively evaluated with only limited reference to the context within which it takes place and against a backdrop of abstract and incontrovertible principles which apply in all situations (Bender, 1988, p. 32; 1990a, p. 767; 1990b, p. 861). This form of reasoning has been identified as 'male' and contrasts with a more context-based approach to problem-solving which assesses situations of conflict with full regard to their particular context including the web of relationships which underlie them.[2] In this sense, the feminist critique of the reasonable man echoes a more widespread preoccupation in feminist scholarship with the concept of reason itself. Indeed the idea that reason might be gendered is a familiar theme in much feminist writing (for leading examples, see Lloyd, 1984; Anthony and Witt, 1993).

It therefore follows that it will not answer simply to abandon the gendered nomenclature of the traditional standard of care in tort and invoke instead the notion of 'the reasonable person' or a standard of reasonableness devoid of its anthropomorphic garb (as, for example, in the most recent edition of Atiyah's classic, Cane, 1993, pp. 28–31). Arguably, such a solution remains problematic because it relies upon the idea of a single standard and continues to deny the very real possibility of diverging concepts of reasonableness. In this context, some feminists have argued for the deployment of a gender-specific 'reasonable woman' standard, at least in relation to the assessment of behaviour about which men and women are likely to disagree (for example, what kind of conduct constitutes sexual harassment, Forell, 1992; Lester, 1993).[3] However, this suggestion has also proved controversial because it appears to imply that there is a single *female* viewpoint which represents the perspective of *all* women, howsoever situated. Not only does this invoke the notion of an 'essential' and immutable woman (with whom all must conform or have their 'womanness' denied) but it inevitably stereotypes and disempowers (Finley, 1989; Cahn, 1992).

At bottom, feminist debate about the reasonableness standard in tort law can be located within a broader philosophical enquiry into the possibility and desirability of invoking universal standards (Conaghan, 1996), a significant preoccupation of much postmodernist and feminist scholarship (Stanley and Wise, 1983; Anthony and Witt, 1993). For our purposes, it remains only to observe that the standard of care which is invoked and applied in the courts is likely to be both contingent (in the sense of representing a partial and subjective viewpoint) and controversial (in the sense of being a standard about which 'reasonable' people might well disagree). Most importantly, it is a standard which has no real claim to objectivity and no particular claim to authority beyond the fact that it is within the power of the judge to invoke it and call it reasonable.

Indeed, any lingering belief that there remains a significant measure of objectivity in the assessment of prudent and sensible behaviour is quickly dispelled by close examination of some of the leading cases in this area. The facts and decision in *Bolton* v. *Stone* (1951) are a good example. In the case, a member of a visiting team drove a cricket ball out of the ground on to an unfrequented adjacent public road where it struck and severely injured Miss Stone, who was standing on the road outside her house. Cricketers will be impressed (but not over-impressed) by the fact that she was nearly one hundred yards from where the ball was struck: the hit was a substantial but not exceptional one, in spite of the court's finding to the contrary. One question (*inter alia*) which fell to be answered by the court was whether the defendants (the committee and members of the club) were in breach of any duty of care owed to Miss Stone. Lord Radcliffe responded as follows:

If the test whether there has been a breach of duty were to depend merely on the answer to the question whether this accident was a reasonably foreseeable risk, I think that there would have been a breach of duty, for that such an accident might take place some time or other might very reasonably have been present to the minds of the appellants. It was quite foreseeable, and there would have been nothing unreasonable in allowing the imagination to dwell on the possibility of its occurring. But there was only a remote, perhaps I ought to say only a very remote, chance of the accident taking place at any particular time. (868)

Thus, said Lord Radcliffe, a reasonable man, taking account of the chances of the accident occurring, was entitled to do nothing and if the unlikely event did occur 'and his play turn to another's hurt, he would have thought it equally proper to offer no more consolation to his victim than the reflection that a social being is not immune from social risks' (869)! The crucial question then, according to Lord Radcliffe, was not 'was the harm foreseeable?' but rather 'was the conduct unreasonable?' and, in this context, the mere foresight of the possibility of some harm was not in itself sufficient to evidence a breach of duty.

When the *Law Quarterly Review* (1951, p. 460) commented critically upon the course and outcome of the case, pointing out that the injured Miss Stone was not only without compensation (she had sought £104) but was faced with legal costs in excess of £3000 simply for asking a court to determine whether or not the defendants had been negligent, they raised a question of some significance.[4] How can judges impart to this area of law a degree of certainty which avoids such a waste of endless and contentious litigation? *Bolton* v *Stone* (1951) achieves no such result. Although the case is well established and frequently cited,[5] other decisions do appear to contradict it, confirming the impression that the final decision of the court in such circumstances is very much a matter of judicial discretion. Indeed *Overseas Tankship (UK) Ltd* v. *The Miller Steamship Co Pty Ltd, The Wagon Mound (No 2)* (1967) provides an authority which is difficult to distinguish from *Bolton* but which offers a clear legitimation to any judge who chooses to disagree with it. Although the facts seem very different, they are analogous and give rise to more or less the same question. Through the carelessness of the engineers on the vessel *The Wagon Mound*, a large quantity of heavy oil overflowed from the vessel into Sydney Harbour. Some hours later, the oil ignited causing damage to *The Wagon Mound*, the plaintiffs' vessel and the wharf at which they were both moored for repair. Apparently, the owners of the wharf had been carrying out oxyacetylene welding and cutting on the repair of the plaintiffs' vessels. When the manager of the wharf saw the oil in the water he had been apprehensive and so discussed the matter with the manager of Caltex Wharf from which *The Wagon Mound* had been bunkering. He was assured that it was safe to proceed with the welding because, as bunkering oil has a very high flash point, it was not thought that it would be ignited when spread on water. Therefore he continued, with disastrous results. At trial, the court held that the officers of *The Wagon Mound* 'would regard furnace oil as very difficult to ignite on water'; that their experience would probably have been that this had very rarely happened; and that they would have regarded it as a possibility but one which could become an actuality only in very exceptional circumstances. From these facts the judge found 'that the occurrence of damage to the plaintiffs' property as a result of the spillage was not reasonably foreseeable by those for whose acts the defendant would be responsible' (426). Consequently he held that the claim in negligence failed.

Rightly or wrongly this finding seems consistent with *Bolton* v. *Stone*. However, on appeal to the Privy Council, the claim in negligence was upheld, their Lordships holding that the risk of ignition, though small, was, in the circumstances, a risk which the reasonable man should have and would have acted upon. In this context Lord Reid, while acknowledging that 'too much reliance was placed on some observations in *Bolton* v. *Stone*', asserted that

> *Bolton* v. *Stone* did not alter the general principle that a person must be regarded as negligent if he does not take steps to eliminate a real risk which he knows or ought to know is a real risk and not a mere possibility which would never influence the mind of a reasonable man. (at 642–643)

What *Bolton* did, argued his Lordship, was to exemplify those circumstances where it was justifiable not to take steps to eliminate a real risk because it was small and because the circumstances were such that a reasonable man would think it right to reject it. *The Wagon Mound (No 2)*, however, presented a risk, which, although so small that it 'could only happen in very exceptional circumstances' (at 643), was nevertheless one which could *not* justify inaction.

We have then, on the one hand, cases where it is justifiable to take no steps to eliminate a real risk if it is sufficiently small and/or is not one which, in the circumstances, requires a response and, on the other hand, total liability if the risk is *not* sufficiently small or if circumstances *do* exist meriting preventative action by the reasonable man. Clearly, a lot hangs on what criteria are applied to determine which risks may be regarded as sufficiently small or what circumstances are such as to justify action even when the risk *is* small. Yet, it is equally obvious that there are no answers to these questions except as subjectively determined by the court with the exercise of hindsight.

The above discussion suggests that the standard of reasonableness inherent in the concept of breach is in fact fairly indeterminate. It does not follow logically from the rules applied. At the same time, if there is any degree of consistency, it is ideological not logical. Confronted with the question of what standard to apply, judges invariably choose their own – the standard of the reasonable member of the Bar, not that of the traveller on the Clapham Omnibus. Far from being a neutral or even average standard, the standard of care reflects the views of a very narrow and select class in our society. This is particularly evident in judicial attitudes toward medical negligence.

In relation to operations with catastrophic and tragic results the standard invoked is that of the reasonable surgeon (someone with whom the judge may have had dinner or drinks at his club). The view of the reasonable patient is rarely considered and judges seem content to accept that in the course of surgery there is a category of errors distinct from the category of carelessness. Thus, in *Whitehouse* v. *Jordan* (1981), where the plaintiff alleged that an obstetrician was negligent in misusing forceps and thereby injuring her, the House of Lords held (with some regret given the gravity of the plaintiff's injuries) that the defendant's action did not depart from generally accepted standards of medical practice. Although it probably did amount to a 'mere error in judgment' (*per* Lord Russell, at 284), it did not constitute negligence.[6]

Whitehouse illustrates the 'hands-off' approach which British judges have traditionally adopted in relation to the medical profession (see generally Brazier, 1992, pp. 80–92). By allowing a wide margin of error in the absence of negligence, the courts produce results whereby many severely injured patients go uncompensated. Moreover, *Whitehouse* is indicative of a judicial tendency to defer to professional standards (a tendency which is by no means confined to the practice of medicine) rather than to seriously scrutinise them.

This tendency has been legally enshrined in the so-called *Bolam* rule (*Bolam* v. *Friern Hospital Management Committee* (1957)), applied by the House of Lords in *Maynard* v. *West Midlands Regional Health Authority* (1985) to hold that where there is a conflict of opinion between medical experts as to what constitutes a preferred practice, it is not open to the judge to choose one practice over another and on that basis hold the defendant negligent. If a defendant can show that she followed 'a general and approved practice' then she will generally be absolved from negligence even if a school of opinion exists in opposition to the practice.

This seems a very strange position to take towards professional negligence. Where a practice has obviously harmful consequences to patients and where such consequences can easily be avoided (for example, by giving the patient a warning of the risks, *Gold* v. *Haringey HA* (1988)), it is surely unreasonable not to seek to avoid those consequences. Moreover, just because a practice is common, does not make it reasonable. Yet the *Bolam* rule goes some way towards saying exactly that. Although the recent House of Lords decision in *Bolitho* v. *City and Hackney Health Authority* (1997) confirms the judicial right to hold a medical practice unreasonable and therefore negligent even where it satisfies the *Bolam* criteria, the courts have rarely done so (see, exceptionally, *Hucks* v. *Cole* (1993)). The British judge is arguably far too slow to condemn a practice as unreasonable unless the relevant professional body (in this case the British Medical Association (BMA)) has done so. This contrasts with the more interventionist approach of some American states where the courts have gone some way towards questioning the traditional deference to established practices (see, for example, *Helling* v. *Carey* (1974)).[7] The contrast between the two approaches is well illustrated by looking at how British courts have approached the American 'doctrine of informed consent' (*Canterbury* v. *Spence* (1972)).

According to this doctrine, doctors owe an obligation to plaintiffs to disclose all risks involved in medical treatment which the *prudent patient* would find necessary to give her consent. Although the obligation varies from American state to state, it places a much greater emphasis on the duty of doctors to disclose to their patients the risks of medical treatment than has hitherto been recognised in Britain. In *Sidaway* v. *Bethlem Royal Hospital Governors* (1985) the House of Lords considered whether or not to apply the American doctrine. Mrs Sidaway agreed to have an operation to relieve pain in her arm and shoulder. The operation carried with it a less than 1 per cent risk of damage to her spinal cord but Mrs Sidaway was not told of this risk. When, in fact, it materialised (causing partial paralysis), Mrs Sidaway sued. The House of Lords dismissed her complaint that her doctor owed her a duty to disclose the risk and rejected the doctrine of informed consent as forming no part of English law. Instead the legal standard of disclosure remained that of the 'reasonable doctor' with due attention and deference to prevailing medical practices.[8]

In *Sidaway*, the House of Lords declined the opportunity to tilt the legal balance in negligence in favour of protecting the physical integrity and autonomy of the patient.[9] Moreover, there seems little doubt that their Lordships' unwillingness to recognise the American doctrine was in part governed by (largely unarticulated) policy considerations. These are explicitly laid out by Dunn LJ in the decision of the Court of Appeal (1984), a decision which the House of Lords later affirmed:

I reach this conclusion with no regret. The evidence ... showed that a contrary result would be damaging to the relationship of trust and confidence between doctor and patient ... It is doubtful whether it would be of any significant benefit to patients most of whom prefer to put themselves unreservedly in the hands of their doctors ... The principal effect of adopting [the prudent patient test] ... would be likely to be an increase in the number of claims for professional negligence against doctors. This would be likely to have an adverse effect on the general standard of medical care, since doctors would inevitably be concerned to safeguard themselves against such claims, rather than to concentrate on their primary duty of treating their patients. (*per* Dunn LJ at 1030–1031; see also the judgment of Lord Bridge in the House of Lords at 662)

Sidaway illustrates clearly the policy-based content of the standard of reasonableness. It is not an objective test in the sense of being neutral as to political and social choices but is rather an expression of such choices. In the context of medical negligence, policy considerations abound and legal decisions cannot be understood without reference to them. Such policy concerns include, first, the fear that too much legal intervention (in the form of a stringent test of reasonableness) might impose heavy costs on Health Authorities and NHS trusts and thereby increase the costs of medical treatment (Weir, 1992, p. 157). Bearing in mind that these costs are, in the main, met by the public purse, the political implications are obvious.[10] Second there is a concern that doctors will engage in 'defensive medicine'. This fear has to some extent been borne out by changes in medical practices in the United States (Owens, 1988) although evidence of a similar tendency in the UK is inconclusive (Brazier, 1992, p. 115). Finally, a consideration which receives less attention in British negligence law is the need to balance these broadly medical considerations against a patient's right to physical autonomy and self-determination, 'a basic human right protected by the common law' (*per* Lord Scarman in *Sidaway* at 649). Judges have a responsibility to protect people, through (*inter alia*) the mechanism of tort law, from unwarranted physical intrusions. The danger is that too much deference to the medical profession ('doctor knows best') may constitute an unjustified abdication of this judicial responsibility.

Such policy concerns are undeniable. But is negligence law the best way to accommodate them? And are judges the best people to resolve them? Contemporary concern about the costs of medical litigation and the arbitrary results which it produces have led to calls for the introduction of a no-fault scheme in the context of medical accidents whereby plaintiffs might be compensated without having to prove fault on the part of a doctor or hospital and, indeed, with no need (save in exceptional circumstances) to engage in litigation.[11] There is arguably considerable merit in such a proposal, especially if the principle of compensation is prioritised (McLean, 1988; Brazier, 1992 and see further, Chapter 5). But the case is also strengthened by the contention inherent in the allegedly uncontentious standard of the reasonable man, particularly as applied to medical accidents. Far from assuming a neutral position, the reasonableness standard serves as a device whereby the judiciary can impose their resolution of the deep and conflicting issues which beset medical negligence with neither overt consideration of what those issues are or adequate explanation as to why a particular solution is preferable. Looked at in this light, the characterisation of the question of breach as one of 'fact', which judges can decide on a case by case basis, seems patently absurd. However, by so characterising the issue and thus suggesting that there is a correct factually-grounded answer, the legal conceptual framework disguises the policy operation taking place and the values and assumptions about 'right behaviour' generally which inform that operation.

Finally, in considering the question of breach, it seems appropriate to address (if briefly) the traditional articulation of those criteria which judges are supposed to see as relevant to the question of reasonableness. The identification by the texts of four common 'factors' comprising the enquiry into breach gives the whole process an aura of certainty and mathematical correctness. The four factors usually offered for consideration are: first, the likelihood or probability of the risk occurring (*Bolton* v. *Stone* (1951)); second, the gravity or seriousness of the risk if it does occur (*Paris* v. *Stepney BC* (1951)); third, the practicability of precautions (*Latimer* v. *AEC Ltd* (1953)) and fourth, the social utility of the defendant's risk-creating activity. Together these four interrelated factors are supposed to guide the judge to the 'right' decision. Of course, she is not told how much weight to give these considerations as against each other. The risk may be unlikely but the gravity great (*The Wagon Mound (No 2)*). At what point do these factors combine to denote negligent behaviour? The answer is, wherever the judges choose. Suppose that precautions are costly and the defendant's activity is socially useful. At what point is it non-negligent to do nothing to avoid the accident?[12]

A significant attempt to answer this question in precise mathematical terms is usually attributed to the dictum of famous American Judge Learned Hand in *United States* v. *Carroll Towing Co* (1947), although its elaboration is better understood against the background of a growing tendency in the 1960s and 1970s to analyse law in economic terms (see Chapter 5). According to this approach, the above-cited four factors can be expressed in terms of an economic equation, comprising three variables B, P and L. Assuming that B equals the cost of avoiding the accident, P represents the probability of its occurrence and L is the cost of the accident should it occur, then the following assertions can be made:

First, where B is less than P multiplied by L (PL), it is rational (that is economically efficient) to spend B to avoid incurring the cost of PL. In other words, it is rational (read reasonable) to avoid the accident. On the other hand, where B is greater than PL, that is where more would be spent avoiding the accident than is incurred by letting it happen, then it is rational (reasonable) to let the accident happen. To put it another way, it is not negligent to cause an accident in such circumstances.

According to economists, judicial attention to factors such as probability, cost of precautions and so forth intuitively expresses economic principles of efficiency (Posner, 1972, pp. 32–4). The test of reasonableness, so regarded, is both objective and ascertainable. It is, moreover, rational and in accordance with basic economic principles. The economic approach confers upon the test of reasonableness a great legitimacy. However, as is often the case with economic arguments, the attractions are more apparent than real. First, the goal of efficiency is assumed not argued for. Do we really want to measure human life in efficiency terms? Can we just assume that we do? Second, if the probability of the accident occurring could be accurately assessed the world would be infinitely simpler than it in fact is. Third, variables must ultimately translate into numbers if the exercise is to be worth anything. Cost/benefit analysis is reliant on some assessment of the costs and benefits. Economic analysis presupposes that we can accurately price such intangibles as life, love, nature and the environment, and tort law, in a haphazard sort of way, attempts to quantify them. But is the exercise anything more than (un)informed guesswork? And is our vision of human existence really so wretched that we feel comfortable about reducing everything to questions of efficiency and cost (Gorz, 1989, pp. 107–90; Bender, 1990a, p. 767)?

It is often said that the economic propositions cited above evidence the deterrent value of negligence (Posner, 1972). By imposing an obligation to avoid an accident only where it would be efficient to do so the law ensures that actors are deterred from taking inefficient risks while at the same time not discouraged from efficient risk-taking. But it has been more convincingly argued that, in economic terms, strict liability is a more efficient standard than negligence (Calabresi and Hirschoff, 1972). Moreover, the assumption that negligence law (or indeed any liability rule) will produce an efficient result assumes that all costs can be known and that an actor will be liable for them if they result from her negligence. But this is certainly not the case. The driver who negligently causes a car accident is not liable for the economic loss incurred by other drivers who are delayed because the accident has caused a traffic jam. Nor is the same driver liable for the medical expenses of a relative of the victim of the accident who suffers nervous shock as a result of the accident but does not fall within the criteria in *Alcock* v. *CC of South Yorkshire* (1991). How can the driver be forced to make the correct cost/benefit calculation if she is not required to include all the costs? How, in these circumstances, can she be deterred from socially inefficient activity? In addition, how can we be confident that the court will get its sums right particularly where it is up to the plaintiff rather than the creator of the risk (the defendant) to provide the information by which a cost/benefit calculation can be made?

It is tempting to conclude that economic analysis of negligence offers little in the way of certainty or correctness of outcomes and much that is ideologically objectionable in its shallow and impoverished view of human activity.

CAUSE

The concept of causation lies at the heart of the tort system for, in a broad sense, it determines who wins and loses in 'the forensic lottery' (Ison, 1967). Causation is a key concept in explaining the differential legal treatment of accident and disease (Stapleton, 1986). It also plays a significant role in shaping the organisation of and, indeed, constituting tort as a legal discipline by focusing on the cause of accidents as an important factor in their classification: accidents caused by products; by defective premises; by careless driving. The irrationality of applying different standards of liability depending on whether one is injured by a product or a car is disguised (if thinly) by the way in which such issues are presented and defined by traditional tort scholarship. Cause is a central organising category which compels a particular understanding of the problem of individual misfortune in our society.

In the context of negligence, causation is a necessary but not sufficient condition for liability. The defendant must be taken to have caused the injuries for which recovery is sought. According to traditional textbook formulation, the question of cause comprises two separate enquiries. First, the careless act must be shown to be a *cause in fact* of the injury suffered; and second, it must also be a *cause in law*. The latter enquiry, which involves determining at what point damage resulting from careless activity is too 'remote' to be recoverable is not really a causal issue at all in the sense that damage which is unquestionably caused by carelessness may nevertheless be too remote. Its characterisation, in terms of cause, while confusing, also serves to disguise the essential policy-based nature of the concept of remoteness (see below).

Cause in Fact

Establishing cause in fact, while in most cases straightforward, is by no means free of difficulties, conceptually or politically. The most common approach adopted by the courts and the commentators is to invoke the 'but for' test: if an injury would not have occurred *but for* the defendant's act, then the act can be said to be a cause of the injury. In *Barnett* v. *Chelsea & Kensington Hospital Management Committee* (1969), a man unknowingly consumed arsenic, became ill and was taken to hospital. The hospital failed to carry out a proper examination or to diagnose the poisoning and the man died. When the man's widow sued the hospital alleging that their careless examination had led to her husband's death the court found that the hospital had not *caused* the man's death because, even if a proper examination had been carried out and arsenic poisoning diagnosed, it would have been too late to save the man's life. Thus, it could not be said that *but for* the hospital's carelessness the death would not have occurred. The carelessness was not a cause in fact of the injury.

It is acknowledged wisdom that the 'but for' test cannot resolve all issues of causation and can even, on application, lead to absurd results.[13] But despite the fact that the logic of the 'but for' test sometimes defies common sense, it is generally regarded as a useful if limited guide to causal enquiry. It is important to point out that the plaintiff need not establish causation as a matter of certainty. So long as the defendant's act is, on the balance of probabilities, a contributing cause of the injury, the plaintiff's burden on causation is met. It is also the case that the act in question need not be the sole factor contributing to the plaintiff's harm. So long as it can be said that but for the defendant's careless act, the harm would, on the balance of probabilities, not have occurred, it does not matter that other factors were also present and activating causes.

So stated, the question of cause in fact seems fairly uncomplicated. But case law points to a contrary conclusion. In particular, difficulties arise in proving the necessary causal link where other possibilities compete. This problem is probably nowhere better illustrated than in *Wilsher* v. *Essex Area Health Authority* (1988). The facts are poignant and memorable, not least because the damage for which the plaintiff sued occurred in December 1978 and January 1979 and the House of Lords' decision, ordering a retrial (which never took place), was given on 10 March 1988! The plaintiff, Martin Wilsher, was born prematurely and remained for some time in a special baby care unit. While there he 'succumbed' to a known hazard of prematurity – retrolental fibroplasia (RLF) – which is an incurable condition of the retina, causing total blindness in one eye and severely impaired vision in the other. On the facts, it was unclear whether or not the condition was a result of his treatment by the hospital or an inevitable and unavoidable result of his prematurity. However, he sued the Health Authority alleging negligence, claiming that RLF was caused by an excess of oxygen tension in his bloodstream in the early weeks of life, attributable to a want of proper care and skill. It was accepted that mistakes had been made. In particular, in the first 38 hours after birth, in an attempt to monitor the partial pressure of oxygen in the arterial blood, a catheter with an electronic monitor at the tip was passed through into the aorta. In Martin's case the catheter was inserted into a vein instead of an artery by mistake so that the sensor, together with its sampling aperture, was wrongly located. It is standard practice to check the placement by X-ray but when this was done neither the house officer nor the registrar on duty noticed the mistake. The result was that false readings were provided by the monitor. The plaintiff alleged that the false readings led to excessive administration of oxygen in consequence of which RLF occurred. Peter Pain J, the judge at first instance, found that the failure of the registrar to notice from the X-ray that the catheter had been misplaced and the subsequent administration by the nursing staff of excess oxygen constituted negligence, for which the authority were liable (1984, unreported). In reaching his conclusion, Peter Pain J relied (*inter alia*) on the House of Lords decision in *McGhee* v. *National Coal Board* (1973)[14] which he interpreted as holding that, in a situation where a general duty of care arises, where there is a failure to take a precaution, and the very damage occurs against which the precaution is designed to be a protection, then the burden lies with the defendant to show that he was not in breach of duty and that the damage did not *result* from a breach of duty. In other words, Peter Pain J shifted the burden of proof on to the defendants.

The Court of Appeal (1986), by a majority, accepted Peter Pain J's application of *McGhee* (although they held the authority liable only in relation to the failure to observe the misplaced catheter in the X-ray). However, the House of Lords (1988) overturned the lower courts' decisions, deciding that the question of causation had not been considered satisfactorily and ordering a retrial in accordance with correct principles of causation: either the plaintiff must show that the defendants' actions had, on the balance of probabilities, caused his injuries or relief would be denied. Nor was he to be assisted by any recognition that the necessary uncertainty arising should require the defence to prove the absence of a causal link between their negligent conduct and the plaintiff's injuries.

In attempting to establish the cause of his unfortunate injuries, Martin Wilsher found himself in a difficult but by no means exceptional position (for a similarly tragic case of medical misadventure turning on the issue of causation see *Bolitho* v. *City and Hackney Health Authority* (1997)). Essentially, he faced two problems. First, he needed to establish that the carelessness of the hospital was sufficient to cause his disability; second, and more problematically, he had to show that the careless acts *did* in fact cause it. However, as the carelessness was merely one of a number of possible causes, and the others did not involve culpability and indeed might have been the inevitable result of his premature birth, how was it *possible* to show, on the balance of probabilities, that the hospital's carelessness affected his well-being? Moreover, how was the court to adjudicate upon the voluminous, expensive and conflicting evidence offered on causation?

Clearly, a retrial would not resolve any of these problems. And yet this is the precise solution prescribed (albeit regretfully) by their Lordships, Lord Bridge observing:

> To have to order a retrial is a highly unsatisfactory result and one cannot help feeling the profoundest sympathy for Martin and his family that the outcome is once again in doubt and that this litigation may have to drag on. Many may feel that such a result serves only to highlight the shortcomings of a system on which the victim of some grievous misfortune will recover substantial compensation or none at all according to the unpredictable hazards of the forensic process. (883)

Unfortunately, their Lordships' decision did little to lessen those 'unpredictable hazards' or their damaging effects on the plaintiff. In particular, by rejecting the lower courts' interpretation of *McGhee*, they expressly declined to ease the burden of proof for plaintiffs in complex medical cases.[15] Granted, this position is not in traditional negligence terms illogical, but not only does it highlight the shortcomings of the system overall, it also expresses a preference, in cases irresolvable by evidence, for the defendant (who, unlike the plaintiff, will often be insured). The result is that in such cases the loss will lie where it falls (upon the individual plaintiff) rather than being redistributed via the defendant to an insurance company (or the taxpayer). The outcome is a particularly grotesque manifestation of the fault principle because it might well be the case that Martin Wilsher's injuries *were* in fact caused by the hospital's negligence. Sadly, he could not prove it.

It might be asked, however, if the position (in general) would be substantially improved if the House of Lords had decided otherwise. The answer must be that the basic ability of the negligence system to provide a satisfactory method of compensation would be little altered. That the ability of a blind child and his family to obtain compensation should depend solely upon the proof of a causing careless act in no way relieves the need of victims whose identical disability is attributed to 'natural' causes even though the suffering will be indistinguishable.

Moreover, it is not entirely clear what approach to causation the House of Lords in *Wilsher* are directing courts to adopt. Certainly, it in no way directs itself towards solving, in any real sense, the extraordinary range of complicated questions which Martin Wilsher's case evidences. While their Lordships affirmed *McGhee*, they offered a very different interpretation from that adopted by the lower courts. *McGhee*, they stated, was simply an application of the principle established in *Bonnington Castings* v. *Wardlow* (1956): that where a defendant's negligence *materially contributes* to a plaintiff's harm then the defendant is a cause of it, even if he is not the exclusive cause. In *Wilsher*, had the plaintiff shown that the defendant's negligence materially contributed to his injuries (as distinct from merely increasing the *risk* of their occurrence) then causation would have been established.[16]

Yet, this is arguably an unnecessarily narrow interpretation of *McGhee*. It seems that, once again, the House of Lords declined the opportunity (provided in this case by the lower courts) to adopt a legal approach which would resolve an obvious injustice arising from the worst excesses of the fault principle. While couched in terms of discovering the true legal principle in *McGhee*, it was in fact a policy decision to protect health authorities rather than patients from 'the unpredictable hazards' of tort litigation. This is essentially the controversy at the heart of the *Wilsher* case from trial level to final appeal.[17]

Cause in Law (Remoteness)

There is an old nursery rhyme which runs as follows:

> For want of a nail, the shoe was lost,
> For want of a shoe, the horse was lost,
> For want of a horse, the king was lost,
> For want of the king, the battle was lost,
> For want of the battle, the war was lost. (Traditional)

Is the blacksmith, who failed to place a nail in the horse's shoe, responsible for the loss of the war? This is a question of remoteness.

Despite the rhetoric of full compensation, the law has always hesitated to make the blameworthy defendant pay the full cost resulting from his harmful acts. Winfield and Jolowicz observe that 'no defendant is responsible *ad infinitum* for all the consequences of his wrongful conduct ... for otherwise human activity would be unreasonably hampered' (Rogers, 1994, p. 155). The question is at what point should the line be drawn between damage for which the defendant must pay and damage from which he is absolved? One difficulty in drawing the line beyond which a tortfeasor should have no responsibility is that utterly blameless victims falling on the wrong side of the line will receive no compensation. The most important criterion the courts use for determining this line is, of course, foreseeability. A defendant will only be liable for damage which could have been reasonably foreseen (*Overseas Tankship (UK) Ltd* v. *Morts Dock & Engineering Co, The Wagon Mound* (1961)). Street, in stating that the courts have accepted the test of foreseeability laid down in *The Wagon Mound*, so that the harm suffered must be of a kind, type or class foreseeable as a result of the defendant's negligence, concludes that case law now makes it 'possible to a considerable extent to expound the law of remoteness with precision' (Brazier, 1993, p. 254). Curiously however, there then follows a brief but significant discussion of the contrast between two cases which highlights the shameful unpredictability of the test.

In *Bradford* v. *Robinson Rentals Ltd* (1967) the plaintiff was required by the defendant employers to drive an unheated van on a lengthy two-day trip. The weather was extraordinarily cold and the plaintiff suffered frostbite. The court held that the defendants, by exposing the plaintiff to severe cold and fatigue in the face of his protests and advice on the radio that only essential journeys should be undertaken, were liable. The defendants had wilfully exposed the plaintiff to a risk (severe cold and fatigue) which was likely to cause a common cold, pneumonia or chilblains, and frostbite was of the same type and kind as the harms foreseeable (even though of course frostbite while driving in England is an exceptionally rare phenomenon). Two years later, in *Tremain* v. *Pike* (1969), the plaintiff was employed as a herdsman on a farm owned by the defendants. He alleged that he had contracted a comparatively rare disease – Weil's disease or leptospiroses – as a result of the defendants' farm being overrun with rats – the carriers of the disease. The disease was in fact probably transmitted via rats' urine into water troughs or hay with which the plaintiff had contact. Payne J held that even if it were to be held that the defendants were in breach of their duty of care in not attempting to eliminate or control the rat population, and even if they ought to have foreseen that the plaintiff was, or might be, exposed to some general hazard involving personal injury, illness or disease in consequence of the infestation, they were nevertheless not liable because Weil's disease 'was at best a remote possibility which they could not reasonably foresee, and that the damage suffered by the plaintiff was, therefore, unforeseeable and too remote to be recoverable' (1307). He went on to add, in clear contrast to *Bradford*, that Weil's disease is not comparable to other human disabilities which may flow from an infestation of rats:

> The kind of damage suffered here was a disease contracted by contact with rats' urine. This, in my view, was entirely different in kind from the effect of a rat bite, or food poisoning by the consumption of food or drink contaminated by rats. I do not accept that all illness or

infection arising from an infestation of rats should be regarded as of the same kind. (1308)

The contrast between the two decisions is stark, yet each is decided in recognition of the principle that the damage sustained must be of the same kind as the foreseeable damage.

Furthermore, as has often been pointed out, there is at least an immediate tension between the *Wagon Mound* doctrine of foreseeability and the so-called 'thin skull' rule of *Smith* v. *Leech Brain & Co Ltd* (1961) – that is, there is an apparent conflict between a rule which requires that damage be reasonably foreseeable and one which provides that a tortfeasor must take her victim as she finds her. It is true that the two rules co-exist but their co-existence is uneasy since the defendant, whose victim is especially but invisibly vulnerable, may be liable for damage which, at least in quantity, it is quite impossible to say was foreseeable. Indeed the very kind of the damage which occurs might, except in the very broadest sense, be unforeseeable. For example in *Robinson* v. *Post Office* (1974), the plaintiff had suffered an injury at work for which the defendant employer was admittedly liable. Consequently, he was injected with antitetanus serum but, because of an allergy to the serum, developed encephalitis (an inflammation of the brain). To the argument that this was not a reasonably foreseeable result of the negligence Orr LJ simply stated:

> In our judgment the principle that a defendant must take the plaintiff as he finds him involves that if a wrongdoer might reasonably foresee that as a result of his wrongful act the victim may require medical treatment he is, subject to the principle of *novus actus interveniens*, liable for the consequences of the treatment applied although he could not reasonably foresee those consequences or that they could be serious. (750)

Indeed in *Smith* v. *Leech Brain & Co Ltd* (1961) itself the difficulty was dealt with by the court simply asserting that the *Wagon Mound* decision was given without having the thin-skull cases in mind, which consequently remained good law. In *Smith*, the plaintiff's deceased husband was injured at work when a piece of molten metal struck and burned his lower lip. The burn was treated at the time but did not heal. When the deceased was sent by his doctor to hospital, cancer was diagnosed and three years after the original injury he died. Holding the defendant employers responsible, the court decided that the burn was responsible for promoting cancer in tissues which were already in a pre-malignant condition as a result (according to the court) of the plaintiff's previous employment in a gas works where he would have been in contact with tar or tar vapours. Whatever one thinks of the court's medical analysis of the facts, the problem of reconciling reasonable foreseeability with the principle that a tortfeasor must take her victim as she finds her was resolved by simply asserting that this principle predated the *Wagon Mound* and must therefore be regarded as an exception to the rule. Quite why is not discussed, nor, indeed, are the consequences of this exception. What is clear, however, is that the justification of the foreseeability doctrine receives a mortal blow from the thin-skull rule.

The position is no different when one considers foreseeability and the *means* by which the harm was caused. The dominant position is expressed in *Hughes* v. *Lord Advocate* (1963). In *Hughes*, the plaintiff and his friend, aged eight and ten, entered a manhole in Edinburgh over which Post Office workmen, working on underground cable, had erected a shelter tent. When the workmen left the area after dark they placed red paraffin warning lamps by the shelter and took the ladder from the manhole and placed it on the ground. When the boys began meddling with the equipment the plaintiff, while swinging one of the lamps stumbled over it and knocked it into the hole. The result was an explosion which threw the plaintiff into the hole and severely burned him. The explosion occurred because paraffin from the lamp had spilled, vaporised and ignited. It was held that although this particular development of events was not foreseeable, the defendants were nevertheless liable for the negligence of the workmen because the type or kind of accident which occurred could reasonably have been foreseen even though the workmen could not have been expected to foresee 'all the possibilities of the manner in which allurements – the manhole and the lantern – would act upon the childish mind' (*per* Lord Guest at 714). Thus, states Street, 'the workmen's conduct created a risk of the kind of harm, i.e. personal injuries by fire, which materialised', producing a principle of law which holds that 'if harm of a foreseeable kind occurs it will normally be no defence that the precise mechanics of the way in which the negligent act results could not be foreseen' (Brazier, 1993, p. 255). However, *Doughty* v. *Turner Manufacturing Co Ltd* (1964) suggests that this principle is by no means clear.

In *Doughty*, the plaintiff was injured when the defendant's employees carelessly dislodged an asbestos cement cover over a cauldron of sodium cyanide which was at a temperature of 800° centigrade. The cover sank into the liquid and less than two minutes later caused the molten liquid to explode from which the plaintiff suffered burns. The explosion was unexpected and occurred because of a chemical change in the cover caused by heat. In the light of knowledge at the time, this explosion was accepted as unforeseeable. The plaintiff nevertheless argued that the accident was 'merely a variant of foreseeable accidents by splashing'. Given the authority of *Hughes* this would seem reasonable but it was held that the risk which materialised was so different in kind from the one that was foreseeable that the facts were distinguishable and Harman LJ stated that the actual damage 'was of an entirely different kind from the foreseeable splash' (102). It is obvious then that either *Hughes* or *Doughty* could have been decided differently without abusing precedent. Moreover, this is the point which is crucial. It should not be of concern to determine which, if either, was correct. The point is rather that each constitutes a subjective decision taken by the court and merely legitimated by precedent.

Sometimes, however, the courts do a very bad job of legitimation. Nowhere is this more evident than in the extraordinary judgments of the Court of Appeal in *Lamb* v. *Camden London Borough Council* (1981). This case flounders in confrontation with the sticky question of intervening acts, a question which has long left the law student (and the judiciary) in a state of complete bewilderment. In *Lamb*, the plaintiff's house was damaged by a burst water main for which the defendant council was responsible. As a result of the damage Mrs Lamb's tenant had to vacate the premises which, once empty, became occupied by squatters who inflicted further considerable damage on the premises. It was clear that the local council was negligent in relation to the damage inflicted by the burst water main. The issue was, was it also liable for the damage inflicted by the squatters, the intervening actors? Certainly, it could be said that but for the council's negligence the damage inflicted by the squatters would probably not have occurred. But was the council's negligence a cause in law of the damage or was it too remote by virtue of the intervening act of the squatters?

Approaching this question on the authority of *Hughes*, one might conjecture that although the 'precise concatenation of events' was not foreseeable, the damage was of a kind which was, in fact, foreseeable. However, there is authority to suggest that the question posed by the intervening act of a third party should not be resolved according to ordinary principles of remoteness. In *Home Office* v. *Dorset Yacht Co Ltd* (1970), Lord Reid suggested that a person should only be liable for the acts of another where they were very likely to happen. In other words, where an intervening act combines with the defendant's negligence to cause further damage a higher degree of probability of outcome is required before that damage will be attributed to the initial negligent actor. This approach was considered by the Court of Appeal in *Lamb*. Although unanimous in agreeing that the council was not liable for the damage inflicted by the squatters, the three judges differed drastically in their reasoning.

Oliver LJ made it clear that liability for intervening acts could not be resolved by ordinary principles of foreseeability. That would lead to too wide a range of liability. He therefore warmed to Lord Reid's test but considered it might not be stringent enough, suggesting in some cases the defendant should only be liable for the acts of another where they amounted 'almost to inevitability' (644). Lord Denning, on the other hand, was unimpressed either with reasonable foreseeability or Lord Reid's formula. He considered it best to approach the question as a straightforward issue of policy. On this view, he considered that as Mrs Lamb was primarily responsible for protecting her property from trespassers and as she was in the best position to insure against such a risk she, and not the council, should bear the loss.

Finally, Watkin LJ's musings tended towards a standard of reasonable foreseeability, while admitting that this test could not 'in all circumstances ... conclude consideration of the question of remoteness' (646). Undeterred however, he went on to suggest that 'a robust and sensible approach to ... remoteness will, more often than not, produce an instinctive feeling that the event or act ... is too remote' (647).

Weir describes these opinions as 'pretty desperate' (1988, p. 206). They certainly provide little guidance to subsequent courts as to how tricky questions of remoteness should be resolved. It is not therefore surprising, given the inconclusiveness of *Lamb*, that there followed a spate of cases very similar to *Lamb*'s facts, producing different results.[18] *Lamb* is surely evidence enough to the confused student that the question of intervening acts is not a mystery to be penetrated by sharpened legal skills and assiduous study. The fact is that judges simply do not know how to justify drawing the line on recovery where they do. They only know that they are comfortable drawing the line at that point. Watkin LJ's 'instinctive feeling' or Staughton LJ's invocation of 'common sense' in *Wright* v. *Lodge* (1993) (where the Court of Appeal were required to allocate responsibility in a motorway pile-up) expresses an intuitive sense among judges that to hold a person liable for the acts of another is essentially unjust and to be avoided. Individual responsibility requires that we are responsible for our own activities but not those of others. Moreover judges are often suspicious of attempts to bypass a tortfeasor in order to reach for a 'deeper pocket', a common enough feature of suits involving intervening actors. It is precisely because the actor immediately responsible for the harm (the vandal, the borstal boy) is not worth suing that the plaintiff seeks to recover from someone else further along the chain of causation.[19] There is a sense that such actors are less 'at fault' (even though they have been clearly negligent) because there is a greater distance between them and the harm done. But why should we assume that the greater the distance between act and consequence, physically, temporarily or otherwise, the less the responsibility? Is the director of a company any less responsible for the health and safety of her employees than the manager at site level? The tortious focus on individual responsibility tends to suggest that she is. By conceiving of human activity in individual rather than social terms (except when it suits the court to do otherwise – see note 12), by analysing harm in terms of the separate causal contributions of individuals rather than as the outcome of a social process, tort law not only fundamentally misrepresents the nature of social activity but provides a legitimacy for denying compensation to those who are harmed as a result of such activity. It is within this ideological framework that judicial (mis)handling of the problem of intervening acts must be understood.

More generally, we are suggesting that the position taken by most texts, in portraying questions of breach, cause and remoteness as ones to which the answers are reasonably clear, is essentially and critically misleading. The order they impose on the cases is an order which without fine and contrived distinctions (and the occasional convenient silence) would not exist. It is important to realise that, in a sense, the very existence of law reports evidences the considerable uncertainty of law. No case will proceed to appeal unless the appellant and/or her counsel believe that she has a reasonable prospect of success. So, whenever we have an appeal upon a point of law we have two parties each of whom is able to provide a substantial argument as to how the case might be decided in her favour consistent with the relevant authorities. The method of the appellate courts, to pronounce in a way which makes their decision seem an inevitable outcome of the issues, is beguiling. Almost paradoxically (and even if there are dissenting judgments), the apparent inexorability of the decisions is maintained.[20] For this reason, it can be a salutary lesson for a law student to consult the official reports which contain at least brief summaries of the arguments advanced by the unsuccessful side.

In turn, the courts' apparent perspective, which we suggest is demonstrably misleading, is reflected by the tort texts. They too tend to proceed as though the cases (usually) fit within an established pattern and their correctness is only questioned if it is argued that the wrong conclusion has been reached. Even in these rare cases, however, the argument is usually about the interpretation of precedent rather than about the policy which the cases represent. The recognition that the correctness of decisions lies not in their logic, wisdom or policy but in the power of those who make them, is seldom observed. But, by so viewing legal decisions, the game being played becomes transparent and the order of the textbooks and, indeed, of negligence appears contingent and contrived.

REMEDYING NEGLIGENCE

The primary remedy in negligence law is damages. In this context, there is an obvious distinction between damages for personal injury and damages for property harm in that, because property usually has a value in money terms, damages can be more readily ascertained.[21] While the aim of damages in tort is to place the injured party (as far as money can) in the position she was in immediately before the tort occurred, in cases of personal injury this often requires the most abstract calculations based upon premises which are quite uncertain. Few tort texts are without criticism of the process of calculation and many also express misgivings about the 'logic' pursued. But it is arguable that the process of calculation in which the courts engage is worthy of more than just misgivings but, on consideration, makes no less than a nonsense of what is done, providing a system which is quite indefensible. The intellectual tools used by the law to arrive at a final figure of compensation have few parallels outside the world of witchcraft and sorcery. Here, however, the bones which are cast to obtain a solution bear such names as 'notional loss of earnings', 'pain and suffering', 'loss of expectation of life' and 'loss of amenities'.

This process would probably have been replaced long ago if the full illogicality had been understood by the public at large. But it is important to remember that only a small percentage of accident victims recover any damages at all. The Royal Commission on Civil Liability and Compensation for Personal Injury (Pearson, 1978), chaired by Lord Pearson, concluded that only 6.5 per cent of accident victims actually recovered damages in tort. However, when these damages are added to the cost of other accidents in terms of social security, occupational sick-pay and private insurance, it was observed that this 6.5 per cent of victims received some 45 per cent of the total cost of compensation paid out (Pearson, 1978, Vol. 1, Table 4; Vol. 2, Table 158, discussed in Cane, 1993, pp. 17–18). It is clear then that tort victims who are successful in their claim do significantly better than those compensated in other ways.[22] A later survey carried out by the Oxford Centre for Socio-Legal Studies[23] found that 12 per cent of the survey sample of accident victims succeeded in a negligence claim. The success rate however was not uniform – 29 per cent of road accident victims received compensation in tort, 19 per cent of work accident victims, but only 2 per cent of all other types of accident victims, even though this represented the largest category of accidents suffered (Harris et al., 1984, p. 51). The tort of negligence, although obviously not central in the process of loss redistribution after accidents, is thus not insignificant.

The Oxford survey also discovered that only 14 per cent of accident victims reached the stage of consulting a lawyer, of whom a further one in seven then failed to obtain any damages (Harris et al., 1984, p. 46). The main reason for abandoning claims concerned the problem of proving the fact of the defendant's negligence. Of those who did obtain compensation, very few resulted in a contested court hearing

(Harris et al., 1984, p. 112; see also Pearson, 1978, Vol. 2, para. 516). Moreover, it was clear that the process of negotiation leading to an accepted offer often had little to do with the real damage suffered (thus fatally undermining the textbook claim that 'full compensation' is the primary remedy under the tort system). These facts led the authors of the Oxford survey to describe a claim for damages as a

> ... compulsory long distance obstacle race. The victims, without their consent, are placed at the starting line, and told that if they complete the whole course, the umpires at the finishing line will compel the race-promoters to give them a prize; the amount of the prize, however, must remain uncertain until the last moment because the umpire has discretion to fix it individually for each finisher. None of the runners is told the distance he must cover to complete the course nor the time it is likely to take. Some of the obstacles in the race are fixed hurdles (rules of law), while others can, without warning, be thrown into the path of a runner by the race-promoters, who obviously have every incentive to restrict the number of runners who can complete the course. (Harris et al., 1984, pp. 132–3)

If anything this underestimates the problems, the most significant of which is probably the time factor. Although the ten years between incident and order for retrial in *Wilsher* is exceptional, it is not unusual for cases to take years to settle. The average length of time from incident to settlement was 19 months according to the Oxford survey (Harris et al., 1984, p. 105) and although the figures in other surveys vary widely, the general impression of lengthy delays is confirmed (Cane, 1993, p. 233). Indeed, so great is the perceived problem of delay in the context of civil justice that it has spawned a wide range of proposals for reform (there have, in fact, been 60 reports in England on aspects of civil procedure since 1851!), including Lord Woolf's recent report to the Lord Chancellor on *Access to Justice* (Woolf, 1996). Woolf recommends the adoption of a three-tier system of civil justice comprising small claims, a 'fast-track' system for claims under £10,000 and a 'multi-track' system for other cases, with a significantly more active role for the presiding judge as a 'case-manager' – drafting timetables and eliciting information from the parties for the purposes of managing the case. The idea is to reduce delays and costs by channelling a larger number of claims into the lower courts and limiting the control of the parties over the pace set. However, the proposals have been criticised (*inter alia*) for paying too much attention to lawyer/litigant delays and too little to court-based delays (Watson, 1996). It is also alleged that they pay insufficient attention to the costs of such a significant shift of responsibility to the courts (Smith, 1996, pp. 23–5). Nevertheless, the Labour government is pursuing the implementation of the Woolf proposals, most of which are scheduled to be introduced in the spring of 1999.[24]

Difficulties associated with the financing of civil claims also limit the ability of accident victims to obtain redress through tort. Eligibility for legal aid absorbing or cushioning the financial risk has steadily fallen in recent years (Smith, 1995, p. 20) and is set to be virtually abolished in the context of personal injury litigation in the near future, to be replaced by an expanded application of the conditional fee system.[25] The costs rule (whereby costs generally follow the loser) further deters many claimants wary of incurring the risk of serious financial loss. Given, as the Oxford study reveals, that many of the sums recovered in settlement are surprisingly small – nearly three-quarters were under £1000 (in the years 1973–77), with half the amounts under £500 (Harris et al., 1984, p. 87) – it is likely that in many cases legal costs far outweigh the sum agreed in settlement.[26] Moreover, there is generally little point in suing an uninsured defendant; this goes a long way towards explaining why road accident victims, for example, are more likely to benefit from the tort system than those injured at home (Atiyah, 1997, pp. 102–3).

The recent introduction of conditional fee arrangements in the context of personal injury claims (whereby plaintiff solicitors agree not to charge costs unless the case is won) may go some way towards reducing the financial risks involved in civil litigation but the continued application of the costs rule means that plaintiffs, even under such arrangements, will still be exposed to (often very substantial) financial risks. In *Whitehouse* v. *Jordan* (1981), for example, the combined costs included the evidence of six eminent specialists and litigation costs over eight years, involving three Queen's Counsel, two junior counsel, and of course solicitors on both sides, with the injured plaintiff finally unsuccessful in the House of Lords.

But because the prize *may* be substantial and considerably more than is available through social security, it is unlikely that potential claimants will always be dissuaded from entering the obstacle race. But as we have said, even if the cause in negligence is established and the defendant is insured or able to bear the loss himself (as for example health authorities), still neither the plaintiff nor the legal advisers can predict the damages which will be received with any certainty. Such certainty as there is arises from consistency rather than logic. This point can be exemplified most clearly by considering the method by which the different heads of damages in personal injury claims are assessed.

The assessment of 'special damages' is far less problematic than general damages. Special damages are usually simply quantifiable. They include particular damage resulting from the tort including quantifiable lost earnings up to the time of the trial, and other expenses which the plaintiff has in fact incurred as a result of the tort, for example, medical expenses. They are thus distinguishable from general damages by virtue of their relative certainty. The loss has occurred and redress will be available upon proof.

The assessment of general damages is incomparably more difficult and less precise. The problems are twofold. First, there is the problem of translating such intangibles as pain and suffering, future loss of amenity, the loss of expectation of life, and even lost body parts into money terms. In considering the problem of attaching a money figure to losses not in the nature of things convertible into legal tender, Lord Hailsham rightly observed that 'Nor, so far as I can judge, is there any purely rational test by which a judge can calculate what sum, greater or smaller, is appropriate' (*Cassell & Co Ltd* v. *Broome* (1972) at 823). Second, there is the problem of predicting future events. Because the majority of negligence settlements are by way of a lump sum, an exercise in clairvoyance is demanded of the courts which can only rarely be accurate.[27] Thus, the court is often required to attempt an estimate of the plaintiff's future loss of earnings (an exercise not helped by the growing prevalence of job insecurity) and, indeed, her future medical condition. If this improves more quickly than is predicted the victim may be overcompensated; if the improvement is less or does not occur, she will be undercompensated. Although the latter difficulty can be avoided, to some extent, by the imposition of a 'provisional' settlement at the plaintiff's request whereby the court awards a provisional sum in damages but leaves open the possibility of a further award should the plaintiff's medical condition deteriorate (s. 32A Supreme Court Act 1981), such an arrangement will only be made where the plaintiff has specified in some detail the deterioration anticipated. Thus, its availability is still to a large degree conditional upon the ability of the plaintiff and her advisors to accurately foresee the future and, unsurprisingly, is rarely utilised (see further Lewis, 1993, para. 3.06 and Law Commission, No 224, *Structured Settlements and Interim and Provisional Damages* (1994)).

The approach of the courts to the uncertainties involved in assessing the loss of future earnings is illustrated in the well-known case of *Lim Poh Choo* v. *Camden & Islington Area Health Authority* (1979). At the time of the negligence (1973), the plaintiff, Dr Lim, was 36 years old and a senior psychiatric registrar. While in hospital for a minor operation, she suffered a cardiac arrest due to the negligence of persons for whom the health authority was vicariously liable. As a result, she became, in the words of Lord Scarman 'the wreck of a human being' (913), suffering from extensive and irremediable brain damage which left her only intermittently, and then barely, sentient and totally dependent upon others. Liability having been admitted, the only question for the court was the assessment of damages. In calculating these, Lord Scarman gloomily commented that

The award is final; it is not susceptible to review as the future unfolds, substituting fact for estimate. Knowledge of the future being denied to mankind, so much of the award as is to be attributed to future loss and suffering (in many cases the major part of the award) will almost surely be wrong. There is really only one certainty: the future will prove the award to be either too high or too low. (914)

The variables and imponderables which were nevertheless 'calculated' in assessing the net loss of the plaintiff are obvious. How long would Dr Lim have lived but for the accident? How long might she now be expected to live? Would she have continued working? Would she have been promoted? Would she have lost her job? How would inflation have affected her income? What taxation changes might occur that would have affected her future earnings? The court's approach in *Lim* and in general is to try to discover as far as is possible the net annual loss suffered by the plaintiff (the multiplicand) and then to multiply this sum by a notional figure (the multiplier) which reflects the predicted number of years of loss bearing in mind both the imponderables and the fact that the plaintiff will receive a lump sum which can then be invested. The expectation is that with investment income and with use of part of the capital each year, the sum awarded will accurately compensate the plaintiff for the number of years of loss so that at the end nothing will remain. As a consequence, the multiplier will not, obviously, equal the (anticipated) number of years lost but will in fact be a notional figure reflecting both the generation of income through investment of the lump sum and all those possibilities which might affect the plaintiff's future earnings (such as unemployment, premature death, career change and so forth). In other words, the sum *per se* does not express the years times loss but is rather an attempt to place a present value on future losses.

In Dr Lim's case, it was decided as a general principle that the effect of inflation upon the award should be ignored unless it was clear that such an assessment would produce an unfair result. Inflation up to the time of the decision could be taken into account but the court argued that there was no reason why tort victims receiving a lump sum should be better protected against inflation than others relying on capital for their future support (but see, in this context, the advantages of a structured settlement (Lewis, 1993)). Consequently Dr Lim recovered, in respect of her future loss of earnings, a capital sum which, after 'all proper discounts', represented her net loss of earnings over a period of years after allowing for working expenses, relevant tax and social security deductions (which may or may not be an accurate reflection of future rates) and other factors likely to affect her future income. A separate sum was also awarded for her 'cost of future care' including nursing/medical expenses but with an appropriate deduction for those 'domestic' expenses of which she was relieved by virtue of her dependent state.

Had Dr Lim had a reduced expectation of life (which, so far as could be accurately calculated, was not the case), the court would also have been faced with the problem of whether to compensate her for earnings during the period in which she would have been earning, were it not for the accident, but, in which she was now likely to be dead, as a consequence of the accident. Clearly, for this period she would have no need of earnings. In fact the courts have vacillated over whether or not to compensate for 'the lost years', finally deciding in *Pickett* v. *British Rail Engineering Ltd* (1980), that a *living* plaintiff (the right of action here does not survive the plaintiff's death) can recover the value of earnings over the lost years, less those living expenses which the plaintiff would have incurred by being alive.

It will be clear, then, that the assessment of future pecuniary loss is a haphazard business. The formula applied merely objectivates what is in fact a thoroughly subjective process. This problem of subjectivity becomes even more considerable when attempting to assess non-pecuniary loss. How does a court quantify pain, suffering and loss of amenities? Can and does money in any real sense compensate a victim for such harm (particularly in circumstances where she is more or less permanently unaware of it)? The tort system is unequivocal in awarding damages under this head – the greater the pain and suffering and perhaps appreciation of a future early death, the greater the award. Moreover, even in the case of the permanently unconscious, loss of amenities will attract a large award. In Dr Lim's case the sum deemed appropriate was £20,000 but the figure seems to have been one effectively plucked out of the air. Some commentators vehemently defend awards for non-pecuniary loss (Weir, 1996, p. 642) and greatly oppose proposals for their reduction, but others feel that a retrospective award for pain and suffering which has already been endured is in no real sense compensation but merely a windfall after an unfortunate experience fortunately caused by a tortfeasor.[28]

Damages for loss of amenity basically redress the plaintiff's inability to continue her lifestyle as enjoyed before the tort. The sums may be quite variable depending also on the age and lifestyle of the plaintiff. However, there is generally an approximate 'tariff' for particular losses based on the current level of awards being made by the courts which, through dissemination in practitioners' manuals (and more recently via the Internet), acts as a guide to parties in the course of settlement. The tariff for non-pecuniary losses is supervised by the Court of Appeal which, while producing consistency, is no less irrational. There is, in particular, a clear problem of judicial uncertainty as to the purposes of compensation for non-pecuniary loss: whatever the money provides, it in no sense puts the plaintiff into the position she would have enjoyed had the tort not occurred.

Thus, even if a decision is taken to fully compensate the victim of negligence, such is the impossibility of an adequate future prediction of the loss suffered and such is the impossibility of calculating non-pecuniary loss that the resulting calculation is scarcely defensible. Clearly, a rational method of compensation, if it is to have any relationship with reality, requires a move away from the crystal ball towards the continuing reality of the plaintiff's suffering and loss. It is in this context that moves to extend the availability of forms of periodic payments can only be welcomed (see note 27 above).

Finally, it might be useful to question the apparently universally held view that money 'compensates' for human suffering, a view which the tort system undoubtedly reflects and reinforces. It might be argued that this correlation between suffering and money is highly questionable. The assumption is that money will enable the victim to purchase the quality of life which might have been enjoyed but for the tort. Ironically, while most people acknowledge that money can never really compensate for injury, they continue, with the aid of lawyers, to concentrate exclusively upon money as a means of redressing the loss, as if those who are *disabled* physically can be *enabled* financially.

Implicit in this process is the assumption that the condition of disability flows from the injury since that is why the victim is compensated. In other words, tort law defines disability solely in individual and medical terms, as a personal tragedy which may or may not attract compensation, depending upon how it has arisen. By contrast, many 'disabled' people locate their disability primarily in social arrangements (Oliver, 1990) – in workplaces which deny wheelchair access, in modes of communication and entertainment which make little or no provision for those with hearing or sight impairments, in forms of transport which are designed only to accommodate the 'able-bodied'. Disabled people often feel that their greatest disability is being perceived by others as disabled and therefore 'different' even though they live in a world full of people of varied abilities. Thus, while it would be foolish to deny that the fact of impairment contributes to the experience of disability, it is also the case that disability is significantly the product of social perceptions and practices. Yet tort law, by focusing exclusively on individual impairment, reinforces a view of disability as a private, personal matter, not as a social product requiring a social response.

Likewise, the tort victim's acceptance of disablement as deriving from her physical (or mental) injury and her efforts to purchase social integration through an award of damages paradoxically prevents her integration except as a disabled person. Thus, the very concept of disability (as represented in tort law) is disabling in that it represents an acknowledgement of inability which is self-fulfilling. Tort law, by 'pricing' injuries for the purposes of compensation, judges and creates the victim as a truly disabled person.

More generally, tort damages represent the commodification both of parts of the body and of health in general. The reason the victim of personal injury is being compensated is because she is deemed to have lost *what she has owned*, whether it be an arm, a leg or the potential to work (labour-power). This translation of what one is into what one owns reduces people to their 'exchange-value' and their suffering to mere 'property damage'. As such it evidences a cheap and fundamentally impoverished view of human life.

4
Historical Perspectives on Negligence

> We must have factories machines dams, canals and railroads. They are demanded by the manifold wants of mankind and lay at the basis of all our civilisation. (*Losee* v. *Buchanan* (1873))

WHY NO HISTORY?

A marked characteristic of most conventional accounts of the tort of negligence (and, indeed, of legal doctrine generally) is the complete absence of any historical perspective. Leading textbooks (for example, Rogers, 1994; Brazier, 1993) make little or no reference to the historical origins of legal doctrine. Even texts which purport to be in some sense 'critical' (Fleming, 1987, p. v) or 'contextual' (Hepple and Matthews, 1991, p. v) lack any significant historical dimension. Such a seemingly glaring omission raises a number of important questions. First, and most obviously, *why* is history regarded as so completely irrelevant to an account of legal doctrine? Second, why is this neglect of history not more often noticed, criticised and commented upon? Finally, and perhaps most importantly, what is the effect of presenting legal doctrine in a timeless ahistorical way?

The most manifest effect of a traditional legal neglect of history is to render insignificant dates and times. Reading a contract text, it makes little difference to the student whether *Hyde* v. *Wrench* (1840) was decided in 1840 or 1940. What matters is that it supports the rule that a counter-offer does not make a contract. Likewise, in tort, the student of negligence attaches no particular significance to the timing of the finding in favour of the consumer against the manufacturer in *Donoghue* v. *Stevenson* (1932). She is not provoked to ask why the House of Lords decided then, and not before, to eschew the doctrine of privity and its dubious relevance to the availability of a tort claim. She is not encouraged to explore the wider 'social context' of *Donoghue* in terms of, for example, the huge expansion in the market for consumer goods in the twentieth century and the observable shift away from protection of industry (the manufacturer's immunity) towards protecting the consumer. For the student of the expository legal

81

tradition, dates are little more than a useful mechanism for organising and absorbing the relevant material.

In this way, law and legal doctrine are presented as timeless and ageless. The doctrine of consideration in contract appears not as a historical product of the social and economic conditions of the nineteenth century (for a different view, see Simpson, 1975), but rather as a universal principle of reciprocity reflecting man's underlying human nature. Likewise, the fault principle in tort emerges as the common sense embodiment of a concept of social justice which is good for all time. In other words, the absence of a historical perspective on legal doctrine tends to reinforce the view of law as consisting of a series of universally accepted and uncontentious principles of common sense rather than as comprising and promulgating historically and politically specific policies and values. To the extent that changes in legal doctrine *are* located historically – *Donoghue* v. *Stevenson*, for example, is often presented as laying to rest the 'older' principle of privity 'originating' in *Winterbottom* v. *Wright* (1842) – they are usually presented as the *application* of a general and universal principle (in this case the fault principle) to a novel situation. In other words, the 'history' of legal doctrine which is employed by conventional texts is not so much a history of the adoption and evolution of a principle or maxim but rather of its *discovery* and subsequent application.[1] Essentially, then, a neglect of history depoliticises law by robbing it of context. At the same time it deifies law by making it immortal.

A further effect of ignoring history is that it gives the student a sense of law as static rather than dynamic. Law is experienced as a set of relatively fixed rules which are simply 'there' to be applied. Thus, for example, no duty is owed in the absence of a relationship of proximity; a plaintiff can recover damages for nervous shock but not for ordinary grief; economic loss is generally not recoverable in negligence. Such highly rule-oriented assertions of legal doctrine in no way communicate the essential fluidity of the common law, its existence and manifestation as a living, moving thing. The textbook tendency to present a picture of the law 'as is' simply fails to provide students with the knowledge and understanding of legal discourse necessary to the process of 'lawyering'. By perceiving law as a framework of rules rather than as a series of arguments the weight of which varies according to time and circumstance,[2] students develop a rigid and unimaginative approach towards case law. They experience case analysis as a mechanical rather than as a creative exercise which, in the end, breeds technicians rather than advocates. It is only by viewing law historically that it can be understood as progressive rather than static; and it is that experience of law's dynamism and vitality which facilitates both an understanding of the system and an ability to manipulate it successfully.

Thus, the absence of any historical perspective in conventional pre-sentations of tort law has a significant effect on the way in which it is experienced and understood. It constitutes a particular 'knowledge' of law, but not one which easily admits to its partiality or to its imperialistic tendencies.[3] At the same time, by so constituting itself, the expository tradition has no need to explain or defend its cavalier disregard for the past because by its very nature, as a set of timeless and universal principles of which the cases are a mere elaboration, it has defined itself as ahistorical except in the narrowest sense accorded by the doctrine of precedent.

What is more curious, however, is the seeming failure of allegedly 'contextual' books to take history seriously. Hepple and Matthews' casebook for example, while quite self-consciously contextual, has no noticeable historical input whatsoever (Hepple and Matthews, 1991). Likewise, Stanton self-consciously addresses 'the modern law of tort' (Stanton, 1994) while Howarth devotes a (by textbook standards) generous five pages to the historical emergence of negligence (Howarth, 1995, pp. 26–30). In our view the failure by contextualists to address this gap in the expository legal tradition suggests that the 'law-in-context' approach to legal education itself operates with too narrow a conception of 'law' and, indeed, an equally limited conception of 'context'.[4] The idea of 'law' underlying most contextualist approaches is 'law-in-the-books', that is, rules. The idea of 'context' which they then superimpose on the textbook version is 'law-in-action', a euphemism which captures a wide variety of different enquiries and activities mostly concerned with the legal process: how law operates in the wider society and how it affects peoples' lives. While contextualists seek to divert attention away from strict obeisance to 'law-in-the-books' by bringing on to the agenda the issue of 'what really happens', they do not in any significant way undermine the understanding of law propounded in the traditional textbooks. Instead of redefining what constitutes law, contextualists merely surround it with a more attractive and digestible packaging. Thus, 'law-in-context' becomes a series of cases intermingled with bits and pieces of information about the background facts with additional random references to the social, economic and political setting. Above all, the concept of context most commonly employed is both immediate and contemporary. The focus is not, for example, on *why* we deny compensation to the victims of medical accidents in the absence of fault but whether we should, in fact, act differently. It is an essentially rationalist exercise which proceeds on the basis that a correct understanding of the nature of the problem (including its 'wider social context') will yield the correct solution. The mistake is to think that any understanding of the nature of the problem can be attained in the absence of an exploration of its history (including the history of why we understand it as we do).

Thus, 'law-in-context' is a misnomer in so far as it inexplicably excludes any attention to the historical context of law; consequently, it reinforces rather than undermines the timeless quality which legal doctrine assumes.

It seems obvious, then, that history is absent from both traditional and contextualist accounts of legal doctrine because they rely on a notion of law as essentially ahistorical. Is this in fact the case? Is there a history of negligence worth exploring?

HISTORY OR HISTORIES?

History is popularly perceived as a collection of facts. It is viewed as what *actually* happened in the past, as evidenced by dates and times, places and events, kings and queens. Equally popular is the idea that history is 'there' to be discovered and then absorbed as a form of knowledge which is essentially uncritical and unreflective. This idea of history as something relatively fixed and uncontentious attracts some powerful proponents. In the early 1990s, for example, in debates about the character and content of the proposed history syllabus in the National Curriculum, the Conservative Party emphasised the educational importance of teaching history as facts to be absorbed.

But, despite such high-ranking allies, the idea of history as fact has always been subject to considerable scepticism – certainly by historians and social scientists who realise that it is the *interpretation* of events and the *selection* of relevant facts which makes history meaningful. Indeed, it is arguable that history must always be partial both because it can never be more than an abbreviation of what has occurred and also because in necessarily omitting so many sources, a selection process will have been employed, a process which is invariably informed by the goals and values of the researcher.

More recently, the deconstruction of history as popularly understood has led to the emergence of a much more complex and multi-textured approach to understanding the past (where even 'the past' is not a concept whose meaning can be readily taken for granted). In the context of legal history, this means approaching the subject not in order to 'discover the truth' but perhaps with a view to exploring different layers of understanding as to how and why the law emerged and took the shape and form it currently occupies. There is, then, no *history* of tort but rather many different histories which stand in relation to each other not as competing accounts of the truth but rather as complementary pieces of a jigsaw so complex it can probably never be completed.

Let us look then at some of the histories which illuminate the law of negligence.

INTERNAL HISTORIOGRAPHY: PROFESSOR PERCY H. WINFIELD

In the 1920s and 1930s, Percy H. Winfield, original author of the eminent and enduring *Winfield & Jolowicz on Tort* (now in its 14th edition, Rogers, 1994), wrote a series of articles on the historical emergence of negligence. Most of what he wrote then still informs conventional legal approaches today. His definition of negligence as 'the breach of a legal duty to take care by an inadvertent act or omission which injures another' still reigns supreme (Winfield, 1926b, p. 184), and his presentation of the tort in terms of three component parts – duty, breach and consequence – is still the mainstay of most texts and syllabuses on the subject in the 1990s (Winfield, 1934, p. 41).

In his work, Winfield had an agenda: he was addressing a number of issues which were the subject of controversy at the time he was writing. His chief 'adversary' in this context was Sir John Salmond (Salmond, 1924). Thus, Winfield was at pains to establish the status of negligence as an independent tort as opposed to (in Salmond's opinion) 'merely one of the modes in which it is possible to commit most torts' (Winfield, 1926b, p. 184). Elsewhere he focused on the 'duty' component in negligence, questioning its utility as a separate requirement in establishing the tort of negligence (Winfield, 1934). He was also concerned with debunking 'the myth of absolute liability', that is, the idea that in legal terms 'medieval man generally acted at his peril' and was governed by a much stricter standard of liability than that which prevailed in the enlightened days of the early twentieth century (Winfield, 1926a). Finally, he engaged in a famous debate with Salmond about the foundation of liability in tort. While he favoured the view, propounded by Pollock, that tort law was based on some general theory of liability, Salmond inclined to the view that tort consisted of a number of specific and separate wrongs, the ingredients of which had to made out in order to establish a cause of action (Winfield, 1927).

The issues which Winfield addressed are still controversial even today. For example, Rogers, current editor of Winfield's classic text, inclines more to Salmond's view as to the basis of tortious liability, though he scrupulously avoids conceding this by observing that 'the difference between them is perhaps less than is sometimes supposed' (Rogers, 1994, p. 18).[5] However, the controversies themselves are not nearly as interesting as the general approach employed by Winfield in his endeavours to examine and resolve them.

Winfield's approach to uncovering the history of negligence was to focus solely on case law. From medieval to modern times he bounded back and forth from case to case, citing instances in support of an argument here and against a claim there (for example, in relation to the emergence of the concept of duty – Winfield, 1934, pp. 44–58). What emerged was a long and meandering narration mapping out what he perceived to be the 'relevant' cases and a story of negligence's birth and development which was in no way informed by or informative of the society in which those disputes arose.

The story which Winfield related ran something like this. The modern tort of negligence emerged from the old writ of trespass on the case. Until well into the nineteenth century private law actions were dominated by two cumbersome and mutually exclusive procedures known as trespass and trespass on the case (case). One essential difference in the use of the two procedures, certainly in the later period of their operation, was that trespass was deemed the appropriate form of action for injuries inflicted *directly* while case was the route to be pursued where harm was *indirectly* inflicted by another.[6] According to the old writ system, to use the wrong form of action, trespass instead of case or vice versa, was fatal to a plaintiff's claim regardless of the merits of the case. However, to proceed by way of case, particularly after the decision in *Williams* v. *Holland* (1833), was to incur less risk of issuing the wrong form of action (Winfield and Goodhart, 1933, p. 365).[7] Hence the emergence of negligence through an action on the case rather than through the writ of trespass and its eventual assumption of a status of independence quite distinct from the tort of trespass.

Winfield located the emergence of negligence as an independent tort in the early nineteenth century, although judges of the time, he maintained, had no more than 'sub-conscious appreciation of it' until Lord Esher's leading judgment in *Heaven* v. *Pender* (1883), (Winfield, 1926b, p. 196). At the same time he was anxious to establish its pedigree in terms of much earlier origins. Thus, he pointed out that certain persons by reason of their status, for example as common carriers and innkeepers (collectively described as 'those who profess competence in certain callings'), were liable for 'inadvertence' from medieval times, a liability which had extended by the time of Elizabeth to the 'farrier' although the cases of other professionals such as 'the ferryman, barber and carpenter' were more 'doubtful' (Winfield, 1926b, pp. 186–8). Thus, Winfield argued that negligence had always been present in English law as a mode of committing certain torts but that its independent status was of more recent origin.

Winfield's story of the birth of modern negligence, proceeding as it does on the basis of reading and interpreting case law (an interpretation which has not gone unchallenged – see, for example, Pritchard, 1964), can be described as an 'internal historiography' in its exclusive focus on 'distinctive-appearing legal things' (Gordon, 1975). Winfield's entire concern is with the technical aspects of doctrinal legal development – the exploration of precedent, changes in procedure, pleading and jurisdiction – in isolation from the society in which these changes and developments take place. Winfield's history thus defines itself very narrowly. The role of the legal historian is to uncover and articulate 'the law' as it has stood over different periods, as if that law can, somehow, stand self-evidently comprehensive and meaningful in abstraction from the context in which it was formed, operated and impacted on people's lives. Implicit in such an approach is the assumption that law need not and ought not to be assessed according to any external standards or values. The social and distributional impact of the rules, for example, is plainly irrelevant. Law measures itself – its frame of reference is its correspondence to the requirements of logic, rationality and coherence in rules. The legal historian can play an important role in discovering the 'order' beneath the apparent chaos of ancient cases. So Winfield sets about the task of 'ordering' his material, and what emerges is an apparently clear and sequenced picture of the relentless rise of negligence.

That such an 'ordering' can be selective and distorting is only part of the reason for approaching Winfield's work with considerable scepticism and doubt. More generally, it must be asked what does the internal historiographer tell us about law? The answer is, it seems, not a lot. Much more can be said about what such a history does *not* tell us. It tells us nothing, for example, about the kinds of society within which legal doctrines like negligence emerged and took shape. It tells us nothing about *why* a doctrine emerged or what role or function it served or what effect it had or was intended to have. An inevitable focus of history is on the nature and process of change yet the internal legal historiographer has little to say about legal change except to observe its occurrence.

Percy Winfield's history, moreover, tells us nothing whatsoever about the point of view, the values, the interests of the society which he is almost inadvertently entering and exploring. Looking at medieval life through 'modern' eyes, he approaches cases in a way which shows no awareness of the very different world his medieval litigants occupy. For example, Winfield, bent upon establishing 'the myth of absolute liability' in medieval law, points to many instances where the inflictor of harm was *excused* from penalty:

> A man may fight on behalf of his lord and a lord on behalf of his man. Such fighting is also permissible where a blood relation is unjustly attacked ... and where a man finds another with his wife within closed doors or under the same blanket or with his daughter, sister or mother. (Winfield, 1926a, p. 39)

For Winfield to posit these as examples of situations where *individuals* are immune from liability for inflicting harm on other *individuals*, thus evidencing his contention that absolute liability was a myth, seems extraordinary. The social world which he is describing is not one inhabited by 'individuals' at all but is rather a complex web of hierarchies and statuses, of masters and servants, husbands and wives, oppressors and oppressed. In such a world there is no single rule, or even a series of rules to which all individuals – separate, equal, independent – are subject. It is, therefore, arid to discuss in general terms whether the rule in medieval times was one of absolute liability or otherwise. The duties and obligations which fell upon the shoulders of the inhabitants of medieval society were determined by status or class and were not, in any case, predominantly 'legal' in the sense that Winfield would have understood the term. Winfield never for a moment considers the medieval world from the perspective of those who occupied it. Nor does he seem to be aware that to look at social arrangements from the viewpoint of the individual separate from society is a perspective of relatively recent origin and not one necessarily shared by 'medieval man'. Winfield misleadingly projects the present on to the past. At the same time he implicitly posits a relationship between law and society which is scarcely a relationship at all – their meetings, it seems, are as random as ships passing in the night. The fact is that the operating categories which we employ today are not necessarily the operating categories governing legal approaches in the seventeenth or eighteenth centuries. To doggedly employ them in our exploration of the past simply serves to distort rather than to illuminate.

Winfield's clouded vision of medieval law is characterised by a number of other questionable assumptions. Chief among these is the idea that the law is slowly but inevitably *progressing* where 'progress' is understood in terms of a gradual movement towards a principled coherence, a unity of form. His perception of the development of negligence bears all the hallmarks of an essentially teleological approach to history.[8] Negligence emerges from the chaos of the discredited writ system to form a new order based upon the apparent and self-evident soundness of the principle of reasonable care. Cases are examined and assessed according to their correspondence with this principle and decisions which fail to follow it are either wrong or distinguishable. The goal is to put the case law into some kind of 'scientific' order. Earlier case law is derided as 'unscientific' and liable to produce 'inconsistencies' (Winfield, 1926a, p. 42). Nineteenth-century judges are presented as moving 'subconsciously' towards the negligence principle while scarcely aware of it, directed inexorably and unerringly by the demands of logic and reason (Winfield, 1926b, p. 196).[9]

To regard law as inevitably and indiscernibly changing for the better is a common assumption of classical common law thought (Cotterrell, 1989, p. 24). It is also traditionally associated with judicial conservatism. After all, if judges are moving *subconsciously* towards the right decision there is no need to take any deliberate or conscious steps to bring about legal change. Indeed, the common law is celebrated by conservatives precisely because of its slow and piecemeal adaptation of the law to changing social conditions and is favourably contrasted to legislation which, in its attempt to impose change on the existing order, carries a high risk of failure (Hayek, 1982, Vol. 1, pp. 94–145). Thus, Winfield is no proponent of radical legal change. Confident in the knowledge of law's invisible process, he is loath to recommend judicial abandonment of a well-established rule even where he acknowledges that the rule in question serves no useful purpose (for example the 'duty' component in negligence (Winfield, 1934, p. 64)). As the common law weeds out that which is superfluous or redundant as a matter of course, there is no need to propose the need for any hasty gardening.

Winfield's perspective is conservative in another sense. It confers greatness on that which *is* on the grounds that if it were not, it would not be there. The existence of a rule is evidence of its wisdom and departures from it should in general be resisted. Radical departures are regarded as nothing less than subversive. This attitude has modern parallels. For example, what makes *Junior Books* v. *Veitchi* (1982) a primary candidate for judicial derision is its failure to properly respect the long-established rule against economic loss recovery (Chapter 2). The merits of the rule against economic loss recovery in negligence – whether in fact it serves any useful purpose – are largely irrelevant to any assessment of that case. It is the departure from the rule which is heretical. Thus, the perspective which characterised Winfield's approach to legal and, in particular, judicial change is still of great significance today, acting as a formidable brake on the process of legal reform whether judicial or parliamentary.

NEGLIGENCE AND ECONOMIC SUBSIDISATION: PROFESSOR MORTON J. HORWITZ AND THE TRANSFORMATION OF AMERICAN LAW

Although it is scarcely evident in the venerated texts of Britain's most famous tort scholar, Percy Winfield, his story of the rise of negligence coincides in time very closely with the course of the Industrial Revolution. Nor is this coincidence generally regarded as accidental or peripheral. Millner acknowledges the debt owed by negligence to 'the favourable climate of the industrial revolution' (Millner, 1967, p. 10), while the American legal historian, Laurence Friedmann makes the even stronger claim that 'the explosion of torts law and negligence in particular must be entirely attributed to the age of engines and machines' (Friedmann, 1972, p. 261). It is thus relatively undisputed that industrial development in the late eighteenth and nineteenth centuries is of crucial significance in understanding the rise of modern negligence.[10] More significantly, it appears that the idea of a causal connection between law and economic activity enjoys widespread if tentative acceptance. What is more controversial is the precise nature of this causal connection.

It has frequently been maintained that demographic changes accompanying the transition from a primarily agricultural to an increasingly industrial society, changes which brought the population out of the towns and villages and into much larger and more ephemeral urban settlements, had a significant impact on the incidence and character of accidents occurring and on law's role in relation to them. The legal historian, A. H. Manchester observes that improvements in transport from the mid-eighteenth century led to 'more people travelling more quickly' and, inevitably, increased the number of accidents on the roads, while the advent of the railway in the nineteenth century resulted in nothing less than 'carnage' (Manchester, 1980, p. 283).[11] It has been further maintained that the Machine Age generated the more frequent occurrence of accidents among strangers; that is, accidents between people who had no prior social relationship with each other and correspondingly no pre-existing, socially defined set of rights and obligations to resolve any likely disputes arising from such accidents (Ison, 1967, p. 2). This, it has been alleged, impacted on the legal system because, in the absence of any existing social mechanism for the resolution of disputes arising from such accidents, accident victims would increasingly turn to the legal system for redress (Abel, 1982, p. 19). In an era of increasing technology, and with the emergence of the factory system and mass production, even the relationship between master and servant was a relationship between strangers governed, increasingly, by the legal mechanism of contract rather than by traditional social obligations and entitlements derived and determined by status (Fox, 1974, Chapter 4; Selznick, 1969, Chapter 4).

At the same time, the advent of complex and dangerous machinery in the workplace and on the roads and rivers brought with it the potential for killing and maiming people in new and horribly inventive ways. The machines of the Industrial Revolution had, as Friedmann wryly observes, 'a marvelous capacity for smashing the human body' (Friedmann, 1972, p. 409). Thus, the legal system was confronted with increasingly complex causal questions, such as, for example, the difficulties in determining who, in the case of two joint actors involved in a collision on the roads, was the *cause* of the occurrence in circumstances in which both were active in relation to it (Horwitz, 1977, p. 95). How could a distinction be drawn between directly and indirectly inflicted injuries in such circumstances? The ancient writ system was forced to the limits of its flexibility in the confusion generated by the increasing difficulty of knowing by which form of action to proceed (*Lloyd* v. *Needham* (1823); *Williams* v. *Holland* (1833); see Epstein et al., 1984, pp. 70–3).

It is against this background of industrial accidents that Horwitz addresses the question of how and why negligence emerged and flourished in nineteenth-century American law. Of course, Horwitz's history is North American history and there are limits to its applicability in the British context (as Horwitz himself acknowledges – Horwitz, 1977, p. 89). But Britain, too, was in the throes of radical industrial change during the nineteenth century, although arguably at a different stage. There are certainly many parallels between the path of negligence in Britain and in North America, and Horwitz draws them (for example, Horwitz, 1977, p. 88; see also Cornish and Clark, 1989, pp. 483–538, for a similar analysis of the development of negligence law in Britain). At the same time, Horwitz is addressing a particular American agenda, one where fault and strict liability compete with each other for possession of the field of torts and his analysis is arguably highly coloured by this perspective. It remains nevertheless an excellent example of what Gordon calls 'external' legal history in its focus not just on 'the boxful of legal things' (such as cases), but also on the wider society within which 'legal things' are located, and for this reason, more than any other, it is a useful perspective to explore (Gordon, 1975, p. 11).

Horwitz's starting point is to see law in instrumentalist terms. For him, the period between 1780 and 1860 witnessed a 'transformation' in American law characterised by an increasing willingness on the part of judges to use law for particular ends; to shape the common law in pursuit of particular goals and to view decision-making as involving not just a consideration of the dispute at hand but of its wider social, economic and political implications also (Horwitz, 1977, pp. 1–3). Law, according to Horwitz, became an *instrument* in the hands of judges, a tool for the promotion of certain interests and objectives. In the context of negligence, this general contention takes the form of a particular allegation, namely that the fault principle prospered in nineteenth-century tort law because it was perceived by, *inter alia*, judges as a means of protecting nascent industry from the huge costs, in terms of accidents, generated by their activities. According to Horwitz, during the course of the nineteenth century, negligence ousted the 'ancient' principle of strict liability, expressed in the maxim *sic utere tuo ut alienum non laedas* ('use your land so as not to injure another'), from its pre-eminent position under the old writ system, gradually assuming a position of dominance in the field of unintentional injuries.[12] In this way, industrialists were relieved of the crushing burden which strict liability would have imposed upon their enterprises and it was carried instead by the accident victims themselves.

Horwitz goes to some lengths to show that negligence in the sense of carelessness was not a part of pre-industrial law. He acknowledges the occurrence of a concept of negligence in eighteenth-century cases involving the carrying out of public duties (for example the duty of a sheriff charged with the custody of a prisoner), and in some instances in relation to contractual duties (for example the duty of a common carrier towards his passengers and their property), but asserts that the meaning of negligence so employed is *not* that of carelessness but rather that of neglect or failure to perform a duty, that is nonfeasance rather than misfeasance (Horwitz, 1977, pp. 85–9). Carelessness, he maintains, may often have been alleged but was not a key component of the complainant's claim.[13] The shift from a concept of nonfeasance to a concept of carelessness was, Horwitz argues, almost imperceptible and occurred initially in the context of collision cases ('the running-down actions') at the beginning of the nineteenth century. Because they invariably involved 'strangers' who were also 'joint actors' (and thus not easily fitted into the traditional causal distinctions drawn by the writ system which presupposed an active tortfeasor and a passive victim), they directed judicial enquiry away from a simple investigation of cause towards a more complex examination of responsibility (Horwitz, 1977, pp. 88–9). Millner identifies a similar tendency in the English traffic cases (Millner, 1965, p. 23). In other words, judges increasingly tended to resolve the question of liability by asking *not* who caused the accident but rather who was *responsible* for it – who was at *fault*? Until around 1840 fault continued to be confined largely to highway accidents and collisions at sea but around that time it is suggested that judges began to recognise its liability limiting potential and began to use it more vigorously to challenge the 'settled' standard of strict liability. The history of negligence from this period onwards is, for Horwitz, a period where the fault principle increasingly encroached upon the terrain of strict liability as a direct result of its instrumental application by judges, with unjust and indefensible results in the field of personal injuries:

The law of negligence became a leading means by which the dynamic and growing forces in American society were able to challenge and eventually overwhelm the weak and relatively powerless segments of the American economy. (Horwitz, 1977, p. 99)

The imposition of a fault standard of liability on industrialists, in conjunction with a range of other common law doctrines such as contributory negligence (barring a plaintiff's claim where she had in any careless way contributed to the injury), *volenti non fit injuria* (barring a claim where the plaintiff was deemed to have accepted the risk) and the doctrine of common employment (whereby the plaintiff could not sue her master for injuries inflicted by a fellow-servant in the course of employment, see below), ensured that the cost of accidents was carried, in the main, by the victims rather than by the perpetrators of such accidents. Thus the legal liability rules effectively *subsidised* industry during this period by shifting the costs of entrepreneurial activity away from industry and on to workers, consumers and bystanders. In making this argument, Horwitz's identification of the dominance of strict liability in the pre-industrial era assumes considerable significance (see note 12). It is the *transformation* from a strict liability to a fault-based standard which is the focus of his attention and the basis of his claim that the judges applied the law in an instrumental fashion to promote the interests of industrialists. In addition, Horwitz raises questions about the social efficiency of 'legal subsidisation'. Did it, in fact, generate more benefits (in terms of industrial investment and production) than it imposed social costs (in terms of accidents) or did it promote 'an overinvestment in technology' and a consequent misallocation of resources? In economic terms, was legal subsidisation efficient? This is a question Horwitz feels ill-equipped to answer on the information available. He also asks why the subsidi-sation of industry took a legal form rather than by implementation through a system of direct taxation. While acknowledging that direct taxation was not then regarded as it is today – that is, as the obvious way of raising revenue – he also suggests that an equally significant reason for the use of legal rules rather than taxation was the desire to conceal the objective being pursued:

> What factors led antebellum statesmen generally to turn to sub-sidisation through the legal, rather than through the tax, system? One explanation seems fairly clear. Change brought about through technical legal doctrine can more easily disguise underlying political choices. Subsidy through the tax system, by contrast, inevitably involves greater dangers of political conflict. (Horwitz, 1977, pp. 100–1)

Thus, in his view, it was no mere accident that industry was subsidised by common law rules rather than by a system of taxation. The common law offered the best means of promoting the interests of capital over those of labour while at the same time avoiding the overt appearance of doing so. At the same time, it ensured that the main burden of promoting industrial activity fell not on the propertied classes, who would more obviously bear the costs of a system of taxation, but rather on those who could least afford to absorb the costs of industry and had least to gain from its protection.

How should we regard Horwitz's history? Unsurprisingly, Horwitz's analysis has been variably received. While many regard it as a

significant contribution to American legal history, it has also been the
focus of considerable attack and animus (see for example Schwartz,
1981; Simpson, 1979). Even worse, it has been treated by some as barely
worth acknowledging (see for example its conspicuous absence from
Prosser's leading casebook, Prosser et al., 1988). Undoubtedly, it is a controversial book. But where does the source of the controversy lie?

As Grant Gilmore, reviewing Horwitz, observes, much of what it
contains is scarcely new or contestable (Gilmore, 1977, p. 791). As has
been pointed out, the close and intimate connection between the
emergence of negligence and the Industrial Revolution is commonly
accepted. Of course, Horwitz goes further than merely observing an
intimacy. Adopting an explicitly 'instrumentalist' stance, he places the
formation of nineteenth-century torts law, shaped to the needs of
industrialists, right at the door of judges and 'antebellum statesmen'
(Horwitz, 1977, p. 100). The law has functioned to serve and perpetuate
the needs and interests of one class (capitalists) over another (workers)
and judges have willingly conspired in effecting this end. Even in
making this claim Horwitz is not without company. Wex Malone had
previously observed how nineteenth-century judges deliberately
fashioned the defence of contributory negligence in order to keep
negligence cases out of the hands of plaintiff-sympathetic juries
(Malone, 1946). Malone describes the process by which judges develop
doctrines to, in effect, control outcomes as 'judicial ingenuity', and far
from regarding it as controversial takes its existence very much for
granted:

> Courts wanted to control juries during the last century, they want
> to control them today, and they will probably want to continue to
> control them in the future. If we take away contributory negligence
> from the judges, they will find some other way. It's hard to beat
> judicial ingenuity. (Malone, 1946, p. 182)

Charles Gregory is similarly casual about judicial instrumentalism,
stating uncompromisingly (though without attribution), that many
judges of the nineteenth century embraced the fault principle as a way
of stimulating private enterprise (Gregory, 1951, p. 365), describing the
process as one of 'judicial subsidies ... to youthful enterprise' (p. 368)
which conferred on industry 'an immunity from liability for accidental
harm to others' (p. 382).[14]

What evidence is there to support these contentions? It is certainly
the case, both in England and America, that many judges and statesmen
of the day were aware of the way in which the fault principle and other
associated doctrines served the interests of industry. In *Ryan* v. *New York
Central Railway Co* (1866), a New York judge refused to apply even the
fault principle to a situation involving a negligent railroad company

whose carelessness started a fire which destroyed a number of properties, on the grounds that the burden inflicted by liability would be so great as to ensure 'the destruction of all civilised society'. He further observed that 'in a commercial country each man, to some extent, runs the hazard of his neighbour's conduct and each, by insurance against such hazards, is enabled to obtain a reasonable security against such loss' (*per* Hunt J, reproduced in Epstein et al., 1984, p. 311).

Thus, in *Ryan* the commercial climate was clearly relevant to judicial consideration of the imposition of liability. In England also there is evidence of an awareness of the impact of tort doctrine on entrepreneurial activity. In 1871 a Select Committee to the House of Commons, considering the doctrine of common employment (whereby a servant, injured by a 'fellow servant' in the 'common employment' of the master was unable to avail himself of the doctrine of vicarious liability entitling him to sue the master, but was confined to an action against his 'fellow servant'), concluded, in favour of the doctrine:

> There can be no doubt that the effect of abolishing the defence of 'common employment' ... would effect a serious disturbance in the industrial arrangements of the country. Sooner or later the position of master and workman would find its level by a readjustment of the rate of wages, but in the meantime great alarm would be occasioned, and the investment of capital in industrial undertakings would be discouraged. (cited in Manchester, 1980, p. 291)[15]

Thus the direct impact of particular tort doctrines on industrial activity was recognised and indeed considered to be a legitimate rationale for their continuance.

Nor is there any doubt that the combined effect of various tort doctrines around in the nineteenth century *was* to limit the liability of industrialists for accidents caused by their activities. In addition to the fault principle, which imposed liability only when the defendant was careless – and even then subject to limitations such as the legal recognition of a duty *(Winterbottom* v. *Wright* (1842)), and the proximity of the damage *(Ryan* v. *New York Central Railway Co* (1866)) – the doctrine of contributory negligence which barred a plaintiff's claim where she herself had contributed to the occurrence of her injuries (*Butterfield* v. *Forrester* (1809)), and the doctrine of *volenti non fit injuria* (consent) which prevented a plaintiff from suing where he was deemed to have accepted the risk, for example, by working for an employer he knew to be engaging in unsafe practices (*Lamson* v. *American Axe & Tool Co* (1900)), ensured that in many situations the accident victim had no redress even where there was evidence of fault. Other doctrines which further hampered the pursuit of legal redress included the doctrine of common employment which, when applied strictly, virtually eliminated the possibility of a suit against an employer by an employee for an accident at work, and the common law rule extinguishing a tort action on the death of the plaintiff and denying any claim to other persons affected by the death (*Baker* v. *Bolton* (1808)).

But to show that nineteenth-century tort doctrines had the *effect* of subsidising industry is not to establish that they were *designed* for that express purpose. To show that the law functioned in a particular way is not to demonstrate that it was devised to function so. Thus, Horwitz and others may be claiming too much when they assert that judges used the law instrumentally to serve the needs of the capitalist classes. That is not to say that they did not. It is simply to assert that it cannot be assumed from the evidence of a class-biased effect that they *consciously* did. Horwitz certainly lacks the evidence to make a claim that 'antebellum statesmen' deliberately chose 'legal subsidisation' over a system of taxation to disguise their class-based intentions. At the same time, the very obvious coincidence of law and ruling class interests in the nineteenth century does beg the question(s) – what is the relationship between law and class and power in society?

For those who adhere to an essentially formalistic view of tort law as a neutral and systematic expression of common sense, Horwitz's arguments are anathema because they politicise law and present it as biased and one-sided. For those who accept that law is not a neutral body of rules but is, indeed, inherently political, the problem which Horwitz's analysis presents is its arguably crude and unsophisticated approach to law's partiality. To view law as merely an expression of ruling class interests is to present a reductionist account of the relationship between law and the wider social and economic environment within which it operates. While law may not be separable from society in the way in which traditional scholars such as Winfield tend to perceive it, it has, it is alleged, a certain internal dynamic which confers upon it a kind of 'relative autonomy', limiting its effectiveness as an instrument of class oppression. The historian E. P. Thompson describes the rule of law as an 'unqualified human good' because of the constraints it inevitably imposes upon the exercise of arbitrary power (Thompson, 1975, p. 266 and see generally pp. 258–69). Similarly, it has been pointed out that law, through both judicial and parliamentary mechanisms, came to the aid of nineteenth-century accident victims through the development of various doctrines and exceptions mitigating the harshness of the system still emerging. So, for example, *Davies* v. *Mann* (1842) introduced a doctrine which prevented the application of contributory negligence where the defendant had the 'last clear chance' to avoid the accident. The development of *res ipsa loquitur* ('the thing speaks for itself') in *Byrne* v. *Boadle* (1863) allowed the court in certain circumstances to shift the burden of proof from the plaintiff to the defendant who was held to be negligent unless he could show that he was *not* at fault. Statutes such as the Fatal Accidents Act 1846 alleviated the heavy burden of misfortune cast upon the dependants of fatal accident victims by permitting them, in limited circumstances, to sue for their loss, while the doctrine of common employment, although not formally abolished in Britain until 1948, was relaxed judicially by various devices and was in any case much less potent after the introduction of Workmen's Compensation in 1897. Similarly mitigating trends emerged around the same time in American law (Friedmann, 1972, pp. 417–27). Thus, as Friedmann observes, 'the law of torts was therefore never a perfect engine of oppression' (p. 417).

Why the legal system built an edifice brick by brick and then almost simultaneously dismantled it is a matter of some complexity. In part, it can, of course, be explained in terms of the changing political climate brought about by the extension of the franchise during the course of the nineteenth century, culminating in the granting of universal male suffrage in Britain in 1867. But it may also be the case that the dominance of the fault principle worked to some extent in favour of accident victims by gradually chipping away at pockets of tortious immunity from which the early industrialists benefited. In this sense, Horwitz may have been wrong to have focused so exclusively on the transition from a system of strict liability to one of negligence. While strict liability may well have occupied considerable space in pre-industrial torts law, it is also the case that in many situations the rule was one of no-liability. Robert Rabin, exploring historical approaches to tort law, argues that immunity was a much more significant device utilised by judges to protect nascent industry than the fault principle, which they regarded as more appropriate to 'inter-personal conduct' (Rabin, 1969, p. 58). More generally, Gilmore suggests that Horwitz tends to overstate the advantages of pre-industrial law at some stages, even going so far as to suggest that it embodied a system of values which reflected the needs and interests of the community as a whole in a way that the emerging capitalist legal system did not (Gilmore, 1977, p. 794). If Gilmore's point is that the feudal society which preceded capitalism was equally oppressive, equally ordered to favour the interests of the powerful over the weak, then it is incontestable. But there is, of course, another point which Gilmore appears to miss and which Horwitz *is* making, however obliquely. Law did assume a new significance in ordering people's affairs with the emergence of capitalism. Whereas in pre-industrial society, order was heavily reliant upon status and the social obligations which attached to it, law in the nineteenth century emerged as the primary expression of social order and tort law played a role in constituting and defining that order in the context of industrial accidents. In this sense, then, it may be possible to say that law takes a particular form and character in capitalist society or even that it is an expression of capitalist social relations. In this context, Horwitz's analysis goes some way towards revealing the nature and specificity of legal relations under capitalism.

NEGLIGENCE AS AN INDEPENDENT LEGAL CATEGORY: G. E. WHITE AND THE INTELLECTUAL ORIGINS OF TORT LAW

For Horwitz, the emergence of negligence and the reshaping of tort law in the nineteenth century was closely bound up with the process of industrialisation. His primary focus is on the relationship between legal doctrine and economic relations, in particular the relations of commodity production and exchange. G. Edward White challenges this almost exclusive focus on the economic determinants of change and points to the importance of intellectual trends in shaping and restructuring nineteenth-century tort law. While industrialisation played a role in developing a notion of fault in the sense of carelessness to resolve the increasing number of disputes between strangers (White, 1985, p. 16), he argues that the emergence of a *fault principle*, a principle which captured and expressed the basic essence of liability in a vast number of private law cases not governed by contract, was the result of intellectual analysis and synthesis of the existing case law by leading legal academics in 1870s America. Moreover, the same intellectual trend towards 'conceptualisation' led to the emergence of tort as an independent legal category as opposed to the collection of miscellaneous, non-criminal wrongs catalogued by Blackstone a century earlier (Blackstone, 1765–9, Vol. 3). Thus, White asserts that 'the emergence of torts as a distinct branch of law owed as much to changes in jurisprudential thought as to the spread of industrialisation' (White, 1985, p. 3).

To what 'changes in jurisprudential thought' is White referring? It is certainly the case that the second half of the nineteenth century witnessed a growing intellectual interest in a category of civil wrongs commonly if haphazardly subsumed under the mantle of tort. Indeed, until that period one could not accurately speak of tort as a category at all if the idea of a category implies some immediately identifiable and unifying characteristic(s). The existence, however, of a residual categoryless number of non-contractual, non-criminal wrongs encompassing the writs of trespass and case gradually generated some intellectual attention. Thus, the first American Treatise on Torts appeared in 1859 (Hilliard, 1859). Yet, in 1870, the famous American jurist Oliver Wendell Holmes Jr was still insisting that 'torts is not a proper subject for a lawbook' (Holmes, 1871, p. 341), although only two years later he was attempting to write his own 'Theory of Tort' (Holmes, 1873). Moreover, in 1874, Ames produced the first American tort casebook (Ames, 1874), and by the end of the century tort was a firmly established legal category with a fast-increasing literature to bolster its credentials (for parallel developments in England see below).

According to White, the intellectual popularity of torts in general and negligence in particular at the end of the nineteenth century was a result of an increasing academic trend towards 'conceptualisation', which he defines as 'the transformation of data into comprehensive theories of potentially universal applicability' (White, 1985, p. 6). In the context of torts, the vast disarray of case law became the 'data' and fault emerged as the 'comprehensive theory of universal applicability'. With the collapse of the writ system (abolished in most American states by the 1850s but already discredited by that time), the need arose to produce a new method of ordering and classifying the legal rules and principles generated by the system which had disintegrated, and in the course of the intellectual restructuring of this body of law, mainly encompassed by the old writs of trespass and case, negligence as fault emerged as the primary standard of liability.

If one can imagine a jigsaw puzzle with the pieces scattered, the role of the academic, as perceived by Holmes and his contemporaries, was similar to that of the solver of the puzzle. The scholar gathered together the pieces (cases) and ordered them in such a way as to complete the picture (the general basis(es) of liability). In 1873, Holmes wrote that the law of torts could be sub-divided into three categories corresponding with absolute liability, liability based on intentional acts, and liability based on negligence (Holmes, 1873). In subsequent years his attention focused more on negligence as 'the common ground at the bottom of all liability in tort', questioning the historical existence of a standard of absolute liability (Holmes, 1881; Winfield, 1926a). In eight years Holmes had reinterpreted existing case law to eliminate or marginalise all vestiges of a strict liability standard while elevating fault to a position of unquestionable pre-eminence.[16]

The method of Holmes and his contemporaries was self-consciously 'scientific' and 'philosophical' (White, 1985, p. 8). It was scientific in that it brought a particular analytical approach to the study of case law (where law was subject to the same form of enquiry as natural phenomena), and philosophical in its quest for general principles, for a set of universal moral standards by which law could be understood and evaluated (just as the 'laws' of natural science provided a means of understanding the natural world). This scientific scrutiny of law included the formulation of hypotheses, their exploration among the available legal material and their verification and presentation in learned legal articles and casebooks. Eventually, it produced the rigid formalistic approach to law which characterised the American legal academy during the early years of the twentieth century (White, 1985, pp. 20ff), an approach not dissimilar in style and in substance to the British formalist tradition exemplified (above) by Percy Winfield.[17]

White argues that the emergence of this new jurisprudence reflected broader intellectual and philosophical trends sweeping the 'Victorian' American intelligentsia. He emphasises, in particular, the diminution in 'the role of religion as a unifying force' and the growth of secularism and scientificism as a source of intellectual and moral unity through the systematic and methodologically scientific 'ordering of knowledge'. Additionally, he points to a 'growing awareness of the value of individual autonomy' and an increasing societal attraction to the idea of individual freedom, making the fault principle with its moralistic tone and individualistic focus the 'natural' answer to the philosophical search for a universal principle of tort liability (White, 1985, pp. 4–6, 12, 19). Elsewhere, in examining the judicial tradition of the period, White draws connections between the academic search for 'scientific' principles and the political ideology of the day with its particular emphasis on the need for social stability and regularity to facilitate the making of market decisions (White, 1988, pp. 121–2, 126). In *The Common Law*, Holmes expressly espouses a *laissez-faire* approach to state regulation ('state interference is an evil where it cannot be shown to be a good') as a reason for letting losses from accidents lie where they fall unless they result from the fault of another (Holmes, 1881, p. 96). White is thus contending that both the emergence of tort as a separate legal discipline and the growth of negligence as the primary basis of tortious liability can be understood in terms of the intellectual trends of the day both within law and more generally.

Can similar claims be made about English legal development? It must at first be pointed out that in the area of tort theorisation, America led the way. Indeed, the first English treatise on tort, by Addison, appeared in 1860, a year after its American counterpart, while the first attempt to articulate a general theory of tort in England did not occur until Sir Frederic Pollock produced the first edition of his textbook in 1887 (Pollock, 1887). During the early years of the twentieth century, tort was as popular a subject for legal scholarship in Britain as in America. Indeed, although by the close of the nineteenth century Pollock's *Law of Tort* was in its fourth edition (1895), the idea of a general theory of tortious liability was still contentious when Winfield was writing in the 1920s, as was the claim that negligence operated as an independent tort (Winfield, 1926b; 1927). On the other hand, as early as 1883, Brett MR was attempting to devise a formula to capture the concept of the duty of care in negligence, thus suggesting that judicial attention was focused on the need for a rationalisation of the case law through the articulation of general principles (*Heaven* v. *Pender* (1883)).

It is also clear that during the period 1850–1907, a period which Sugarman describes as the 'classical period of legal education and scholarship' (Sugarman, 1991, p. 35), British jurists were similarly engaged in articulating a scientific approach to the study of law. Sugarman locates the emergence of such an approach in Oxford and identifies Pollock as one of its leading proponents (Sugarman, 1986). Indeed, in a lecture given in 1886, Pollock describes the task of the law teacher as guiding the student 'to the distinction of that which is accidental and local from that which is permanent and universal', self-consciously comparing the role of the jurist to that of the mathematician (Pollock, 1886, p. 463, cited in Sugarman, 1986, p. 30).

It is Sugarman's contention that the development of a legal scientific approach to the study of law was an attempt by legal academics to justify their existence by 'peddling' a 'special expertise' (Sugarman, 1991, p. 38), and he credits the Oxford jurists of the late nineteenth century (including the leading tort scholars Pollock and Salmond) with the construction of the 'black-letter tradition' with its emphasis on 'exposition, conceptualisation, systematisation and analysis of existing legal doctrine' (Sugarman, 1991, p. 38), which he maintains has continued to inform British approaches to legal education ever since (see Thomson, 1987). Like White, Sugarman does not view the exposition of law as science as a neutral exercise, but rather as rooted in the political ideology of the times. He points in this respect to the relationship between law, nationalism and imperialism (Sugarman, 1991, pp. 56–8), and identifies the juristic project as in part a response to problems of social order generated in particular by the extension of the franchise and the middle-class fear of 'majoritarianism' (p. 56). The scientific approach to law as to other disciplines provided the middle class with a cultural and intellectual basis by which to legitimate their continued control of the social order.

The presence of similar intellectual trends in the study of law in England and America does go some way towards explaining the approach taken towards tort law in particular by academics in both countries during the relevant period. But the evolution of an identifiable body of legal obligations based on relations other than contract, with the principle of no liability without fault at its heart, can also be located within the much broader framework of the essentially liberal values and assumptions informing the Victorian period. Arblaster has identified the rise of individualism as one of the earliest characteristics of modern liberalism (Arblaster, 1984, p. 95). The eighteenth and nineteenth centuries witnessed the emergence of philosophical perspectives based generally on individualism, that is, on the ideas that the individual can be conceived of and understood in isolation from others and from society as a whole (abstract individualism), and that his needs and goals possess value and legitimacy independent of society (individual rights). This tended to produce a version of liberal political philosophy which defined the limits of the state in very narrow terms and extolled the virtues of individual freedom from state interference (see, for example, J. S. Mill's 1859 *On Liberty* – Mill, 1974).[18] In addition, the work of 'classical' economists of the late eighteenth century and early nineteenth century (in particular Adam Smith and David Ricardo), which was widely interpreted as propounding the virtues of a free self-regulating market society, led to the popular espousal of 'political economy' with its concomitant championing of freedom of contract and the pursuit of individual self-interest (Taylor, 1972, pp. 18–31).

The emergent body of rules and principles which formed the content of the new independent legal discipline of tort, and, in particular, the judicial and intellectual emphasis on the fault principle, fit neatly within this broad framework of ideas. First, one can identify a strong consensual theme running through the tort of negligence. In 1931, Winfield identified a tortious obligation as one 'imposed by law' and thus distinguishable from an obligation which was 'freely assumed' by the parties themselves through the mechanism of contract (Winfield, 1931a). Although this definition implies that tort may be seen to run counter to the general nineteenth-century emphasis on consent as the source of legal obligation (exemplified most notably by the idea of freedom of contract), it is in fact misleading. Atiyah points out that early instances of tortious wrongs often took place in a 'relational' context where agreement between the parties was deemed, to a considerable extent, to define and limit the scope of the legal obligation (Atiyah, 1979a, p. 502). This is nowhere more obvious than in the context of work-related accidents where the doctrine of common employment and the defence of *volenti* might prevent the imposition of liability on a careless employer on the grounds that the worker had consented to the risk (see above). According to Atiyah, the legal obligation of due care was one which was initially viewed by the common law as 'something for which a man had to pay' (Atiyah, 1979a, p. 501). However, he identifies a shift in this view in the late nineteenth century as judges began to recognise that 'due care was something which a person was generally obliged to show anyway' (p. 505). Thus, he maintains that the tort of negligence can be viewed as evolving from a concept of legal obligation which was essentially contractual.

The relationship between negligence and consent is also highlighted by Holmes. In *The Common Law*, in the course of praising the virtues of negligence over strict liability, Holmes points to the advantage of negligence in presenting the individual with a choice as to the imposition of liability. A negligence standard allows the actor to avoid liability by *choosing* to be careful. Moreover, if he opts for carelessness he is deemed to have accepted the imposition of a legal obligation. The adoption of a strict liability standard allows no such room for individual choice. The actor is liable regardless (Holmes, 1881, pp. 88–96). Thus, negligence can be viewed as consonant with the general emphasis on consent as the source of political and legal obligation in liberal theory.

Negligence is also highly individualistic. Reflecting a view of individual responsibility, it carefully delineates the limited situations in which an individual should be liable for the misfortunes of another. Only when an individual is in some sense morally culpable should she be required to assume responsibility for the effects of her activities on others. This moralistic component in tort law is nowhere more evident than in Salmond's remark that 'reason demands that a loss shall lie where it falls, unless some good purpose is to be served by changing its incidence; in general the only purpose so served is that of punishment for wrongful intent or negligence' (Salmond, 1924, pp. 12–13).

Salmond's statement reflects not only the view that an appropriate reason for imposing a legal obligation includes 'punishment' but also the perception that absent some such 'good purpose' the law should not interfere at all. He thus articulates a point of view which places tort in general and negligence in particular within an abstentionist framework, that is a framework which posits the notion of a limited relationship between the state and the individual. This echoes the comments of Holmes (see above), and is suggestive of a strong correspondence between the espousal of the fault principle and the *laissez-faire* tradition. The limited imposition of obligations on the individual frees her to pursue her legitimate self-interest, and at the same time improves the lot of all (or most) by contributing to the total maximisation of wealth and happiness in society (but see note 18, drawing attention to the complex relationship between utilitarianism, as exemplified by Benthamism, and the principle of *laissez-faire*).

Thus does tort fit like a glove within an entrepreneurial spirit which swept the newly industrialised world in the nineteenth century. Thus also does White's history (and that of similar writers such as Atiyah and Sugarman) complement rather than compete with Horwitz's account. Indeed, even the approach of Winfield and his predecessors takes on a new and somewhat more valuable role when understood as a highly influential, fundamentally ideological product of its time. Perhaps the most important lesson to be learned from this brief tour of tort's history is the contingency and cultural specificity of ideas (such as the fault principle) which continue to retain an almost uncanny hold on modern consciousness.

What we have tried to show then, is the various ways in which the history of negligence may be perceived. At its least radical, it indicates that there is undeniably and unsurprisingly a relationship between the ideology of those with power in society and the content and operation of law. At its most radical, it serves to exemplify the proposition that, even in tort, one sees the exercise of power reflecting the interests of capital at the expense of labour. In any case, history demonstrates most powerfully the fragility of the ideology which is still expounded via 'the black-letter tradition'. For that reason, it is the first and foremost weapon of the subversive, in this case, the critical lawyer.

5
Negligence as Accident Compensation

The absence of history from conventional accounts of the tort of negligence is powerfully expressive. By saying nothing, tort texts are, in fact, saying something. By selecting what issues to address (and how to address them), the text directs the student towards these issues and away from others which, by virtue of their neglect, are passed over and forgotten. In this sense, traditional legal knowledge is highly coercive. Yet the student does not necessarily experience such knowledge as directed or coerced. Thus, while she steadily and conscientiously steers her course over well-trodden ground in accordance with a map which has been rigorously plotted, she is apt to miss much of what might pass as knowledge of negligence, were it drawn to her attention.

Clearly then, traditional legal approaches to law present a partial and incomplete picture. One solution to this problem of partiality is to generate and present a series of 'counter-images' of law, whether drawn from history (as in Chapter 4) or from contemporary political and social contexts. One such counter-image involves a consideration of negligence as a mechanism of accident compensation.

MEANS AND ENDS

If the compensation of accident victims is a social goal worth pursuing (Chapter 8), then the tort system in general and negligence in particular (as the primary tort concerned with compensation for personal injury) can be evaluated according to how well or how poorly it realises this goal. Negligence is thus viewed as a means to a particular social end – it becomes a function of the goal of compensation, relocated and 'contextualised', among other existing systems of compensation including social security and private insurance.

This reconceptualisation of negligence in terms of accident compensation does not fit easily into the existing scheme of traditional legal exposition. The texts do not concern themselves overtly with any particular goal which tort law is supposed to serve. Indeed the exposition and analysis of case law, the examination of decisions in terms of their legal 'correctness' (such as whether they comply with precedent or whether they successfully distinguish themselves from conflicting decisions), is presented very much as an end in itself. This is not to say that the texts or the writers of learned journals do not address the question of tort law's function (Williams, 1951). Indeed, much controversy has been generated over this issue between, for example, those who conceive of tort primarily in terms of compensation and those who attribute to it the very weighty responsibility of deterring anti-social behaviour.[1] Generally, however, although conventional texts do give some attention to competing accounts of tort's function, usually in an introductory chapter (Rogers, 1994, pp. 16–45; Brazier, 1993, pp. 3–13; Markesinis and Deakin, 1994, pp. 35–40), the themes there identified are not commonly integrated into textual discussion of individual cases throughout. In other words, most textbooks proceed on the assumption that case law can usefully be examined without particular reference to tort's competing goals. Thus, at the very outset, it becomes clear that the re-interpretation of negligence as accident compensation is at odds with the textbook approach, for while the former views negligence as a means to an end, the latter proceeds on the basis that ends are, for the most part, irrelevant.[2]

THE EMERGENCE OF AN ACCIDENT COMPENSATION PERSPECTIVE IN GREAT BRITAIN

In 1970 Patrick Atiyah published his landmark text *Accidents, Compensation and the Law*, the first title to be published by Weidenfeld and Nicolson as part of their 'Law in Context' series (Atiyah, 1970). The series, edited by Robert Stevens and William Twining, was a response to a perceived need to broaden the traditional perspective brought to bear on law and legal education by looking at law in its 'political, social and economic context' (Atiyah, 1970, p. xi). The idea was to explore 'law-in-practice' as well as 'law-in-the-books', to give students a much clearer picture of the role and operation of law in society.

Atiyah's book reflected this concern. In his Preface, he voiced doubts about the coherence and utility of that body of knowledge presented to students as tort law, pointing out that the traditional tort text had scarcely changed its format or approach since *Donoghue* v. *Stevenson* (1932), despite a subsequent 'revolution' in the law of negligence. Moreover, the traditional approach was unrealistic in its failure to take on board and explore policy issues. Atiyah suggested that torts should be presented in their different social contexts, a suggestion which carried with it the prospect of carving up and dismantling tort as then delineated, parcelling off different torts into other legal categories. For example, the 'economic torts' could be taught in labour law; defamation could form part of a civil liberties/constitutional law course; negligence could be taught as part of general accident law. In other words, negligence was best viewed as part of a complex structure of compensation mechanisms which included, *inter alia*, social security and private insurance. Only in this context could the tort of negligence be properly understood or assessed. Atiyah then proceeded to develop this interpretation of negligence which he hoped would bring about a significant change in the teaching and general perception of tort law (Atiyah, 1970, pp. xvi–xviii).

Unfortunately for Atiyah and without prejudice to his unique and monumental contribution to legal literature, the revolution in legal education which he hoped to bring about has never taken place. Most tort textbooks today are not significantly different in approach and organisation from texts in the time of *Donoghue* v. *Stevenson* (1932)[3] and, although 'law-in- context' has become something of a cliche in legal circles (far from revolutionary, it is regarded by many as comparatively tame), the general approach to legal education found in the academic texts, learned journals and nutshell 'crammers' continues to be predominantly non-contextual, formalistic and rigidly doctrinal. Although most tort scholars accept the validity or at least relevance of Atiyah's approach they have not significantly absorbed or utilised his insights. At the same time, when the case is urged for radically changing traditional approaches to teaching tort, it is commonly (but wrongly) assumed that significant change has already taken place. The perspective which Atiyah presented as novel and innovative in 1970 is now regarded as commonplace and self-evident (so much so as to require little attention in the leading texts).

Atiyah's evaluation of negligence as a mechanism of accident compensation was in keeping with the preoccupations of the times. In particular, he acknowledged the influence of American law reform and legal scholarship in shaping and informing his views (Atiyah, 1970, p. xviii).[4] The 1960s heralded a period of unprecedented tort law reform in the United States. Of particular significance was the introduction of strict products liability (liability for defective products causing harm, without proof of fault), by the Californian Supreme Court (*Greenman* v. *Juba Products Inc* (1963) *per* Traynor CJ), and its subsequent adoption by the Second Restatement of Torts, s. 402a in 1965.[5] The emergence of strict products liability generated a considerable body of literature about the goals and functions of tort law (for example, Calabresi, 1961; Fletcher, 1972; Epstein, 1973).[6] Significantly, the primary rationale given by Chief Justice Traynor for introducing strict products liability was compensatory. In *Greenman*, he relied on his concurring judgment in *Escola* v. *Coca Cola Bottling Co of Fresno* (1944) where he had asserted that

The cost of an injury and the loss of time or health may be an overwhelming misfortune to the person injured, and a needless one, for the risk of injury can be insured by the manufacturer and distributed among the public as a cost of doing business. (462)

Thus, Traynor's main objective was to *spread loss* by using manufacturers' liability and the price mechanism. His judgment in *Greenman* together with his reliance on *Escola* provided the precedent for the extension of strict products liability to most of the United States (Nolan and Ursin, 1995, pp. 88–105).

America in the 1960s also witnessed the emergence of economic analysis of law, a school of thought which assessed legal rules according to criteria of efficiency and wealth maximisation. Economic theorists, such as Calabresi, favoured the introduction of strict products liability but were less enthusiastic about the compensation rationale (Calabresi, 1961). Thus, for Calabresi, the principal motive for introducing strict liability was to bring about a more efficient allocation of resources by forcing the producer to internalise the cost of accidents (Calabresi and Hirschoff, 1972). By contrast, Richard Posner, another economic theorist, disagreed with Calabresi's advocacy of strict liability (Posner, 1973). Certainly it is clear that neither writer was enamoured with Traynor's loss-spreading goal and it is probable that their distaste stemmed from a deeper antipathy towards the concept of social insurance, which many saw as the logical political direction of Traynor's arguments (Calabresi, 1961). In any case, the economic analysis school, by bringing to bear on tort law a standard of evaluation which was external to rather than generated by legal doctrinal analysis, further added to the debate about the role and function of tort in American legal writing.[7]

Additionally, the rise in car insurance premiums in the United States had stimulated a search for cheaper alternatives to the litigatory model in the context of road accidents. In 1965 Robert Keeton and Jeffrey O'Connell published their *Basic Protection of the Traffic Victim* attacking the operation of the fault system in car accident cases and proposing a new 'no-fault' approach to accident compensation based on private insurance (Keeton and O'Connell, 1965). The insurance industry reacted favourably to the idea of no-fault auto insurance and proposed its own plan in 1968 (American Insurance Association (AIA), 1968). The political ball was now rolling and in 1970, Massachusetts adopted the first no-fault auto accident statute in the United States. By the mid-1970s, half of the American States had adopted some modified form of no-fault scheme in relation to car accidents.[8]

However, American influence cannot take all the credit for Atiyah's innovative approach to British legal education. His antipodean origins are also very much in evidence. Both Australia and New Zealand considered the question of accident compensation in the 1960s and early 1970s and in 1967 the Report of the Royal Commission of Inquiry into Compensation for Personal Injury in New Zealand, (Woodhouse, 1967) recommended the introduction of a state accident compensation system to replace tort law in the area of personal injuries. Variations on these proposals formed the basis of the New Zealand Accident Compensation Act 1972 which created a social insurance scheme for accident compensation in New Zealand.[9] Atiyah was of course well aware of the Woodhouse Report when he published his text in 1970. He was also aware of and indeed acknowledged the steady growth of a body of literature on accident compensation in Britain during the 1960s, particularly Terence Ison's *The Forensic Lottery* (1967) (which proposed a social insurance scheme for accident victims in the United Kingdom) and Elliot and Street's *Road Accidents* (1968), which proposed a state road accident compensation scheme (see note 8). Atiyah's particular contribution was to bring this 'new' approach to the study of tort law.[10] His book brought the accident compensation perspective into the classroom. It also, undoubtedly, reinforced the growing pressure on the political system to consider the question with a view to reform.[11]

In 1972, the story of the thalidomide tragedy exploded in the *Sunday Times* and the political momentum for change quickened significantly. Thalidomide was a drug taken by pregnant women in the early 1960s to relieve symptoms of nausea. The drug was marketed in Britain by Distillers Ltd who became the subject of suit by hundreds of children born with severe congenital deformities which, they alleged, had been caused by the thalidomide pill. The *Sunday Times* investigation highlighted the legal difficulties which the thalidomide children faced in their attempts to obtain compensation. There were doubts, first, as to whether a person could sue at common law for injuries inflicted *in utero*.[12] There were also innumerable problems involved in establishing negligence on the part of Distillers or the manufacturers. As a result of the public outcry which the *Sunday Times* story elicited, the children eventually obtained a settlement after ten years of negotiation. But the affair as a whole strengthened the call for an enquiry into the provision of accident compensation in Britain and the then Prime Minister, Edward Heath, responded in December 1972 by announcing the setting up of a Royal Commission on Civil Liability and Compensation for Personal Injury, chaired by Lord Pearson.

During the period of the Commission's investigation (it finally reported in 1978), the issue of accident compensation did not stray far from the political agenda. Britain's membership of the EEC in 1973 stimulated new debate about the question of products liability. Moreover, in 1976, the Congenital Disabilities (Civil Liability) Act was passed, vesting a right to sue in tort for damage inflicted *in utero*.

The mid-1970s also saw the emergence of another public outcry, this time over the alleged effects of the whooping cough vaccine, pertussis. Concern among parents about the possibility of brain damage resulting from the vaccination led to a dramatic reduction in the number of babies being vaccinated, from 79 per cent in 1973 to 38 per cent in 1976. Much of the publicity which the issue attracted arose from a vigorous campaign by the Association of Parents of Vaccine Damaged Children (APVDC) who drew attention both to the risks of the vaccine and to the legal difficulties faced by parents seeking compensation from the government. The question was referred to the Commission, which recommended in its final Report that the government or local authority should be strictly liable in tort for severe brain damage suffered by anyone as a result of vaccination recommended by them in the interests of the community. However, in the meantime, public pressure on the government to act was so strong that they introduced, as an interim measure, payment of £10,000 to anyone who had suffered vaccine damage. The authority to make the payment was created by the Vaccine Damages Payment Act 1979. Although described as an 'interim' measure, the Act has not since been replaced by any longer term strategy nor was Pearson's recommendation of strict liability ever adopted. The government's response to the vaccine damage scare was to find a palliative to quieten the dissenters and to postpone more serious consideration of the question to another day. Inevitably, neither the needs of the children the Act was intended to benefit were properly addressed nor were the anomalies which the singling out for special treatment of a particular group inevitably created, resolved or even acknowledged.[13] Instead the Vaccine Damage Payments Act 1979 (the payment is currently set at £30,000) represents a piecemeal, reactive and essentially incoherent response to the question of compensation. Ironically, its genesis and destiny provide a singularly fitting background to an exploration of the approach and conclusions of the Pearson Commission to which we now turn.

It is at once important to point out that the Commission saw its role as restricted by its terms of reference which were as follows:

> ... to consider to what extent, and in what circumstances and by what means compensation should be payable in respect of death or personal injury (including ante-natal injury) suffered by any person:
>
> a) in the course of employment
> b) through the use of a motor vehicle ...
> c) through the manufacture, supply or use of goods and services
> d) on premises belonging to or occupied by another or
> e) otherwise through the act or omission of another where compensation under the present law is recoverable only on

proof of fault or under the rules of strict liability, having regard to the costs and other implications of the arrangements for the recovery of compensation, whether by way of compulsory insurance or otherwise. (Pearson, 1978, Vol 1, para. 1)

The Commission interpreted these terms as excluding consideration of accidents taking place in the home and not the result of an act or omission of another. It further contended that such exclusions precluded it from considering the general question of whether the tort action should be abolished in cases of personal injury and replaced with a universal accident compensation scheme such as New Zealand had adopted in 1972 (see note 9). Thus, it viewed itself as unable to consider the merits or demerits of a New Zealand-type scheme. Such a narrow interpretation of the Commission's remit has been challenged (Atiyah, 1979b, p. 233) and indeed it certainly seems at odds with the general intention behind the setting up of the Commission which expressly acknowledged that the New Zealand scheme could be a subject of consideration. As the Lord Chancellor commented in the House of Lords in December 1972:

Of course I am familiar with the New Zealand work. As the noble and learned Lord is aware, there they have hit upon a particular scheme. So, in America has the State of Massachusetts and certain other States ... obviously the Royal Commission will want to examine both these and other types of possible model. (Official Report (HL) 19.12.72. Vol. 337, cols 974–5, reproduced in Pearson, 1978, Vol. 1, Annex 1, p. 391)

It seems difficult to accept in the light of this comment that the Commission was compelled to adopt such a narrow interpretation of its terms of reference. In any case it was not inhibited from straying outside its terms of reference where it perceived it was necessary to do so. For example, in the context of vaccine-damaged children, it recommended that *all* severely handicapped children (regardless of cause) should be entitled to an extra social security benefit, because it was often so difficult to ascertain the cause of such a disability (Pearson, 1978, Vol. 1, para. 292). The fact remains that after five years of effort, investigation and exploration, this Commission had nothing whatsoever to say about the viability or otherwise of a general accident compensation scheme.

If the Commission was not prepared to consider the abolition of tort actions in the field of personal injuries generally, neither was it prepared to present tort as the sole contender in the field. Its strategy was to promote a 'mixed system' where tort, social insurance and private insurance all played a part. Moreover, within the context of tort litigation it favoured an extension of the concept of strict liability to a limited number of areas such as products liability and a rather amorphous category of harms described by the Commission as 'exceptional risks' (Pearson, 1978, Vol. 1, Chapter 31).

The Commission took some pains to emphasise the need to see accident compensation in terms of a complex structure of provisions and entitlements which could be viewed and assessed as a whole. In this sense its approach mirrored Atiyah's pioneering reinterpretation of negligence as an aspect of accident compensation law for the purposes of legal study (Atiyah, 1970). However, the Report as a whole does not indicate that it took this interpretation particularly seriously. While the evidence reveals that only a small percentage of Britain's three million accident victims per year receive anything from the tort system (Chapter 3), suggesting that tort actions play a relatively minor role in the 'complex structure' being examined, the Report devotes a remarkable amount of time and space to the operation and vagaries of the tort system. For example, a large section of Volume 1 focuses on the assessment of damages in tort, while, elsewhere, the Report directs considerable energy towards examining the case for retaining tort in particular instances (industrial injuries – Pearson, 1978, Vol. 1, Chapter 17; road accidents – Pearson, 1978, Vol. 1, Chapter 18), invariably leading to the conclusion that an action in tort should be retained. Moreover, as Atiyah points out (Atiyah, 1979b, p. 233), in coming to such conclusions, the Report makes little use of and pays scant attention to its own evidence suggesting that tort is an expensive and cumbersome system which fails to produce value for money (Pearson, 1978, Vol. 1, para. 83). Thus while Lord Allen, one of the Commission's members has described tort as merely 'a junior partner in a joint operation' (Allen, 1979, pp. 7–8), the general tenor of the Report is to promote tort to the exalted position of Managing Director.

The influence of a tort vision of accident compensation is no more evident than in the way the Commission approached the classification of accidents, defining them in terms of how they are caused – by products, at work, in the air and so forth. This approach, which resulted in a multitude of chapters examining the adequacy of the compensation process in a series of discrete areas, is again a product of the way in which the Commission chose to interpret its terms of reference, and the end result is a text not significantly different in its general structure and organisation from the traditional tort textbook. Inevitably then, the Report echoes rather than critically explores the arbitrary and illogical divisions in tort law which determine the existence, scope and extent of entitlements.

The Report's main conclusions and recommendations illustrate this. For example, the Report recommends a social insurance scheme for road accidents (and the retention and improvement of a social insurance approach to industrial injuries); it recommends strict liability in the areas of dangerous products, 'exceptional risks' and in relation to vaccine-damaged children; it rejects the introduction of a no-fault scheme for medical accidents, leaving this contentious and troublesome area relatively untouched and likewise with respect to occupier's liability. The Report even shies away from recommending any significant extension of compulsory insurance. The result is a sense of confusion as to exactly what position the Report adopts and a feeling of unease about the varied and divergent methods by which accident victims are supposed to acquire compensation. Not surprisingly, the Report has been accused of being unprincipled, incoherent and 'the ultimate in the modern trend to "ad-hockery"' (Atiyah, 1979b, p. 227). At the same time, those whose allegiance lies wholly behind the tort system viewed it as a vindication of tort over the creeping evil of social security. As Tony Weir has commented: 'The law of tort has thus been subjected to a critical examination and has passed it' (Weir, 1979, p. 3).[14]

It is interesting to observe that those, like Weir, who advocate a principle of individual responsibility according to which 'people must put up with the harm they suffer in this life unless someone else is to blame for it' (Weir, 1979, p. vi) should have received the Report relatively warmly despite the Commission's own affirmation that it sought to shift the emphasis away from tort towards social security (Pearson, 1978, Vol. 1, Chapter 11). It is also significant that, although the Commission was at pains to emphasise that no-fault compensation was not a novel or alien creature to English law but was indeed a fundamental aspect of the English system of social security (Pearson, 1978, Vol. 1, paras. 176–7), it was nevertheless extraordinarily unwilling to embrace it in any extended sense. It seems impossible not to conclude that, aside from the statistical evidence which the Report generated (but barely used) and which subsequent writers have sought to promote more vigorously (Atiyah, 1980; Harris et al., 1984), the Pearson Commission was little more than a political charade and a tragic waste of a rare opportunity to promote and secure social justice.

If commentators of the time prophecied that its recommendations would not be implemented because of the inadequacies of the Report itself (Atiyah, 1979b, p. 227), the emergence of 'Thatcherism' in the 1980s proved more than strong enough to fell such a weak adversary. Conservatism in the 1980s proved antithetical to the compensation goal under consideration in Pearson in almost every conceivable way. Most obviously, the Thatcher government asserted from the outset its determination to cut public expenditure (Gamble, 1988, pp. 105–6) rather than extend it as 'a shift in emphasis from tort to social security' implied. More fundamentally, the government was committed to a reduction in the state's sphere of influence, an expansion of the private sector and the promotion of the 'free market'. This in turn reflected a growing disillusionment with Keynesian economics and with conceptions of the state's virtual economic omnipotence which had dominated British politics in the post-war period (Hindess, 1987, especially pp. 13–32). This hegemony of social democratic ideology with its concomitant assumption that government could and should intervene to regulate both the economy and the standard of living of its citizens, was exploded by the Thatcherist philosophy of the 1980s, which emphasised the limited role which government could play in both these spheres.[15] The idea of limited government is also echoed in Hayek's writing which expounds a theory of knowledge purporting to demonstrate the inefficiency of state 'organisation' promoting instead the 'spontaneous orders' of the market and the common law (Hayek, 1982).

Given the resurgence and popularity of such 'neo-liberal' perspectives in the 1980s and their adoption at least rhetorically by the government of the day, it is unsurprising that the quest for an improved system of accident compensation made little headway. As Atiyah enigmatically observed in 1980 'the political climate is unpropitious for any radical advances in the welfare state' (Atiyah, 1980, p. 18). Moreover, it is often said that the Thatcher era produced an 'uncaring society', a society where the promotion of the market and the emphasis upon individual economic rights led to the dismissal of poverty and misfortune as, at best, 'bad luck' and, at worst, a reflection of individual inadequacy for which neither the society nor other individuals should be held responsible. Indeed, it might be argued that a society which neither rewards individual enterprise nor encourages a sense of community responsibility for the misfortune of others, but instead invites all of its members to try their luck in the lottery of the market whose random distributions can neither be challenged nor condemned, inevitably produces a sense of indifference towards the project of realising justice and the good society.

ACCIDENT COMPENSATION AND THE WIDER SOCIAL AND POLITICAL CONTEXT

The discussion so far suggests a strong correlation between political and ideological trends and perceptions of negligence and the tort system. The emergence of a post-war democratic consensus about the power and responsibilities of government produced a climate within which the debate about accident compensation and tort's role in relation to it flourished. But already by the 1970s poor economic indicators, particularly high inflation and rising unemployment, called into question the perception that the state could and should solve the problems of its citizens, including those resulting from accidents and other misfortunes. In this context, the tort system reasserted itself as an attractive and well-established mechanism for allocating loss in such circumstances, avoiding excessive reliance on the state and facilitating individual resolution of disputes as they arose.

However, it must not be assumed that the political sensitivity of tort law is a particularly modern phenomenon. Nor did tort scholars and lawyers suddenly relate tort and the social goal of accident compensation for the first time in the 1960s. Indeed, in 1881, Oliver Wendell Holmes recognised the possibility of a social insurance system, remarking that 'the state might conceivably make of itself a Mutual Insurance Company against accidents and distribute the burden of its citizens' mishaps among all its members', but dismissed the idea as an unjustifiable intervention by the state in the affairs of the individual (Holmes, 1881, p. 96). Moreover, at the beginning of the twentieth century, debates in England and America about the provision of compensation for industrial injuries inevitably raised questions about the need for compensation in the case of accidents generally, leading to complex attempts to distinguish different types of accident for purposes of compensation. Thus, Professor Jeremiah Smith, a sworn disciple of the fault principle, when confronted with the Workmen's Compensation Acts at that time being enacted in many American states, gloomily observed that

> The result reached in many cases under the Workmen's Compensation Acts is absolutely incongruous with the results reached under the modern common law ... For this difference there is no satisfactory reason ... In the end one or other of the two conflicting theories is likely to prevail ... there may be an attempt to bring about State Insurance, not confined to hired labourers ... A State Insurance law may not merely insure against accident, but also against disease ... It may include damage wholly due to a natural cause, such as a stroke of lightning. (Smith, 1914, pp. 363–4)

Smith was concerned that the introduction of strict liability, compelling employers, through the medium of third party insurance, to absorb the cost of injuries at work, would unavoidably create problems because the situation of the worker could not satisfactorily be distinguished from that of other accident victims or even sufferers of disease. He viewed the erosion of the fault principle in the Workmen's Compensation Acts as leading inevitably and regressively to a system of universal social insurance for accidents and diseases (Nolan and Ursin, 1995, pp. 21–30).

In Britain also, the privileging of industrial injuries over other misfortunes raised questions of equity in relation to the boundaries of social insurance. In 1942, the 'Social Insurance and Allied Services, Report by Sir William Beveridge' (Cmd. 6404) considered the arguments for and against the industrial 'preference', concluding that it should be retained (Beveridge, 1942, para. 81).[16] This example shows that the question of how far the social security system should extend and assume responsibility for what has traditionally been the province of the tort system has never been very far from the surface of debate about the nature and scope of the welfare state. Yet there is no doubt that the question assumed a particularly high public profile in the 1960s and 1970s. Why?

One way of understanding such a change in legal focus might be in economic terms. Can we explain the emergence of an accident compensation perspective in terms of changes in the nature of the relations of production and exchange under capitalism? Negligence as fault, it can be argued, emerged in the shadow of an 'exchange model' of social relations embodied in nineteenth-century 'classical' contract law. Such an exchange model, based upon the idea that obligations are assumed voluntarily and for consideration, was well suited to the immature markets of early capitalism but ill-equipped to fit the increasingly complex web of economic relations emergent in the late twentieth century. An increasing division of labour, the expansion of technology and the specialisation of knowledge, all led to an interdependence in modern business transactions which could not easily be captured by a simple exchange model. The expansion of economic loss recovery in tort in the 1970s and early 1980s (*Anns* v. *Merton LBC* (1978); *Junior Books* v. *Veitchi* (1982)) can be cited as symptomatic of a general tendency of tort to encroach on the territory of contract in order to regulate economic relations which contract law could no longer contain. Inevitably such shifts in boundaries raised questions about the role and scope of private law and, with the emergence of increasing public regulation of business transactions, questions also about the role and scope of public law. The growing focus on accident compensation and its preoccupation with the merits and demerits of a public compensation scheme fit squarely within these more general concerns.[17]

An additional focus might emphasise the complexity of modern technology which inflicts injuries which are often either undetectable or unavoidable. Technology brought us thalidomide and pertussis. Both raised complex questions of fault and causation in the wake of which the tort system proved itself to be entirely inadequate. It has been argued by Morton Horwitz that the concept of fault was adopted by judges in the early nineteenth century to resolve questions of responsibility in accidents generated by the revolution in transport technology (Horwitz, 1977, p. 95). One might similarly argue that much of the modern disillusionment with fault stems from its growing irrelevance in the context of complex technology, with its ever-increasing ability to injure and maim in circumstances where its responsibility can never be properly attributed.

Another possible explanation for the emergence of an accident compensation perspective might be located in changing conceptions of social justice. Hugh Collins has argued that the modern law of contract can be understood in terms of a shift in the concept of justice away from values of liberty, equality and recipocrity ('the justice of exchange') towards an increasing emphasis on values based on state paternalism, fairness of outcome and social cooperation (Collins, 1993). Modern contract law, he suggests, has been reinterpreted and adapted as a distributive mechanism. Can similar claims be made about tort?

Clearly the conception of justice underlying tort law in the nineteenth century (expressed by the fault principle) placed a premium on individual responsibility and free choice and in this sense reflected a contractarian view of social relations by which an individual was only bound when she chose to assume an obligation in relation to another. The criterion of fault enabled such a choice to be made because, by choosing to be careful liability might be avoided, whereas by acting carelessly an individual could be said to have voluntarily assumed responsibility for the consequences of her act (Chapter 4). The individualism of nineteenth-century contractarianism contrasts starkly with the development and (limited) realisation of a welfarist model of social organisation in the twentieth century, strongly reliant upon ideals of community. The concept of social responsibility implicit in welfarism rendered negligence and the fault system visibly dated. Indeed, Millner, writing in 1967, observed that 'fostered by the individualism of the nineteenth century, whose needs and spirit it accurately reflects, negligence is in some ways basically unsuited to the paternalistic society of the twentieth' (Millner, 1967, p. 234). Modern reconceptualisations of tort as a mechanism of accident compensation invoke a conception of justice which assumes a certain social or community responsibility for accident victims. Tort becomes part of a model of justice concerned, not simply with assigning individual responsibility and safeguarding the supremacy of freedom of choice, but with ensuring that losses in society are fairly distributed and not borne disproportionately by some individuals over others. In so far as a concern with the social goal of accident compensation reflects a more general acceptance of the principle of community responsibility, the emergence of the accident compensation perspective is inextricably linked to the expansion of the welfare state. Likewise its decline coincides with a major assault on the welfare state in the period after 1979.

One ideological link between welfarism and accident compensation is the concept of entitlement based on citizenship. Marshall, writing in the 1950s, articulated a reinterpretation and expansion of the concept of citizenship to include not just civil and political rights but also social rights including the right to a 'modicum of economic welfare and security' (Marshall, 1950, p. 11, cited in Hindess, 1987, p. 34). This emphasis on the economic entitlements of citizenship, allied with a belief in the power and responsibility of government to intervene and regulate the lives of its citizens to a hitherto unprecedented extent, inevitably raised the issue of the state's role in compensating accident victims. Moreover, so viewed, the question of accident compensation became not just a matter of state benefits but rather of citizen's *rights*. It is not easy to comprehend this way of conceiving of welfare in an age where the dominant view is to regard social security as 'handouts' to the largely lazy and undeserving. From the perspective of writers such as Marshall, far from feeling ashamed or inhibited about claiming social security benefits, we should regard them as a natural entitlement of citizenship, a formal collection on an insurance policy which covers all citizens as the need arises.

Obviously such a view of welfarism encourages consideration of the role of the state in providing for accident victims and points strongly to mechanisms of social insurance as the preferred solution. At the same time, it generates a strong sense of community which reinforces people's responsibilities for and towards each other, what Marshall describes as 'a direct sense of community membership based on loyalty to a civilisation which is a common possession' (Marshall, 1950, p. 40, cited in Hindess, 1987, p. 37). In this way, the emergence of an accident compensation perspective can be linked to a general acceptance of the social philosophy underlying the welfare state. That is not to say that such a philosophy, particularly in its genesis, should be represented in unequivocally positive terms. Saville, for example, has argued that the emergence of the welfare state cannot be attributed solely to benevolent forces or to the 'struggle of the working class against their exploitation' but must be viewed also, at least in part, as a product of the requirements of industrial capitalism and 'recognition by property owners of the price that has to be paid for political security' (Saville, 1975, p. 57). Thus, ultimately, the ideology of welfarism which is so strongly profiled in the accident compensation debate, may take its colour and direction from the underlying economic order and its particular needs. Indeed, when that order is no longer dependent upon welfarist ideology for its legitimation but needs to eschew it in order to reduce a level of public expenditure it can no longer sustain, welfarism is predictably set aside (or, in the case of New Labour, radically and problematically reinterpreted) with accident compensation reform similarly jettisoned.

Finally, the emergence of an accident compensation perspective must also be understood in terms of changing approaches to law and legal education. The 1960s and 1970s saw an increasing tendency among legal academics to view law as an instrument which could be applied to different social goals (Thomson, 1987, p. 185). This was perceived to reflect a more 'realistic' approach to law than the prevailing expository tradition. The increasingly interventionist and goal oriented role of the state as reflected in a fast-growing corpus of public law and administrative bodies, inevitably challenged prevailing conceptions of law's autonomy as expressed by the Rule of Law (Unger, 1976). In a seminal article in 1975, Kamenka and Tay identified in the emergence of public law a significant change in the *form* of law during this period which, they alleged, generated a 'crisis' in law and legal education (Kamenka and Tay, 1975; see also Habermas, 1976). Although subsequent commentators, for example Nelken, 1982, were sceptical about Kamenka and Tay's alleged crisis, the debate as a whole was illustrative of a fundamental rethink by legal academics of traditional approaches to legal education in the light of the emergence of the modern bureaucratic state (Thomson, 1987). In particular, the conventional distinction between private and public law was no longer tenable, leading (*inter alia*) to a re-examination of the boundaries which had hitherto defined tort law and social security as separate and independent areas of study.

So viewed, the emergence of the accident compensation debate in the 1960s and 1970s can be understood against a background of interrelated factors – social, political and economic – all of which contributed to the shape and tenor of the debate.

CONTEMPORARY PERSPECTIVES ON ACCIDENT COMPENSATION

There is no doubt that the publication of the Pearson Report and its barely lukewarm reception represented a turning point in the public debate on accident compensation in Great Britain. The Report's relative timidity, combined with the election of a Conservative government in 1979, ensured that throughout most of the 1980s accident compensation was not on the agenda. However, by the end of the decade there were signs of a revival of interest in the questions Pearson appeared to answer so unsatisfactorily. In particular, the principle of fault-based liability once again came under scrutiny from a variety of directions.

First, in the area of defective products, the UK government was compelled by an EC Directive in 1985 to enact a form of strict liability for defective products under the Consumer Protection Act 1987, Part 1 (enacting the Products Liability Council Directive No 85/374/EEC, 25 July 1985; see generally note 6). The fault principle came under further scrutiny in the early 1990s in the context of the tragic plight of haemophiliacs and other sufferers who contracted AIDS from HIV-infected blood and tissue transfer, supplied by the National Health Service and imported from the United States in the early 1980s. The efforts of those affected to secure satisfactory compensation from the government, who denied fault in the matter, highlighted both the inability of the tort system to cope with such a visible tragedy and the piecemeal and reactive nature of government responses to such tragedies. In particular, the willingness of the government to retreat behind the legal technicality of fault and the arbitrary and capricious allocation of compensation they were prepared to countenance, echoed the tragedy of vaccine-damaged children whose plight had caught the public imagination and sympathy in the late 1970s (see above and note 13). In both cases, keen political campaigning and clever use of the media brought the issue to public attention, forcing a government response despite the vagaries of the fault principle. Yet, while both groups of sufferers were equally in need of compensation it is surely problematic that they had to rely on political means because of inadequacies in the existing systems of compensation. Inevitably too, their ultimate success raises serious questions of equity in relation to the many other daily tragedies which occur but do not catch the public eye or the political imagination.[18]

Such daily tragedies include the victims of medical accidents who face significant problems proving fault, particularly given the traditional highly protective judicial attitude towards doctors. Victims of medical accidents also face problems establishing causation, illustrated most poignantly by *Wilsher* v. *Essex Area Health Authority* (1988) and *Loveday* v. *Renton* (1990). Where a plaintiff *is* successful, she recovers damages and costs from an already underfunded health authority which is not likely to have budgeted for the bill and has to respond by cutting back on health services generally, for example by closing a ward or refraining from purchasing special equipment.

The technical and distributional problems which medical litigation inevitably generates have led to calls from a number of organisations, including the British Medical Association (BMA), for some kind of no-fault alternative. Indeed, a private member's bill (The National Health Service (Compensation) Bill) proposing the introduction of a no-fault scheme in the context of medical accidents (eliminating the need to prove fault or, in most cases, conduct litigation, with damages being assessed by a special Compensation Board) was introduced in the House of Commons in 1990/91, attracting cross-party support but opposed by the government and (therefore) failing in its second reading. The government's grounds for opposition, presented by William Waldegrave, then Secretary of State for Health, included concerns about the lack of accountability implied by the proposed scheme and the extra burden of costs it would (arguably) place on the NHS (*Independent*, 2 February 1991, p. 7). Waldegrave conceded, however, that existing avenues of redress for medical victims were not without their problems and mooted the possibility of an arbitration scheme to smooth the process of litigation. This idea now forms part of a larger series of recommendations contained in the Woolf Report on 'Access to Justice: Final Report' (Woolf, 1996). Fully acknowledging the difficulties facing claimants in the context of medical injury, the Report recommends a two-pronged strategy to deal with the difficulties: the introduction of specialist practices and procedures in the management and resolution of medical litigation on the one hand and the encouragement and development of alternative forms of dispute resolution, on the other (Woolf, 1996, Chapter 17). Some of these recommendations have since formed the basis of a Consultation Paper on 'Proposed New Procedures for Clinical Negligence', issued by the Lord Chancellor's Department in late 1997, focusing on ways of addressing problems in the litigation process. The difficulties associated with medical negligence litigation have also come up in the context of current government proposals to abolish legal aid in the context of, *inter alia*, personal injury claims in favour of a radical extension of the conditional fee system (Chapter 3). Concern has rightly been raised about the likely difficulties with financing medical negligence claims through a conditional fee arrangement. It has, for example, been pointed out that medical cases often require considerable expenditure of costs *before* a lawyer is in a position properly to assess the likely prospect of success. Given the risks and the high cost of legal insurance in medical claims, many lawyers and litigants are likely to be deterred if not practically disabled from bringing a civil claim. However, the recent Consultation Paper on 'Access to Justice with Conditional Fees' (Lord Chancellor's Department, 1998) is, in our view, far too complacent about these difficulties, assuming that they can largely be solved *via* the 'panacea' of procedural reform combined with the introduction of some kind of quality control mechanism to ensure that only 'competent' lawyers represent victims of medical accidents (paras. 3.15–3.19)! It remains to be seen whether or not such recommendations, if implemented, will significantly impact on present problems.

Rosie Barnes's no-fault proposal for medical accidents also presaged (if not precipitated) a new Law Commission investigation into personal injury damages, an investigation which has since yielded a number of reports and consultation papers[19] relating to, *inter alia*, the level of personal injury awards, the types of damages awarded and different modes of payment. However, to date, this has produced no significant change except in relation to modes of payment – the Damages Act 1996 includes new provisions for periodic payments and the promotion of structured settlements (see further Chapter 3) – and collateral benefits

(Social Security (Recovery of Benefits) Act 1997). The research remains indicative of a continued official concern with the vagaries and outcomes of tort litigation.

As things stand, while there appears to be a strong government reluctance to deal with the problems of the tort system by abandoning it, either in whole or in part, in favour of a public no-fault system, there does seem to be a definite political willingness to resolve some of the procedural problems confronting civil litigants, particularly those relating to delay. Indeed, the difficulties generated by prolonged litigation, both in terms of public cost and private redress, have been the subject of a number of official reports in recent years, including the 'Report of the Review Body on Civil Justice' (Civil Justice Review, 1988) and the Woolf Report (Woolf, 1996), both of which envisage significant reform of the role and operation of the court system as the key to the quicker, cheaper and more just resolution of disputes. However, the implications of such proposals for personal injury litigation are perhaps more difficult to guage than is generally thought. On the one hand, the emphasis of Woolf, in particular, on the court's role in *managing* the progress of litigation clearly corresponds, to a large extent, with existing practice in the context of mass litigation, for example, in relation to defective drugs and large-scale disasters. On the other hand, the identification of procedural issues as the primary obstacle facing those seeking 'access to (civil) justice' necessarily diverts public attention away from the substantive problems surrounding the nature and content of tort law which continue to dog claims for compensation in the context of personal injury. The *reform* of civil litigation (for our purposes in the context of personal injury) presupposes that civil litigation is indeed an appropriate way of conceiving of and determining those issues generated by accident and misfortune in our society, that is, as individual disputes requiring resolution. It takes an act of considerable imagination in the bleak and atomistic world of the 1990s to view such issues in terms other than as the expression and product of individual conflict.[20]

Nevertheless, the continued public focus on issues arising from tort in the wake of an apparent recent upsurge in litigiousness (*Guardian*, 3 December 1996) suggests that the questions raised (but never wholly answered) by the accident compensation debate stubbornly persist today. Moreover, the emotive effects of media coverage of mass disasters – the Hillsborough football crush, the Zeebruge ferry accident and the King's Cross fire in the 1980s and a series of high-profile rail crashes in the 1990s – have also heightened public awareness, so much so that the issue of accident compensation, far from being dead and buried, has re-emerged as a legitimate matter for debate.

Yet this political resurgence of an apparently dead issue is barely reflected in tort textbooks (see, exceptionally, Stanton, 1994). Indeed, the texts are unlikely to communicate any serious enthusiasm for or engagement with the issue precisely because they have systematically marginalised it. Not only is it presented as a physically separate and discrete area of study, a *segregated* knowledge of the tort system, but it is a disqualified knowledge – the traditional legal approach to tort law as case analysis ensures that an accident compensation perspective is defined as largely irrelevant to the law of negligence. By rigidly clinging to traditional legal categories, categories which Patrick Atiyah long ago dismissed as obfuscating rather than illuminating, the texts have effectively excluded from the law of negligence much of what passes as knowledge of its operation by those who are affected by it.

6
Nuisance: the Pale Green Tort

INTRODUCTION

Tony Weir, in his *Casebook on Tort*, locates the tort of nuisance squarely within the relationship of 'neighbours', by which he means not persons with a sufficient degree of proximity towards each other in the Atkinian sense of *Donoghue* v. *Stevenson* (1932), but rather *real* neighbours, that is 'the people next door or upstairs' (Weir, 1996, p. 361). To Weir, nuisance regulates the very special relationship between neighbours, defining their mutual rights and obligations with respect to their use of their property. So presented, nuisance poses as a minor tort with no great implications beyond the cosy domestic world of neighbourly squabbles. Such modest claims about the scope and operation of the tort are generally subscribed to by commentators (for example, Hepple and Matthews, 1991, p. 609; Brazier, 1993, p. 345), although *Winfield & Jolowicz* acknowledge that in 'modern parlance' nuisance has become associated with environmental protection (Rogers, 1994, p. 400). Their exposition, however, does little to explore or map the emergence of such a modern approach beyond pointing to the obvious fact that the harms which nuisance has occasion to address and redress are of a broadly environmental character. Thus, in general, the law of nuisance continues to be perceived as defining the rights and obligations of individuals, whose interests in the use and enjoyment of their respective properties conflict, by striking a fair and reasonable balance between them. Closer scrutiny reveals that the dramatis personae of the tort of nuisance extend well beyond neighbours engaging in garden-fence disputes with each other. For example, behind the seemingly innocuous conflict between a cricket club and a houseowner, who objected, reasonably, to the showering of cricket balls in her back garden, appears that rather elusive and potentially dictatorial character – The Public Interest (*Miller* v. *Jackson* (1977), see below). Hovering on the sidelines of a dispute between the occupant of a 'good class residential street' and his next-door neighbours, who were engaged in an activity (brothel-keeping) which allegedly threatened the value of property and the character of the street, lurks the dark and rather ominous shadow of Civilised Society (*Thomson-Schwab* v. *Costaki* (1956) at 654). Most recently, couched in the trappings of an old-fashioned doctrinal debate about the scope of liability under the Rule in *Rylands* v. *Fletcher* (see below) lies a barely concealed judicial dislike of Unnecessary European Regulation (*Cambridge Water Co Ltd* v. *Eastern Counties Leather plc* (1994)). The tort of nuisance tells a story of more than just unneighbourly behaviour. It evokes the past in signalling a crucial aspect of the transition from feudalism to capitalism – the shift from the protection of property to the promotion of industry. It expresses the present in its persistent if cautious confrontation with the activities of an age to which it was not born, for example the advent of television.[1] And it points us to the future by compelling us occasionally to consider the environmental implications of activities which, to date, we have unquestionably characterised as progressive. Moreover, while significantly similar in character and scope to the tort of negligence, nuisance, as the most prominent of the 'land torts', sheds light on aspects of tort law hitherto barely perused.

THE TRADITIONAL EXPOSITION OF NUISANCE LAW

Fleming has complained that the concept of nuisance has become 'so amorphous as well nigh to defy rational exposition' (Fleming, 1987, p. 379). In spite of this, a glance at the textbooks suggests that the writers do a very neat job of expounding and packaging this 'impenetrable jungle' (Dobbs et al., 1984, p. 616). Traditional accounts of nuisance take a predictable form. They begin by defining private nuisance, then proceed to distinguish it from public nuisance, to itemise the criteria which determine what constitutes a nuisance, to identify the defences which can be invoked to defeat a claim of nuisance and, finally, to detail the choice of remedies available, including the scope of their application to particular nuisances. This format is very persuasive, giving the impression that the commentators have brought order and sense to an area of law which, when perused by the untrained eye, appears as a gathering of disconnected and miscellaneous wrongs. Traditional expositions of the tort of nuisance are in fact an excellent example of the rationalisation and synthesisation skills which make up the 'special expertise' of the legal academic.

According to conventional wisdom, there are two kinds of nuisance, private and public, which, although bearing the same name, have, it is said, little in common with each other. Ordinarily, when tort scholars address nuisance, they focus on *private* nuisance, which defines the scope of obligations and entitlements between neighbours in relation to the uses of their property. Public nuisance is regarded as an entirely different creature and, moreover, a complete misnomer, 'a bad pun' (Weir, 1988, p. 363). We will briefly consider both alongside a near relation, the action in *Rylands* v. *Fletcher* (derived from a case of that name (1868)).

Private Nuisance

Private nuisance is usually defined as 'any unlawful interference with a person's use or enjoyment of land, or some right over or in connection with it' (Rogers, 1994, p. 404). The determination of whether an interference is unlawful depends on whether it is considered by the court to be substantial and unreasonable. Over the years a variety of different forms of interference have been characterised as a nuisance, including the emission of noxious fumes materially damaging property (*St Helens Smelting* v. *Tipping* (1865)); the noise of an oil-distributing depot operating at night in a residential area (*Halsey* v. *Esso Petroleum* (1961)); the flooding of the plaintiff's land (*Sedleigh-Denfield* v. *O'Callaghan* (1940)) and the unpleasant smell emitting from a pig farm (*Bone* v. *Seale* (1975)). Thus, nuisance can involve actual physical damage to property (and, perhaps, personal injury, although this has recently been doubted by the House of Lords in *Hunter* v. *Canary Wharf Ltd* (1997))[2] and/or non-physical 'amenity' damage such as noises or smells which unreasonably affect the plaintiff's comfort and enjoyment of her property. Traditional determinations of whether or not an interference is unlawful (substantial and unreasonable) depend upon a number of factors including the nature of the locality (*Sturges* v. *Bridgman* (1879), *St Helens Smelting Co* v. *Tipping* (1865));[3] (possibly) the utility of the defendant's conduct (*Adams* v. *Ursell* (1913) and see Howarth, 1995, pp. 502–4); the duration of the interference (*Halsey* v. *Esso* (1961), *British Celanese Ltd* v. *Hunt* (1969)); whether or not the defendant's act was motivated by malice (*Christie* v. *Davey* (1893), *Hollywood Silver Fox Farm* v. *Emmett* (1936));[4] and, whether or not the plaintiff's reaction to the interference was 'abnormally sensitive' (*Robinson* v. *Kilvert* (1889)). The occurrence of material damage creates a strong *prima facie* presumption of unlawfulness (*St Helens Smelting Co* v. *Tipping* (1865)) whereas, in the case of solely amenity damage, the courts tend to engage in a more complex balancing exercise before deciding that the alleged interference is a nuisance (Buckley, 1981, p. 9).

The House of Lords in *Hunter* has recently suggested that an 'emanation' from the defendant's land is a characteristic (Lord Goff) if not a prerequisite (Lord Hope) of a claim in private nuisance. In other words it may be that an interference, no matter how substantial or unreasonable, does *not* constitute a private nuisance unless it emanates from the defendant's land. Whether or not this is a correct statement of the legal position (there is judicial authority to the contrary, see, for example *Southport Corporation* v. *Esso Petroleum Co Ltd* (1956) *per* L Devlin at 224; see also Howarth, 1995, p. 496), it certainly reflects the practical reality of most private nuisance claims. Moreover, in cases where the interference complained of does *not* emanate from the defendant's land it may be remedied through an action derived from public nuisance – see *Halsey* v. *Esso* (1961) and discussion below.

As the essence of the tort is to protect property, the plaintiff, to bring an action, must have some proprietary interest in the land affected.[5] Moreover, nuisance has traditionally been characterised as a strict liability tort reflecting the maxim *sic utere tuo ut alienum non laedas* ('use your land as to not injure the interests of another'). Thus, it is no excuse that the defendant carries out an activity on his land taking all reasonable care to avoid harming his neighbour (*Rapier* v. *London Tramways Co* (1893). The activity may still be a nuisance by virtue of the interference it occasions. However, it has been judicially observed that 'fault of some kind is almost always necessary' in nuisance even though it might not amount to negligence in the sense of a breach of a duty of care (*per* Lord Reid in *The Wagon Mound (No 2), Overseas Tankship (UK) Ltd* v. *The Miller Steamship Co Pty Ltd* (1967) at 639). In particular, it has been recently affirmed by the House of Lords in *Cambridge Water* v. *Eastern Counties Leather plc* (1994) that foreseeability of harm is a prerequisite of liability in the tort of nuisance.[6]

A number of defences both general and particular can meet a claim in nuisance, most notably the defences of prescription and statutory authority.[7] The principal remedies available if a nuisance is established are damages and an injunction (and, to a limited extent, self-help). As the object of suit is usually to stop some continuing interference, an injunction is normally sought by the plaintiff. However, injunctive relief is not available as of right but is subject to the equitable discretion of the court. Generally, the courts tend to grant an injunction where a nuisance is substantial and continuous, although they may place some limits on its application in order to strike a balance between the conflicting interests of the parties (*Kennaway* v. *Thomson* (1981)). In addition to injunctive relief, a plaintiff is entitled to damages for loss resulting from a nuisance. This includes compensation for physical damage to property, amenity damage such as noises and smells and possibly economic loss in the form of a diminution in the value of the affected property (*Thomson-Schwab* v. *Costaki* (1956)).[8] The court has the discretion (since Lord Cairn's Act 1858) to grant damages in lieu of an injunction (*Shelfer* v. *City of London Electric Lighting Co* (1895) but see *Miller* v. *Jackson* (1977) and *Kennaway* v. *Thomson* (1981)).

Public Nuisance

In contrast to private nuisance, public nuisance is, by definition, not a tort at all but a crime which may, in certain circumstances, generate a civil cause of action. Nor is its object the protection of property rights. Rather it is concerned with recognising and protecting the rights of members of the public. A common example of public nuisance is obstruction of the highway (for example in the course of picketing, *Hubbard* v. *Pitt* (1976)), but public nuisance has also been held to include quarry-blasting (*Attorney-General* v. *PYA Quarries Ltd* (1957));

an ill-organised pop festival (*Attorney-General for Ontario* v. *Orange Productions Ltd* (1971)) and engineering a hoax bomb scare (*R.* v. *Madden* (1975)). The essential character of public nuisance is the infringement of a public right, an interference with the lives and activities of a community rather than an individual, thus making criminal law a more appropriate legal response. It is as Lord Denning states:

> ... a nuisance which is so widespread in its range or so indiscriminate in its effects that it would not be reasonable to expect one person to take proceedings ... to put a stop to it, but that it should be taken on the responsibility of the community at large. (*AG* v. *PYA Quarries* (1957) at 191)

The community, for purposes of a public nuisance, are that 'class of Her Majesty's subjects' who are affected by the nuisance (*AG* v. *PYA Quarries* (1957) *per* Romer LJ at 184), where the question of what constitutes a 'class' for these purposes is a question of fact for the court. An individual can sue in relation to a public nuisance if she can prove she has suffered particular damage over and above that of the community at large (*Tate & Lyle Industries Ltd* v. *GLC* (1983)). In the absence of special damage, the only sanction is a criminal prosecution (triable summarily or on indictment) or, in certain circumstances, an injunction sought by a relator action brought by the Attorney-General.[9] Aside from the name, it might be asked what, if anything, the two forms of nuisance have in common. While conceptually, it seems, very little, factually there may be considerable overlap between them. In *Halsey* v. *Esso* (1961), the plaintiff succeeded in establishing that the defendant's activities constituted both a public and a private nuisance. The case involved the operation of an oil-distributing depot outside the plaintiff's house which resulted in disturbance caused by noise generated, first, by the operation of the depot (held to be a private nuisance) and second, by the arrival and departure of tankers throughout the night which, by virtue of their use of the highway, constituted a public nuisance. This potential factual overlap between public and private nuisance may be of significance where the end sought to be achieved by litigation is environmental protection (see below).

Rylands v. *Fletcher*

Until recently, the cause of action deriving from *Rylands* v. *Fletcher* (1868) was considered by many legal scholars and practitioners to be of little practical significance, being rarely invoked in the courts. However, the decision of the House of Lords in *Cambridge Water Co* v. *Eastern Counties Leather* (1994) has produced a flurry of academic commentary (see, for example, Ogus, 1994; Wilkinson, 1994; Hilson, 1996) which has once again placed *Rylands* v. *Fletcher* on the legal map, a result which is, at least, puzzling, given that the decision itself *appears* to further limit the scope of *Rylands* application and, therefore, its practical significance.

In *Rylands* v. *Fletcher* (1868) the defendant employed independent contractors to construct a reservoir on his land. Due to the existence of disused mine shafts on the site, of whose existence the defendant did not and (it was held) could not have reasonably known, the reservoir flooded the plaintiff's adjoining mines. In the absence of fault on the part of the defendants, the Court of Exchequer dismissed the plaintiff's claim (1865). However, this decision was reversed on appeal (1868) and the defendant's liability was eventually affirmed by the House of Lords (1868). Ruling in favour of the plaintiff, the Court of Exchequer Chamber stated the following principle:

> the person who, for his own purposes, brings on his land, and collects and keeps anything likely to do mischief if it escapes must keep it at his peril, and, if he does not do so, he is prima facie answerable for all the damage which is the natural consequence of its escape. (*per* Blackburn J at 279–280)

This principle was approved by the House of Lords with the added rider that the defendant, to be liable, must also be engaged in a non-natural use of the land (*per* Cairns LC at 338–340).

Rylands v. *Fletcher* has since been applied in a number of cases which have largely been concerned either with the question of what constitutes 'a thing likely to do mischief' – the category has been held to include electricity (*National Telephone Co* v. *Baker* (1893)); oil (*Smith* v. *G.W. Railway* (1926); gas (*Batchellor* v. *Tunbridge Wells Gas Co* (1901)); and even people (*Attorney-General* v. *Corke* (1933) but see, contra, *Smith* v. *Scott* (1973) and *Matheson* v. *Northcote College Board of Governors* (1975)) – or with whether or not the defendant's use of land can be characterised as non-natural.[10] On the latter point, Lord Goff has recently stated in the *Cambridge Water* case that natural use means 'ordinary use' which, although not expressly defined by him, appears to encompass primarily domestic or residential uses rather than industrial practices.[11]

The case law has emphasised the need to show an *escape*, that is, the departure of some harm-causing substance from the defendant's land (or a place over which he exercises control) to somewhere else (*Read* v. *Lyons* (1947)). Uncertainty has arisen over who can invoke the principle and in relation to what kind of damage. In *Rylands* itself, the plaintiff was a tenant of the property affected and the question of his right to sue did not arise but a number of subsequent decisions are at least suggestive of a right to sue beyond the holder of an interest in land (see, in particular, *Perry* v. *Kendrick's Transport Ltd* (1956) *per* Parker J and *British Celanese Ltd* v. *Hunt* (1969) *per* Lawton J). Similarly, authority is divided on the question of whether or not the principle extends to claims for personal injuries – *Hale* v. *Jennings Bros* (1938) and *Perry* v. *Kendrick's Transport Ltd* (1956) suggest that such harm is recoverable while the majority of their Lordships in *Read* v. *Lyons* (1947) are doubtful (although, with the exception of Lord MacMillan, they do not take an express view on the point). Most recently, the question has arisen as to whether or not a defendant can be liable under *Rylands* for harm which he could not reasonably have foreseen. The response of the House of Lords to this question in *Cambridge Water* was resoundingly negative, holding that just as foreseeability of harm is a prerequisite to recovery under negligence and nuisance, it should also be a prerequisite to liability under *Rylands* v. *Fletcher* (for doubt, post-*Cambridge Water*, as to precisely *what* has to be foreseen in order for liability in *Rylands* to arise, see further below). This does not detract from the strict liability nature of the tort, however, in the sense that where foreseeable damage occurs, the defendants will be liable regardless of whether or not they have taken all reasonable care to avoid it (see the judgment of Lord Goff at 77).

Rylands liability is further hedged by a series of defences, many of which derive from Blackburn J's original exposition. Defences include the plaintiff's consent (express or implied) or default; where the source of danger is maintained for the *common benefit* of the plaintiff and the defendant; acts of stranger or God; and statutory authority (for further details, see Rogers, 1994, pp. 454–62). On the whole, the general tenor of the case law on *Rylands* liability has been to restrict rather than to expand the scope of the principle. This is in marked contrast with many US states where it has been 'elevated' to the status of a strict liability tort governing ultra-hazardous activities (Nolan and Ursin, 1987).

It might be asked in what sense *Rylands* can be viewed as establishing a new or separate cause of action. Clearly, it is associated with the escape of dangerous things from land but does it thereby carve out an area of liability which is distinct from private nuisance or is it merely a particular application of it?

It was the view of some commentators that the rule in *Rylands* was best understood as laying down a distinct principle applicable to 'exceptional' or 'unusual' risks (see, for example, Pollock, 1939, p. 386). By contrast, Newark, in his seminal article on nuisance in 1949, argued that *Rylands* was, in fact, a subspecies of private nuisance governing isolated escapes (as opposed to ongoing and continuous interferences which more frequently characterised nuisance claims). In the *Cambridge Water* case, the latter view was preferred carrying with it significant implications for the scope of the *Rylands* principle. Not only did it strengthen the case for applying to liability in *Rylands* the same test of remoteness of damage as governs the tort of nuisance (*per* Lord Goff at 75) but, when considered alongside the more recent House of Lords decision in *Hunter* which, while not expressly concerned with liability under *Rylands*, has plenty to say about the scope of liability in nuisance, the *Cambridge Water* decision is highly suggestive of a more restrictive response to those uncertainties arising in relation to the scope of the *Rylands* principle beyond damage to property interests.

Having briefly summarised the basic framework and substance of the rules and principles governing nuisance liability (broadly construed), let us approach it more critically.

CRITIQUING NUISANCE

Historical Context

Attention to the historical context of nuisance law (sadly lacking in most conventional texts), illuminates its modern social role by revealing the values it reflects and the interests it serves.

The tort of private nuisance goes back a long way. Winfield traces it to the old assize of nuisance, a thirteenth-century remedy which protected interferences with land short of dispossession (for which the assize of novel disseisin was available) and which offered relief only to a freeholder (Winfield, 1931b, pp. 190–1). By the sixteenth century, it was possible to proceed in nuisance by way of an action upon the case (Winfield, 1931b, pp. 191–2). This action could be brought by persons other than freeholders but it was still necessary to have an interest in land. Case rather than trespass became regarded as the more appropriate form of action because nuisance commonly involved an *indirect* interference with property rights while trespass carried with it the requirement of directness (Winfield, 1931b, pp. 201–2). It followed that, unlike trespass, nuisance required a showing of actual harm by the plaintiff (*Aldred's Case* (1611)).

Public nuisance also has an ancient pedigree. In its earliest form, it was concerned with purprestures (encroachments upon the royal domain or the public highway) but during the course of the thirteenth century the concept expanded in a disjointed way to include within its meaning a series of petty crimes involving invasions of the public right (Prosser et al., 1988, p. 810). During the sixteenth century it was recognised that a private action might arise from a public nuisance where the plaintiff suffered greater damage than the 'generality' (*Anon* (1535) *per* Fitzherbert J). The emergence of a civil action, combined with the fact that private and public nuisance shared with each other common features of annoyance or inconvenience, is thought to account for their traditional association despite their very different characteristics. It has also been argued that such association has led to conceptual confusion by suggesting that private nuisance is available to redress personal injuries despite its links with proprietary interests (Fleming, 1987, p. 381; Brazier, 1993, p. 347).

Blackstone identifies the action in private nuisance as governed by strict liability of *sic utere tuo* (Blackstone, 1765–69, Vol. 3, p. 217). In the context of industrialisation, the inevitable conflict between the rights of residential landowners and the interests of industrial developers posed a powerful challenge to the absolute concept of property ownership reflected in the traditional maxim. As Brenner observes, the medieval conception of nuisance was directly concerned with limiting a neighbour's ability to use and develop his land: 'It drew the line around free use and enjoyment of land at that point where another's use and enjoyment were impaired, and the standards for judging impairment were rural, agricultural and conservative' (Brenner, 1974, p. 404). This would suggest that nuisance law was potentially a significant barrier to the process of industrialisation. But research demonstrates that this was not in fact the case (Brenner, 1974; McLaren, 1983).

Significantly, however, the relative impotency of nuisance law in the face of industrial development cannot be explained by any dramatic change in common law doctrine. The principle of strict liability, identified by Blackstone, did not give way to a fault-based standard in this context so easily as it did where personal injury redress was the issue. As late as 1893 the English courts were asserting that the absence of carelessness did not absolve the defendant from liability in nuisance (*Rapier* v. *London Tramways Co* (1893)) and, in relation to the United States, Horwitz observes that 'while other areas of the law were changing to accommodate the growth of American industry, the law of nuisances for the longest time appeared on its face to maintain the pristine purity of a pre-industrial mentality' (Horwitz, 1977, p. 74).

This suggests that nineteenth-century judges were much less willing to permit the 'subsidisation' (see Chapter 4) of nascent industry by compromising the rights of property owners than they were where the harm inflicted was personal rather than proprietary.[12] Nevertheless, the law of nuisance was not unaffected by the Industrial Revolution as judges developed various methods of balancing the conflicting demands of property and industry.

One such tactic, identified by Horwitz, involved blurring the line between public and private nuisance by extending the situations where a requirement of special damage was a precondition to suit (Horwitz, 1977, pp. 76–8). This was possible particularly in situations where landowners claimed a diminution in the value of their property as a result of impaired access created by industrial works (for example, in the case of railway expansion) and the courts, by classifying the wrong as a public nuisance, were able to deny the claimants a remedy (*Smith* v. *Boston* (1851)).

Similarly, the distinction drawn in *St Helens Smelting Co* v. *Tipping* (1865) between inflicting material damage to property and producing 'sensible personal discomfort' (*per* Lord Westbury) was arguably of crucial significance in limiting the liability of industrialists for nuisance. Cornish and Clark observe that in the period immediately after 1865 it was almost impossible to sue for amenity damage (smells, noise, vibrations) if one resided in an industrial area. Inevitably, the distinction had a disproportionate class impact by protecting the primary interests of residential landowners (in the physical integrity of their property) while denying any redress to those who simply wished to live in an environment free from the stench and clamour of industrial activity (Cornish and Clark, 1989, p. 157). The relaxed standard applied to cases of amenity damage, combined with the impact of the locality rule after *St Helens Smelting*, heightened the 'zoning' function of nuisance law. Brenner notes that although nuisance had always operated to some extent as a zoning mechanism and although the locality rule was not new, its application to the effects of industrial development, 'when whole towns could be built, demographic patterns altered, occupations eliminated and created, and skies blackened, all by factories' (Brenner, 1974, pp. 406, 414), was radically different in its impact and effect in the pre-industrial era.[13] Brenner further argues that the impact of industrialisation inevitably changed social expectations in relation to amenities such as air and water quality, which, through the balancing exercise inherent in the concept of reasonableness, allowed for a considerable lowering of judicial standards reflecting the realities of industrial pollution unaccompanied by any significant change in legal doctrine: '*De facto* changes in nuisance law did not, therefore, require *de jure* changes; a drastically different socio-economic milieu and new levels of tolerance of noise and smoke could accomplish the same thing' (Brenner, 1974, p. 409). It should be observed here also that what the courts characterised as amenity damage, in the form of industrial pollution, had inevitably deleterious effects on health, which, because they were not immediately manifest or obvious, were not generally sufficient to found a cause of action (Brenner, 1974, p. 417).[14]

Nor can the role of Parliament in facilitating industrial development by means of statutory authorisation be overlooked. Immunity-conferring 'nuisance clauses' began to emerge originally in the Railway Acts of the early nineteenth century and although the original intention of such clauses was apparently to ensure that the activity could not be subject to injunctive relief rather than to deny a remedy in damages for injury to property, a judicial interpretation of the effect of these clauses gradually evolved to extend a full immunity from private suit in the absence of negligent conduct. As a result, nuisance law was hardly ever applied to activities carried out by public enterprises (Brenner, 1974, pp. 421–2).

Finally, the slow but gradual injection of a fault element into nuisance, despite its historical roots as a strict liability tort, must also be understood against the background of nineteenth-century indus-trialisation. *St Helens Smelting* v. *Tipping* (1865) can be identified as a turning point, launching a modern approach to nuisance which redefined the concept of reasonable use in such a way as to enable the court to take a more relative approach to the conflicting interests of residential landowners and industrial developers (Brenner, 1974, pp. 410–15). However, it would be wrong to suggest that judges were united by a common opinion as to how to strike a balance. Litigation in the 1850s and 1860s, particularly the trilogy of cases composed of *Hole* v. *Barlow* (1858), *Bamford* v. *Turnley* (1862) and *St Helens Smelting* v. *Tipping* (1865), indicate that there was considerable division of opinion among judges on the matter (McLaren, 1983, pp. 170–80). Nevertheless, as judges struggled to articulate the factors which were relevant to a resolution of conflicts about land use, a fault-based element undeniably permeated their reasoning. Although the position still remained that, in law, a defendant could be liable in nuisance despite his adherence to standards of due care (*Rapier*), and an injunction could not be denied because the activity being complained of conferred some public benefit (*Shelfer* v. *City of London Electric Lighting Co* (1895)), increasingly the presence of some kind of fault, judicially perceived, became a factual prerequisite to recovery. This encroachment of negligence into the tort of nuisance (which Millner identifies as a predominantly nineteenth-century development – Millner, 1967, p. 182), via the notion of reasonable use of land, can in part be explained by the intellectual preoccupation with fault-based liability during the crucial period of the late nineteenth and early twentieth centuries (White, 1985, pp. 61, 127–9), but it can also be seen as part of a general legal reassessment of the absolute concept of property ownership which had characterised pre-industrial law and which was no longer appropriate to the modern industrial era. The concept of reasonable use became in the nineteenth century the means by which the conflicting interests of residential land use and industrial development were reconciled.

Within the context of this increasing permeation of fault-based considerations into the determination of liability in nuisance, the decision in *Rylands* v. *Fletcher* (1861–73) seems strangely out of place. After all, the crux of the decision in that case was that the defendants were liable despite the fact that no want of proper or reasonable care in relation to the selection of the site or the construction of the reservoir could be attributed to them (as opposed to their contractors who, it was acknowledged, were at fault in this respect).

Opinion has remained divided as to whether or not the *Rylands* decision struck new and liability expansive ground at a time when the tide was flowing in the opposite direction. Both Winfield and Jolowicz (Rogers, 1979, pp. 399–400, 419–20) and Fleming (1987, pp. 308–10) point out that the *Rylands* decision, while undoubtedly having antecedents in the tort of nuisance (many of the examples cited by Blackburn J as expressive of the principle are examples of nuisance liability), cannot in fact be accounted for by that tort at that time, not just because the facts in *Rylands* involved an isolated escape rather than a continuous state of affairs (see the argument of Newark, 1949, discussed above) but also because the result in the decision was to hold the defendants strictly liable for the acts of their contractors, a result not reached in the context of nuisance until a decade later (in *Bower* v. *Peate* (1876)).

More generally, it has been mooted that *Rylands* evidences a judicial effort to protect the landed gentry from the encroachment of industry (Bohlen, 1911), although such a suggestion is dismissed by Fleming who points out that the effect of *Rylands* was not to protect interests in land as such but rather 'to protect one industry (mining) against another (milling) because the latter was obviously a far better loss avoider' (Fleming, 1987, p. 309; see also Molloy, 1942, who argues that Bohlen's analysis is not supported by the biographies of the judges involved in the decision).

Certainly, although it has been observed that Blackburn J, while articulating the *Rylands* principle, did not seem conscious that it might be considered ground-breaking or revolutionary in its implications, the case was received amidst some controversy, particularly in the US where it invoked strong antithetical opinions (see, in particular, *Losee* v. *Buchanan* (1873) and *Brown* v. *Collins* (1873)). Moreover, its subsequent history largely bears out a judicial perception of the decision as threatening and in need of constraint (no doubt because of its apparent departure from fault), resulting in the gradual grafting of restrictions and exceptions to limit the application of the rule (Fleming, 1987, pp. 309–10). Finally, it must be remembered that the *Rylands* v. *Fletcher* litigation went on from 1861 to 1873 which is clear evidence that the issues raised by the case were far from settled in law.

The development of public nuisance was also affected in various ways by industrialisation. The requirement that a private suit could only be brought where the plaintiff suffered special damage was strictly insisted upon to limit the liability of industrialists for the disruption caused in particular by construction (Weir, 1988, p. 175). Moreover, although the deleterious effect of industrialisation on public health and convenience was apparent, it did not lead to a significant increase in prosecutions for public nuisance. Indeed, Brenner observes a significant diminution in indictments during the nineteenth century which he attributes expressly to a policy favouring the polluters (Brenner, 1974, pp. 420–4). Inevitably, industrial pollution led to the introduction of statutory controls (too often of limited effect – Brenner, 1974, pp. 424–8; McLaren, 1983, pp. 208–9) to replace many common law examples of public nuisance – so much so that in modern times the conception of public nuisance as a random set of 'ill-assorted wrongs' has gradually been displaced by a narrower focus on its particular application to highway obstructions and conditions (see, for example Rogers, 1994, pp. 433–7).

Thus, although its pedigree is ancient, the modern law of nuisance (like negligence) is, in part at least, a creature of the Industrial Revolution. This is of particular interest when we consider, below, its more recent revitalisation in the context of environmental protection. More generally, it suggests that the modern law of nuisance is as ideologically loaded as the tort of negligence.

Ideological Content

The common law is made by judges, and few today would deny the creative nature of the enterprise. Lord Reid observes that only 'those with a taste for fairy tales' would subscribe to the view that judges merely discover law (Reid, 1972, p. 22). But if judges are prepared to acknowledge that they make law, few are prepared to accept that they fashion it in their own image. The belief that judges are *constrained* by existing doctrine, by formal rules of precedent and statutory interpretation and by the nature of legal reasoning accounts for the widely held conviction that they can make law impartially and apolitically without prejudice or bias. As we have already asserted, textbook accounts of legal doctrine do much to reinforce this conviction by locating new judgments within a pre-ordained pattern of rules and principles with which each additional case seems, more or less, to accord. Even judicial decisions involving a departure from principle can be accommodated, on the whole, by the application of a series of analytical techniques: distinguishing the case on the facts; highlighting a hitherto unknown line of authority which lends it support; greeting it as part of the process of incremental doctrinal development necessary to bring the law in line with modern conditions. Thus, the textbook has an important ideological function in legitimating judicial decision-making by presenting it within a relatively stable and coherent doctrinal framework. At the same time, critical approaches to legal doctrine can undermine the ideological impact of textbook exposition by highlighting the instability and incoherence of legal rules.

A closer look at the doctrinal substance of nuisance law bears this out. Of course, commentators will always concede the presence of a degree of uncertainty, but it might be suggested that the purported 'rationalisation' of nuisance leaves more than a few 'furry edges'. Indeed, nuisance law abounds with concepts, tests and standards which are indeterminate, dictating no particular legal outcome and giving almost full reign to subjective judicial preferences. The only significant constraint is that judges must justify their decisions using the language of these wholly indeterminate concepts, tests and standards rather than by reference to the subjective preferences which are in fact determinative (Chapter 2, note 9). Thus, judges decide what kinds of inconveniences a plaintiff should and should not have to tolerate by reference to what is required of the ordinary reasonable person (taking account of her expectations as a resident of Bermondsey or Belgrave Square). The standard of tolerance of the ordinary reasonable person, particularly when allied with the locality rule, has operated as an excellent vehicle for judicial prejudices over the years, while at the same time disguising the essentially class-based nature of the exercise being carried out. Similarly, the 'rule' that a plaintiff cannot recover for reactions to an interference because of abnormal sensitivity 'leaves the court with the scope for the exercise of considerable discretion' (Buckley, 1981, p. 13) in defining what is normal and abnormal. Furthermore, when determining the reasonableness or otherwise of the defendant's act, considerations of social utility allow judges to give activities (playing cricket, selling fried fish to the poor) their own particular weighting, while at the same time, the subjectivity of this judicial exercise appears less obvious when expressed in terms of public benefit. Indeed, the whole balancing exercise which the test of reasonableness implies is arguably a means by which the judges can offer their intuitive sense of the justice of the case as a legal solution.

Not only is nuisance law indeterminate in the sense that many of its concepts command no particular legal solution, it is also open-ended to such an extent that it is difficult to assert any doctrinal proposition with a degree of confidence. For example, even after *Hunter*, uncertainty remains over the application of private nuisance to personal injury (and, perhaps, material damage to property), their Lordships' comments on the subject being *obiter* (above, note 2). Similarly, it is still unclear precisely what the measure of damage is for amenity harm, whether or not malice will make an otherwise lawful activity unlawful (above, note 4) or even whether interference with TV reception can ever constitute a nuisance (above, note 1). The standard of liability in nuisance also remains uncertain: is material physical damage to property sufficient, without more, to establish liability in nuisance, or can the courts still engage in a balancing exercise? In other words, is the standard of liability for damage to property different from that applied to amenity harm? Peter Cane has argued that it is: that while

nuisance involving material damage to property tends to reflect a
'conduct-based' negligence standard of liability, the infliction of
amenity damage is governed by a 'fairness-based' strict liability standard
(Cane, 1982, pp. 56–8). Are the courts utilising two different
conceptions of justice depending on the nature of the alleged harm?
The irony of this conclusion, as Cane himself observes, is that amenity
damage appears to be subject to a stricter standard of liability than
physical damage, representing 'a departure from the spirit of *St Helens
Smelting*' (Cane, 1982, p. 57). While traditional expositions of nuisance
consistently suggest that case law draws a distinction between physical
and amenity damage which is weighted towards a recognition that the
law takes a more serious view of the former than the latter, an interpretation can also be offered, which, in terms of the standard of
liability applied, is suggestive of the opposite conclusion. It is also
suggestive of the view that material damage to property is not properly
the stuff of nuisance at all but is more at home in the tort of negligence
(Gearty, 1989). The extent of doctrinal uncertainty means judges are
less constrained by doctrinal precepts than textbooks would have us
believe. This point is well illustrated by *Miller* v. *Jackson* (1977), a case
involving a nuisance suit against a cricket club by a nearby homeowner
whose back garden was subject to the occasional showering of cricket
balls. Textbooks tend to play down the subversive aspects of this
decision by emphasising the minority status of Lord Denning's
judgment on the question of liability and speculating that *Miller* was
wrongly decided in relying on public interest to deny injunctive relief
(Rogers, 1989, p. 638). Students tend to enjoy the case with its quaint
championing of the 'manly sport' of cricket (*per* Cumming-Bruce LJ).
They view *Miller* as an entertainment which enlivens a rather tedious
topic by its refusal to follow the rules. But such a view misses an
important point, namely, that Lord Denning felt free to *deny* liability
here. Moreover, as a matter of law, such a conclusion, had it
commanded a majority, could hardly be considered wrong given the
nature of the locality and the social utility of the defendant's act. At
the same time, to impose liability, emphasising the degree of inconvenience experienced by the plaintiffs in the enjoyment of their
property (including the threat of physical danger), was not inappropriate or incorrect. Either outcome could be considered consistent
with legal doctrine. The difference between the majority and minority
on the question of liability is explicable largely in terms of the weight
attributable to the social value of cricket. For Lord Denning, cricket is
a game, which in the summertime 'is the delight of everyone'. It is a
game where 'the young men play and the old men watch', a game
which, in this instance, has gone on for 70 years on a green which until
recently was adjoined by 'a field where cattle grazed'. The field has now
become a housing estate occupied by, among others, the plaintiff, 'a

newcomer who is no lover of cricket'. Lord Denning views the closure of the cricket club as a potentially disastrous calamity. The cricket ground might be replaced by 'more houses or a factory. The young men will turn to other things instead of cricket. The whole village will be much the poorer. And all this because of a newcomer who has just bought a house there next to the cricket ground' (at 341).

In this passage, Denning is appealing to a quaint and charming picture of English country life. He conjures up images of green fields, sleepy sunny afternoons, the quiet sounds of a cricket match on a summer's day. His head is populated with old men, young men and grazing cattle. His characters are white, male and English. Threatening this bucolic vision of English men at play is the arrival of a newcomer, the sort of person who lives on a housing estate, who does not appreciate the finer points of cricket, who might even be female and who brings in her wake the threat of social degeneration as the young men are forced to abandon cricket and go to work in factories.

Lord Denning's picture of English social life is instantly recognisable. One would not be surprised if Miss Marple appeared with her knitting needles. As a work of fiction it has charm, but it is hardly representative of contemporary social reality. Yet Lord Denning relies on this fantasy as self-evident proof of the particular public interest in saving the cricket club. Indeed, so great is the public interest at stake that he is prepared to ride roughshod over private property rights without so much as compensating their infringement in the absence of actual physical damage:

> This case is new. It should be approached on principles applicable to modern conditions. There is a contest here between the interest of the public at large and the interest of the private individual. The *public* interest lies in protecting the environment by preserving our playing fields in the face of mounting development ... The *private* interest lies in securing the privacy of his home and garden without intrusion or interference by anyone ... As between their conflicting interests, I am of the opinion that the public interest should prevail over the private interest. (345)

Thus, Lord Denning transforms the law of bickering neighbours into a mechanism for protecting the environment. Nuisance has become a means to a social end, an instrument for the promotion of the public interest. Individual property rights must give way to the greater good.

It is interesting to consider in what circumstances Lord Denning is prepared to disregard private property rights. In *London Borough of Southwark* v. *Williams* (1971), the Court of Appeal (including Lord Denning) refused to accept that homelessness constituted necessity and therefore a defence to the tort of trespass to land. While protecting our 'playing fields' is sufficiently important, it seems, to justify overriding the interests of private property owners in the public interest, housing the homeless is not. Lord Denning regards any concession to the homeless in this context as a threat to law and order. The public interest and the protection of property run together. But in *Miller* v. *Jackson* (1977), it is the property owners who are perceived as the threat to order, where order is the way of life described by Lord Denning in the opening passage of his judgment. Thus, embedded in Lord Denning's articulation of the law is a race-specific, gender-specific and class-specific view of social life which he quite freely brings to bear upon his assessment of the public interest without any scruples or hesitations about whether or not the images he describes and holds dear are matched in the public he purports to represent.

Some might argue that it is a mistake to make too much of this case as Lord Denning's judgment did not command a majority on the question of liability (although he did have the support of Cumming-Bruce LJ in refusing to grant an injunction) and almost certainly does not represent the law. But Lord Denning's world-view did have a lasting effect upon the lives of the plaintiffs. Moreover, although Lawton LJ in *Kennaway* v. *Thompson* (1981) was reproachful of Lord Denning's judgment in *Miller*, the question of what principles should govern the granting of an injunction in nuisance cases remains open. The traditional criteria embodied in *Shelfer* v. *City of London Electric Lighting Co* (1895), which Lawton LJ in *Kennaway* approves, have been trenchantly criticised. For example, Weir questions whether 'a late Victorian decision' interpreting 'a mid-Victorian Act' should continue to determine the granting of injunctive relief (Weir, 1996, p. 456). Moreover, *Miller* v. *Jackson* (1977) significantly undermined the doctrinal proposition that it is no defence that a plaintiff comes to the nuisance. Subsequent decisions, taking their cue from *Miller*, have allowed the issue to influence the question of remedies *(Kennaway* v. *Thompson* (1981); *Tetley* v. *Chitty* (1986)). Indeed, until *Hunter*, *Miller* v. *Jackson* (1977) might reasonably be seen as the most significant modern case in private nuisance.

Our second example of judicial ingenuity in the face of doctrinal 'constraint' is of historical rather than contemporary legal significance (particularly after *Hunter* v. *Canary Wharf* (1997)) but is nonetheless instructive for that. *Thomas* v. *NUM* (1985) involved an incident in the 1984–85 Miners' Strike. A group of working miners (strike breakers) sought an interlocutory injunction against the National Union of Mineworkers to prevent their members (striking miners) from verbally abusing and harassing them as they went into work. Each day a crowd of some 50–70 picketers gathered at the colliery gates as the working miners entered the workplace in vehicles surrounded by a police guard. The difficulty the court confronted was that it was unclear what, if any, civil wrong the picketers were committing. Scott J searched through the whole gamut of torts for some element of unlawfulness in the defendants' acts. Assault, he held inapplicable because of the absence of any imminent threat of harm to the plaintiffs who were, after all, in armoured vehicles and surrounded by a police guard (on the tort of assault, see further Chapter 7). He also rejected public nuisance in the form of obstruction of the highway because even if an obstruction *was* taking place (on the facts it was unclear), as a public nuisance it could give rise to no private action in the absence of special damage. Nor was there an unlawful interference with the performance of the plaintiffs' contracts of employment because the acts of the picketers did not prevent the performance of any primary obligations under those contracts (on the tort of interference with contractual relations, see further Chapter 7). What wrong, then, was being committed?

Clearly Scott J considered that the rights of the plaintiffs *were* being interfered with, observing that 'the law has long recognised that unreasonable interference with the rights of others is actionable in tort'. Nuisance, he suggested, was a good example. Pursuing the analogy he continued:

> Nuisance is strictly concerned with, and may be regarded as confined to, activity which unduly interferes with the use or enjoyment of land ... But there is no reason why the law should not protect on a similar basis the enjoyment of other rights. All citizens have the right to use the public highway ... The tort might be described as a species of private nuisance, namely unreasonable interference with the victim's right to use the highway. But the label for the tort does not, in my view, matter. (22)

Accordingly, because of the 'unreasonable harassment' of the working miners in the exercise of their right to use the highway, an interim injunction was granted.[15]

The judge in *Thomas* was in a difficult situation. Clearly disapproving of the defendants' conduct, he believed that it could not possibly be lawful. The problem was to find a tort upon which to hang the wrong. However, after due consideration, he dispensed with the need for labels, the principle being sufficient to found a cause of action. Surely, the principle underlying the law of torts was the protection of individual rights from unreasonable interference? In one paragraph, Scott J purported to transform the law of torts from a collection of different wrongs into the embodiment of a single, sacred principle. Like Holmes and his contemporaries he pursued the universal and, having found it, used it to invent a new tort (or at least a serious issue to be tried) with which to thwart the strikers.

What should we make of Scott J's judgment as a statement of law? It takes little legal knowledge to recognise that it drives a coach and four through the distinction between public and private nuisance, abandons without a second thought the requirement that a suit in private nuisance requires an interest in land, recognises a cause of action where none has existed before, and makes a series of assertions which are highly contestable and hopelessly vague in application. The reality is that Scott J's sympathies lay with the working miners and, by manipulating precedent, he was able to reach a result which accorded with his views.

It is important to realise that the decision in *Thomas* was not a mere extension by analogy of the tort of nuisance. It arose from a dispute which was overtly political, with press, police and state united in attempts to portray the strike as, above all else, a threat to law and order and the right to work (a right which notably does not extend to the unemployed or, according to Lord Denning, to those who join trade unions – Denning, 1972). This is but one case in which the courts showed themselves ready to reinforce this portrayal by refusing to recognise that the striking miners' exercise of freedom of speech and assembly was lawful. Not surprisingly, the decision was largely ignored by tort scholars, upsetting, as it does, the neat doctrinal framework upon which textbooks rely; yet, by omitting it, the texts continue to reinforce a sense of doctrinal coherence which disguises the underlying *disorder* which spawns decisions like *Thomas*. Interestingly, when the case *has been* given prominence, it has been to illustrate the typical pragmatism of English courts (Weir, 1996, p. 22). For Weir, the case is not political manipulation but extension 'by analogy' and a legitimate exercise in judicial creativity which may or may not be accepted by the appellate courts (as it happens, the thrust of *Hunter* is to wholeheartedly reject it). Students are thereby encouraged to view Scott J's decision as pursuant to a great British tradition and illustrative of tort law's concern, not just for safety and wealth, but also for freedom (Weir, 1996, p. 22). One might be forgiven for harbouring some scepticism about what sort of freedom Weir has in mind. If this case is about freedom, it places the freedom of strike breakers to work without reproach far above the freedom to act to protect jobs and communities. What *Thomas* illustrates is that tort law is able to defend some freedoms while paying scant attention to others.

Our final example of the relationship between doctrinal constraint and judicial creativity is *Cambridge Water Co Ltd* v. *Eastern Counties Leather plc* (1994) which launched itself as a modern restatement of liability under *Rylands* v. *Fletcher*. The case involved the operation of a tannery (ECL) which used perochlorethene (PCE), a chemical cleaning substance, to degrease pelts. Unknown to ECL, the routine spillage of small quantities resulted in the solvent penetrating the concrete floor of the tannery and gradually seeping into the ground below, eventually reaching a source of the local water supply some 1.3 miles down-catchment from the tannery. The contamination was not discovered until the early 1980s when, after the adoption of a European Directive (relating to the Quality of Water Intended for Human Consumption (80/778/EEC)) which specifically addressed (*inter alia*) levels of PCE in drinking water, tests revealed that levels of PCE at Cambridge Water's Sawston borehole were significantly in excess of the new standards. After tracing the contamination to ECL, Cambridge Water sued alleging negligence, nuisance and liability under *Rylands* v. *Fletcher*.[16] At trial, the plaintiff's claims in nuisance and negligence were dismissed on the grounds that ECL could not reasonably have foreseen either that the solvent would escape in the way that it did or that, having done so, it would contaminate the plaintiff's water supply. The *Rylands* claim was also rejected on the ground that ECL's storage of PCE in the manner and quantities established, was 'for the general benefit of the community' and, therefore, a natural use of land (judgment of Ian Kennedy J in the trial court, summarised by Lord Goff in the House of Lords at 78).

In the Court of Appeal, however, the appellant, Cambridge Water, succeeded. Surprisingly, it did not appeal the original judge's findings in relation to negligence and nuisance – surprising because it is far from clear that a failure to reasonably foresee the manner of escape is properly decisive of the nuisance claim (see Mann LJ's comments on this point at 58). Rather, the arguments before the Court of Appeal related primarily to the judge's ruling on the applicability of *Rylands* v. *Fletcher* and the scope of non-natural user. The Court of Appeal, however, had other ideas. Expressly declining to address the 'fundamental questions relating to the rule in *Rylands*' (at 61–62), Mann LJ chose instead to base his decision on a relatively obscure case, *Ballard* v. *Tomlinson* (1885), which, he claimed, established the principle that the owner of land has a 'natural' right to appropriate by abstraction naturally occurring water beneath his land in an uncontaminated condition, a right which is protected by a civil suit against the polluter. This seemed to him to determine the issue in favour of Cambridge Water: 'In our judgment the case (*Ballard* v. *Tomlinson*) is not distinguishable and the judge was wrong not to apply it' (at 61).[17]

In the House of Lords the original outcome prevailed but for reasons which differed from those given by Ian Kennedy J at first instance. Emphasising that the original decisions on negligence and nuisance had not been appealed, Lord Goff, giving judgment for the House, largely confined himself to a consideration of liability under *Rylands* and, in particular, to the relevance of foreseeability of harm in this context. Disposing first of the Court of Appeal's reliance on *Ballard* (which he did fairly swiftly), Lord Goff stated that the finding of liability in

Ballard, whether based on nuisance or on *Rylands*, had nothing whatsoever to say about the relevance or otherwise of foreseeability. *Ballard* was silent on this point (it did not arise) and, therefore, irrelevant to the general consideration of whether or not a defendant can be liable, either under nuisance or *Rylands*, for harm which he could not reasonably have foreseen. Moving directly to this question, Lord Goff held, first, that *Rylands* v. *Fletcher* was best understood as a particular manifestation of private nuisance relating to isolated escapes (at 71); second, that foreseeability of damage is a prerequisite of liability in nuisance (71–72); and third, that foreseeability of damage was also, therefore, a prerequisite of liability under *Rylands* v. *Fletcher* (72–77). As ECL could not reasonably have foreseen that the damage in question might occur, the plaintiff's action should fail.

How can it be that courts can reach such different outcomes on the same set of facts? How can a case which one court regards as 'determinative' of the matter (as Mann LJ observes 'the law which is binding on this court is clear' at 62) be so blithely dismissed by another? Is *Cambridge Water* an example of a 'hard case' at the edge of doctrinal certainty? Mann LJ does not think so, but Lord Goff clearly regards the case as raising matters in need of clarification. What a pity, then, that he fails to provide such clarification.

The area of uncertainty which Lord Goff sets out to address concerns the relevance of foreseeability of harm to a claim under *Rylands* v. *Fletcher*. Prior to 1994, academics acknowledged some doubt as to whether or not the *Wagon Mound* test of remoteness (i.e. reasonable foreseeability of type of harm) applied to a *Rylands* action but the general consensus seemed to be that it did, although without affecting the standard of *liability* which remained strict. In other words, the manner in which the harm arose (the escape) need not be foreseeable but the harm which followed from that escape must, indeed, be so (Rogers, 1979, p. 419; Heuston and Buckley, 1992, p. 325; Dias and Markesinis, 1989, p. 350). Some authority for this position can be derived from the *Rylands* decision itself: Blackburn J's allusion, for example, to 'anything likely to do mischief' suggests that the defendant must reasonably recognise the dangerous nature of the substance under his control but, having done so, he 'must keep it at his peril', implying liability regardless of whether or not he could reasonably have foreseen and/or guarded against an escape.

In *Cambridge Water*, Lord Goff confirms the correctness of the position of academic commentators as to the applicability of the *Wagon Mound* test of remoteness to the *Rylands* principle. Although not actually characterising the issue as one of remoteness, he affirms that 'foreseeability of damage of the relevant type should be regarded as a prerequisite of liability' (at 76). The difficulty is that he is quite unclear as to whether or not the principle of foreseeability also extends to the manner and fact of the escape (Hilson, 1996). On a strict reading of the judgment, one might conclude that the *ratio decidendi* does not extend beyond foreseeability of type of damage. Indeed, it is probable that this is sufficient to conclude the case in favour of ECL. The facts (as presented by Lord Goff) suggest that ECL could not reasonably have known at the time the solvent was spilled that the quantities of PCE later found in the water supply were sufficient to contaminate it (see especially 77). Indeed, it was acknowledged that before the introduction of the European Directive, levels of PCE were not considered relevant to the question of whether or not water supplied for drinking purposes was 'wholesome' (at 64), Lord Goff being at pains to emphasise that 'the water so contaminated ... has never been held to be dangerous to health' (at 66).

However, does this mean that PCE is not a 'thing likely to do mischief'? Can we honestly conclude that it could not reasonably have been foreseen that if a chemical cleaning fluid got into the water supply it would contaminate it? It is in this sense that the manner in which the contamination occurred becomes important. What was unforeseeable was that PCE in such small quantities would escape, permeate the ground and eventually contaminate the Sawston borehole. In other words, the *type* of damage here is intimately connected to the manner of escape. This is clearly recognised by Ian Kennedy J, the trial judge, who held that:

> ... a reasonable supervisor at ECL would not have foreseen ... that such repeated spillages of small quantities of solvent would lead to any environmental harm or damage – i.e. that the solvent would enter the acquifer or that, having done so, detectable quantities would be found down-catchment. Even if he had foreseen that solvent might enter the acquifer, he would not have foreseen that such quantities would produce any sensible effect upon water taken down-catchment. (summary of Ian Kennedy J's judgment *per* Lord Goff at 64)

This elision by the trial judge of foreseeability of damage with fore-seeability of the manner in which the damage occurs is not addressed by Lord Goff. This, in itself, is sufficient to generate confusion as to precisely what Lord Goff envisages must be foreseen. This confusion is compounded by his Lordship's emphasis in his account of the facts of the extraordinary nature of what has occurred – 'the remarkable history of events which led to the contamination of the Sawston borehole' (at 63; see also his identification of 'relevant facts' at 66), suggesting that the manner of occurrence of the harm is as significant as the fact of its occurrence for purposes of his decision. Moreover, Lord Goff's characterisation of the issue is astonishingly imprecise. At

different points he refers to 'foreseeability of harm' (at 72), 'foreseeability of risk' (at 73) and 'foreseeability of the relevant type of damage'
(at 75 and 76) as if these phrases all possess essentially the same
meaning. Yet any student of tort should know that words like 'risk' and
'harm' can embrace a whole host of concerns which go beyond the
relatively narrow enquiry into type of damage for purposes of
remoteness, and embrace a host of questions relating to the manner
in which the harm occurs, the likelihood of its occurrence and the range
of people or things who might be affected by the activity under
scrutiny. It is hardly surprising then that the headnote preceding the
official report of *Cambridge Water* accords to foreseeability a broader
significance than is traditionally envisaged by the *Wagon Mound* test
of remoteness.

Lord Goff's perusal of the *Ryland* decision itself seems somewhat brief,
aside from a passing allusion (at 72–73) to the most quoted aspects of
Blackburn J's judgment for evidence to support his position (whatever
that might be). Yet a return to the facts of *Rylands* v. *Fletcher* more than
suffices to resolve the issue which Lord Goff's judgment seems to
obfuscate. The whole point of *Rylands* was that the defendant was held
liable *despite* the fact that he could not have anticipated the manner
of escape because he did not and could not reasonably have known
about the disused mineshafts through which water from his reservoir
escaped to flood the plaintiff's land.

One is left wondering whether or not Lord Goff's lack of clarity on
this crucial point is deliberate or unintended. We suspect the former.
Lord Goff seems to have fully recognised the difficulty in characterising the harm which occurs as 'unforeseeable' without reference to *how*
it occurred, but, ironically, he might well have been able to reach the
desired result (a finding in favour of ECL) by a straightforward
manipulation of remoteness rules. One could equally argue *either* that
the type of damage which occurred – water contamination – was a
highly foreseeable consequence of the escape of a chemical substance
or that the type of damage, defined more narrowly in terms of the
failure of the water supply to comply with standards which, at the time
of spillage, did not exist, was, thereby, completely unforeseeable (for
a similar sleight of judicial hand, see *Tremain* v. *Pike* (1969); for an
interesting discussion of other problems relating to the characterisation of the 'damage' in *Cambridge Water*, see Steele, 1995, pp. 246–9).

So viewed, the interesting question is not whether *Cambridge Water*
was correctly decided but rather *why* the law lords chose to decide the
case as they did. To some extent, the result can be attributed to good
housekeeping instincts – Lord Goff considered that the application of
a foreseeability criterion to the determination of liability in *Rylands*
would lead to 'a more coherent body of common law principles' (at 76).
It might be observed, given the doubt with which the case has been

received, that this has more the character of aspiration than actuality. More generally, it is instructive to consider the broader social and political context within which *Cambridge Water* was decided. ECL is judicially perceived as a model company which excites the admiration of right-thinking people. Mann LJ observes that it is of 'high repute' locally, taking a proper 'pride in its history' as a business which was first incorporated in 1879 (at 56). Lord Goff commends the company's 'good standard of housekeeping' and its 'modern and spacious' accommodation (at 63). Into this idyllic scene of industrial industriousness comes a European regulation which, for no demonstrable health reason, renders water from the Sawston borehole no longer 'wholesome' and, thereby, threatens the whole future of this well-established business with a damages bill of almost £1,000,000. Anyone could be forgiven for thinking that this offends justice and common sense, particularly in circumstances where the alleged polluters could not possibly have known that their activities would have such expensive consequences (see, for example, Ogus, 1994). However, the effect of placing the cost of the pollution on Cambridge Water is equally disquieting – they will inevitably recoup their loss through raised water rates, but in what sense is it more just to require the residents of Cambridge to foot the bill?

It might be argued that by placing the cost on Cambridge Water, they are in a better position to *spread* the loss (amongst their customers) than ECL is to absorb it. Cambridge residents are thus merely paying a modest amount to save a decent company from bankruptcy: a form of public subsidy to private industry. On the other hand, this is not necessarily the most economically *efficient* result. In economic terms, it might be argued that it is preferable for the costs of an activity to be borne by those who engage in it – by so doing, those costs are *internalised* and a proper (that is, efficient) level of the activity in question will result (see further below). Yet another way to look at it is in environmental terms. Is the protection of the environment better served by imposing liability on ECL or in absolving them? Are such policy considerations relevant to a determination of liability? This point is considered briefly by Lord Goff who concludes that the goals of environmental protection are more properly the concern of legislation than the common law and, in that context, the fact that the legislature has addressed the issue of environmental protection through the implementation of a public regulatory structure is a reason for the exercise of judicial restraint in the development of the relevant common law principles (at 76). In other words, Lord Goff expressly declines to take account of any public policy concern with 'the protection and preservation of the environment'. Yet his decision has momentous implications in this regard and has, inevitably, come to be assessed in these terms (see, for example, Wilkinson, 1994). Moreover, while Lord

Goff may not choose to view the facts before him in terms of the values of environmental protection, it cannot be asserted that his decision is, therefore, value-free. Indeed, perhaps what *Cambridge Water* most evidences is a fundamental judicial unwillingness to openly acknowledge the real issues and conflicts involved in a dispute – in this case a conflict between environmental concerns and business interests – while, at the same time, enthusiastically reaching an accommodation which is undoubtedly informed by their own perceptions of how that (unacknowledged) conflict should best be resolved.

NUISANCE LAW AND THE ENVIRONMENT

The above discussion suggests that nuisance law operates ideologically and politically. Ideologically, it is heavily weighted in favour of the protection of private property, while politically, its indeterminacy renders it vulnerable to doctrinal manipulation by the courts. Invariably, the costs of applying nuisance law have fallen disproportionately upon the relatively poor and the dispossessed. Nevertheless, it is important to recognise that the very *uncertainty* of tort law does provide some scope for using it instrumentally to pursue socially desirable goals. Moreover, it has been argued that private law claims, particularly nuisance claims, may offer an extra 'access' point to decision-making about environmental issues (Steele, 1995); as McGillivray and Wightman observe, the 'unofficial' character of private law (in the sense of being privately initiated) endows it with a unique potential to challenge official definitions of the public interest, thus offering a strategic alternative to more 'official' mechanisms of policy-making (McGillivray and Wightman, 1997).

It has been observed that nuisance often involves disputes about activities which have an environmental impact. The emission of fumes, the generation of noise and vibrations are obvious environmental harms, the seriousness of which can vary. In this respect, private and public nuisance share a common bond as both can render unlawful environmentally harmful activities. Public nuisance, in particular, has historically concerned itself with matters of health and safety (Brenner, 1974, pp. 420–4). Additionally, many anti-pollution statutes have utilised the concept of statutory nuisance to define and proscribe environmentally harmful activities, for example, the Public Health Act 1936, s. 92(1) (now found in modern form in the Environmental Protection Act 1990, Part III, as amended by the Noise and Statutory Nuisance Act, 1993); the Clean Air Act 1956, s. 16; the Control of Pollution Act 1974 ss. 58–59.[18] Thus, a successful suit in nuisance often has the incidental effect of improving the environment because the interference complained of is generally environmental in nature. Of course, a nuisance may *not* involve environmental harm.

A brothel (*Thomson-Schwab* v. *Costaki* (1956)) or a sex-shop (*Laws* v. *Florinplace* (1981)) may be nuisances but they are not ordinarily regarded as pollutants. Moreover, the environmental interest and the interests of the *plaintiff* do not always coincide. In *Miller* v. *Jackson* (1977), for example, it was the *defendant* cricket club who represented the concerns of conservationists in the face of new development. Similarly, in *Leakey* v. *National Trust* (1980), where the court imposed a duty on the National Trust to protect the plaintiff houseowners from a natural hazard arising on their property, the plaintiff's suit arguably burdened rather than benefited the environment by saddling the National Trust with a duty which might undermine their conservationist objectives.

Nor is nuisance the only tort (or family of torts) which has occasion to address environmental issues. In recent years, a number of cases relating to environmental issues have arisen under trespass (*League Against Cruel Sports* v. *Scott* (1985)), negligence (*Tutton* v. *Walter* (1985)), breach of statutory duty under the Nuclear Installations Act 1965, s. 12 (*Merlin* v. *British Nuclear Fuels plc* (1990)) and even product liability under the Consumer Protection Act (CPA) 1987 (*AB* v. *South West Water Services* (1993)). In environmental terms, these decisions have yielded mixed results. In *League Against Cruel Sports*, for example, an environmental group bought up pockets of land on Exmoor and successfully invoked trespass to prevent the hunting of deer on the sanctuaries thus created; in *Tutton* v. *Walter*, a farmer was held liable in negligence for failing to warn his bee-keeping neighbour that the spray he was using on his crops was dangerous to bees. By contrast, in the *Merlin* case, the plaintiffs were denied compensation under the 1965 Act despite the fact that their house was contaminated by radioactive dust particles emitted by a nearby nuclear power station and, therefore, was not only dangerous but drastically reduced in value. The court held that as the house was not physically damaged, no liability should arise for the 'economic loss' sustained by the plaintiffs. (See, by contrast, the recent decision of the Court of Appeal in *Blue Circle Industries plc* v. *Ministry of Defence* (1998) where it was held that radioactive contamination of the plaintiff's soil, resulting in the loss of a chance of a sale of his property, was not economic loss but physical damage because 'the properties' of the land had changed – *per* Aldous LJ at 393. Although distinguishing rather than overruling *Merlin*, the *Blue Circle* decision clearly raises for consideration the correctness of that decision). Finally, in *AB* v. *South West Water Services,* which involved claims against a water company in relation to highly contaminated water consumed by the plaintiffs with deleterious consequences to their health, the suit (invoking multiple causes of action including negligence, public nuisance, *Rylands*, liability under the CPA and even breach of contract) was successful, but a claim for exemplary and aggravated damages failed (see generally Rogers, 1994, pp. 635–43).

All of these decisions raise for general consideration the viability of the tort as an instrument of pollution control. But in relation to nuisance in particular, it must be said that although it can on occasion benefit the environment, it is not always the case that it does so or that it does so exclusively. Indeed, a consideration of the history of nuisance in the context of the Industrial Revolution suggests that, on the whole, it has been an ineffective weapon against pollution, adapting to accommodate it (for example, by invoking the locality rule or drawing a distinction between physical and amenity damage), rather than combating it. Nuisance law has never really reflected a concern for environmental protection as such. Its primary focus has been to define the rights and limitations attaching to the enjoyment of private property. Environmental damage is only relevant in so far as it poses a threat of harm to someone's proprietary interests. The wrong lies in the violation of property rights not in the destruction of the environment.

It has been observed in Chapter 5 that the mid-twentieth century witnessed a growing trend towards viewing the law in instrumentalist terms, as a means to a particular end. As with negligence, legal and academic debate surrounding nuisance law has been transformed by a focus on its instrumental potential as a mechanism for controlling pollution. Litigation in the United States in the late 1960s and early 1970s, for example in *Boomer* v. *Atlantic Cement Co* (1970) (a nuisance action against a large cement plant operating in Albany, New York) and *Jost* v. *Dairyland Power Cooperative* (1969) (a suit by farmers against a power plant in Wisconsin discharging sulphur dioxide gas harmful to the plaintiffs' crops) stimulated considerable debate about the role of law in combating pollution and the effectiveness and appropriateness of nuisance in this context (Calabresi and Melamed, 1972; Rabin, 1977).

Much of the debate which has emerged addresses the issue in economic terms. For many commentators, the goals of pollution control and economic efficiency are one and the same, and their enquiries take the form of exploring to what extent the common law rules comply with an efficiency standard, making recommendations accordingly. Thus, for example, the traditional rule that it is no defence that the plaintiff came to the nuisance has been criticised as economically wasteful (Baxter and Altree, 1972; Calabresi and Hirschoff, 1972). Similarly, the rules governing the choices of remedies have come under considerable scrutiny (Calabresi and Melamed, 1972; Ogus and Richardson, 1977).

The attractiveness of economic analysis in the context of pollution control lies in the fact that it purports to offer an answer to two crucial questions: first, what level of pollution is acceptable; and second, how is it best achieved? If it is assumed that in a society where individuals are productive, some level of pollution is inevitable and acceptable, the question of how that level is determined is obviously important. Economic theory offers one answer. The desirable level of pollution in any given society is the *efficient* level, meaning that level of pollution which allocates and employs existing resources in such a way as to maximise value in that society. It follows that industrial activities which harm our environment should not necessarily be inhibited by the law of nuisance or other mechanisms. Rather, the *costs* of the activity, including the costs of the environmental harm it inflicts, should be weighed against the *benefits* it confers in terms of wealth production. In this way, it becomes possible, theoretically, to determine how much pollution is consistent with the overall goal of wealth maximisation. The object of economic analysis of law then becomes to ensure that legal rules produce efficient rather than inefficient solutions to private conflicts. In this sense, economic analysis of law operates *prescriptively*. It evaluates law according to a given standard or goal (efficiency) and prescribes a framework of rules consistent with that standard or goal. Efficiency becomes a measure of law's worth and value.[19]

Economic theory is also employed *descriptively*, the object of such analysis being to produce a theory of law which 'seeks to explain legal institutions in ethically neutral and ultimately empirical terms' (Veljanovski, 1986, p. 215). Attention thus focuses on the nature of the common law as a body of rules which have evolved in a gradual and piecemeal fashion, the total product of a series of separate individual disputes, the joint yet uncoordinated effort of different judges in different places at different times. Just as markets tend to operate to maximise wealth despite the absence of any planned or concerted effort to achieve it (Adam Smith's 'invisible hand'), so also (it is suggested) does the common law, in some mysterious and spontaneous fashion, evolve in a way which reflects and promotes the goal of economic efficiency (Veljanovski, 1986, pp. 223–4). In this sense, economic analysis purports to expound a unitary conception of the common law. Just as Holmes sought a unifying principle underlying the apparent chaos of the nineteenth-century action on the case, economic analysis offers the notion of efficiency as the underlying impetus governing the elaboration of common law rules (Veljanovski, 1986, p. 223). Legal doctrine, it is contended, reflects to a considerable extent efficiency concerns. Even where judges have no obvious knowledge of economic concepts and have not in any overt way employed them, their decisions often produce a result which is economically efficient. The claim made here purports to be empirical not normative. Economic analysis offers itself as a neutral, factual account of the form and content of legal doctrine. Its legitimacy rests upon its assumed neutrality. Indeed, even where a prescriptive recommendation is made for the adoption or rejection of a particular rule according to whether or not it is efficient, the exercise is presented as a value-neutral calculation of the correct legal solution. Thus, efficiency is a goal whose desirability is assumed, not argued for. In this way, the goal of pollution control merges naturally with the pursuit of efficiency and the law is viewed as an instrument for the achievement of that end.

In 1960, Coase, writing a seminal article exploring the economic effect of legal liability rules, concluded that, in a situation involving a conflict over land use, the legal rules in theory made no difference to the efficiency of the outcome because, regardless of who was awarded the legal entitlement, the parties would strike a bargain which would produce the most efficient solution (Coase, 1960). However, Coase's argument was qualified by the assumption that the process of negotiation involved no significant transaction costs, for example, the cost of identifying the parties involved, getting them together, initiating and managing the bargaining process. The presence of such costs could mean that legal rules *do* affect the efficiency of the outcome because the bargaining process might be affected by a desire to avoid incurring transaction costs. This suggests that in most situations the presence of transaction costs means that the legal rule employed to resolve disputes over competing land use *is* of significance in bringing about an efficient outcome.

Thus, an economic approach to nuisance requires consideration of the impact of legal rules, including where the legal entitlement should lie (the question of liability) and how to protect it (the question of remedy) (Calabresi and Melamed, 1972). This has led to a dissection of the locality rule, criticism of the rules governing the choice of remedies and arguments for the injection of a cost/benefit calculation into the test of reasonableness (Ogus and Richardson, 1977). In the United States, the input of economics has produced some interesting judicial decisions. In *Boomer* v. *Atlantic Cement Co* (1970), the majority of the court, in effect, declined to enjoin a cement plant's operations on the basis of a cost/benefit calculation as to the relative economic harm inflicted on the parties by the granting or denial of injunctive relief. The court made the denial of an injunction against the defendant dependent upon the payment of permanent damages to the plaintiffs to compensate them for the continued effects of the nuisance. Even more novel was the solution preferred by the court in *Spur Industries Inc* v. *Del E Webb Development Co* (1972) where the Supreme Court of Arizona granted an injunction against a cattle feedlot but required the *plaintiff developers to indemnify the defendants* for the costs of shutting down or moving their operation. The court placed particular emphasis here on the fact that the plaintiffs came to the nuisance and could therefore foresee the likely results of developing in that area, including the detriment to the defendants.

In Britain, the courts have been much more reluctant than their American counterparts to self-consciously adopt an economic perspective in resolving legal disputes, although the influence of political economy on nineteenth-century judges is evident, for example in the judgments of Bramwell B (*Bamford* v. *Turnley* (1862)). It might be argued that Denning's approach in *Miller* v. *Jackson* (1977), at least in so far as it bases the denial of an injunction on grounds of public interest, goes some way towards opening up the possibility of some kind of cost/benefit approach to nuisance where the comparative social utility of the competing activities assumes a greater significance. Similarly, the greater weight given to the granting of planning permission by Buckley J (*Gillingham BC* v. *Medway (Chatham) Dock Co Ltd* (1992)) in the context of determining a nuisance claim (see above, note 3) might be viewed as a judicial attempt to ensure that the public interest dimension is properly taken into account in the resolution of conflicts over private rights (Steele, 1995).[20] The point remains, however, that many of the current legal rules governing nuisance in the UK, for example the 'rule' which precludes pleading that the plaintiff came to the nuisance, and the limited criteria governing the award of damages in lieu of an injunction are vulnerable to the charge of inefficiency. At the same time, the judges do not, on the whole, seem inclined to abandon them.

This has led many commentators to conclude that private law (including nuisance) is *not* a particularly efficient means of controlling pollution. Ogus and Richardson, for example, highlight the common law's protection of private property rights over and above the imperative of efficiency (Ogus and Richardson, 1977, pp. 286–8). They also suggest that the limited conception of damage which nuisance law employs, combined with the selective enforcement of standards dependent on the possession of both a proprietary interest and individual initiative, does not tend to produce the optimum economic result in terms of resource allocation (Ogus and Richardson, 1977, pp. 295–8). Other commentators, such as Julian Le Grand, emphasise the importance of more *direct* forms of government intervention to control pollution (Le Grand, 1985, pp. 118–24). The operation of private law, it is argued, must be viewed within the context of a wider range of legal strategies, particularly the public regulation of polluting activities. This may be seen in the context of water pollution. The law addresses this problem partly through a web of common law entitlements attaching to, for example, riparian ownership (Howarth, 1992), and partly through the operation of a consent system, a form of licensing system operated and enforced by a public regulatory body, the Environment Agency (Water Resources Act 1991). Any evaluation of the law as an instrument for controlling water pollution (whether defined in terms of economic objectives or otherwise) must look at the overall range of legal techniques employed, with a view to identifying their comparative strengths and weaknesses, points of intersection and overlap and common omissions. Just as a focus on accident compensation leads to a comparison of negligence with alternative legal strategies such as social security, a focus on water pollution leads invariably to some evaluation of the comparative worth of public and private forms of legal regulation. This, in turn, raises broader questions about the role and effectiveness of the state. The argument slips imperceptibly from an instrumental consideration of different legal strategies to a political debate about the limits of state action. It also raises questions about the proper definition of the public interest. Although public regulation may express the *official* view of the public interest in, for example, curbing water pollution, private law – at least in a 'twin-track' system (that is, one which does not necessarily require the deferral of private to public law but recognises the possibility that they will yield 'different answers' to the question of whether or not an activity is lawful or unlawful) – creates the possibility of alternative, competing definitions of what the public interest requires (McGillivray and Wightman, 1997, pp. 180–93).

At this point an economic approach to the problem of pollution sheds its guise of political neutrality and assumes critical significance in directing the choice of legal mechanisms and defining the limits of state action. In this context, private law poses an attractive mechanism of pollution control in allegedly mirroring the market's ability to produce an unplanned economically efficient result. Those who are politically opposed to extensive state intervention are likely to espouse private law in preference to stronger forms of government intervention in the form of public law regulation. Private law becomes part of a market-based response to the problem of pollution control. Such an approach is particularly evident in EC policy-making (see, for example, the 1993 'Green Paper on Remedying Environmental Damage' (EC, 1993) and the 1996 'Progress Report on the Fifth European Community Environmental Action Programme' (EC, 1996, para. 4.6)) but can also be detected in UK policy development (see, in particular, the 1990 Conservative Government White Paper, 'This Common Inheritance' (Department of Environment (DOE), 1990, Cm. 1200, Annex A) and the UK's 'Response to the Communication from the Commission of the European Communities (COM(93)47 Final Green Paper on Remedying Environmental Damage', December 1993).[21] The essential idea behind market-based approaches to pollution control is to find ways to ensure that prices are a true reflection of a cost/benefit calculation which has taken proper account of environmental factors. Private law is relocated amidst other strategies aimed at achieving the right price signals, including privatisation of polluting industries (for example, electricity and water), taxes and charges on polluting activities and, to a lesser extent, subsidies and administrative regulation. The choice of policy may vary but the overall focus of such an economic approach is to posit the market, not the state, as the primary regulator. In this context, civil liability rules may, in some circumstances, be an appropriate regulatory mechanism, providing polluters with an incentive to minimise costs by carrying out their activities with reasonable care (DOE, 1990, A. 27). This, of course, presupposes a negligence standard but some economists argue that strict rather than fault-based liability may be the more efficient standard of pollution control on the grounds that it internalises some of the costs which the polluting activity generates (Polinski, 1989, pp. 91–6). The price of the activity thus more accurately reflects its true costs (see the EC Commission's 'Green Paper on Remedying Environmental Damage' (COM(93)47 final) and the Council of Europe's 'Lugano' Convention on 'Civil Liability for Damage Resulting from Activities Dangerous to the Environment' for considerations of strict liability in this context).

Of course, an economic approach does not always lead to the espousal of private over public forms of regulation, nor does it necessarily result in the privileging of market-based strategies (see Le Grand, 1985, pp. 106–26). However, as the goal of efficiency is the self-declared aim and virtue of the market system, it certainly lends legitimacy to an approach to pollution which emphasises the limits of state action.[22]

More fundamentally, the reinterpretation of environmental protection as a function of economic efficiency proceeds on the assumption that the environment is a resource, essentially subordinate to human needs and desires and at humans' disposal in pursuit of personal gain. This assumption in turn depends upon a particular view of human nature which perceives the pursuit of individual self-interest as both natural and desirable. It is only by self-motivated individual interaction that wealth is generated. Moreover, the more wealth produced, the more everyone gains in the long run. Such a view of human nature and interaction forms the basis of Adam Smith's defence of the market system.[23] It has also served to legitimate the systematic destruction of our environment by industrial and commercial activity over at least the last 200 years. In its modern, 'environmentally friendly' form, this position finds expression in the concept of 'sustainable development' which Wilkinson describes as 'the fundamental tenet of environmental law' (Wilkinson, 1997). Essentially, sustainable development is a form of inter-generational cost/benefit analysis. Its origins are attributable to the Brundtland Report, *Our Common Future* (World Commission on Environment and Development, 1987) in which it is defined as 'development which meets the needs of the present without compromising the ability of future generations to meet their own needs' (see also Pearce et al., 1989 and Cm. 2426, 'Sustainable Development: the UK Strategy', DOE, 1994). This, in itself, tells us little because everything depends upon the meaning given to the aspiration that future 'needs' should not be 'compromised'. According to Pearce, what is required is that a given generation should not pass on to subsequent generations less capital than it has itself inherited. 'Capital' in this context consists of both human-made and environmental capital (for example, natural resources, the ozone layer). The 1994 Strategy paper is less precise, attributing to the principle of sustainable development merely a concern that 'decisions throughout society are taken with proper regard to their environmental impact' (DOE, Cm. 2426, 1994, para. 3.2). So long as environmental effects are properly taken into account, economic development can continue. Sustainable development is, thus, the modern environmentally friendly legitimation of continuing economic development. As the 1994 Paper comments: 'Sustainable development does not mean less economic development: on the contrary, a healthy economy is better able to generate the resources to meet people's needs' (para. 12).

Difficulties associated with the definition of sustainable development are further compounded by a lack of agreement as to how environmental assets are to be valued for purposes of any balancing exercise. While much of the 1994 Paper focuses on different methods of environmental accounting, it is clear that this is essentially a subjective exercise which depends significantly on the weight which a society chooses to place upon its environmental resources. While sustainable development implicitly assumes that there is a correct answer to the question of what value we place on environmental assets, there *is* no factual value which attaches to a human life or a fine view, only the value which a society or an individual chooses to put on it. The economic solution to the problem of 'valuing' values is to define them in terms of individual willingness to pay. Thus, saving the whales, scenic conservation and water quality are all ultimately quantifiable.

The idea that the moral or aesthetic values and political goals which a given society adopts and pursues can be costed mathematically in terms of individual willingness to pay seems inherently absurd. Apart from the fact that not all individuals are in the same position to express their value preferences because of a comparative or absolute *inability* to pay, many values and aspirations *collectively* expressed and pursued, are not reducible either to individual preferences or to mathematical equations (Sagoff, 1988, pp. 26–42). Cost/benefit analysis, because it is based on the sum total of individual interactions, cannot encompass a conception of society as something more than the aggregation of individuals.

It is also important to understand why we have underestimated the value of the environment in the past. The answer lies not, as is traditionally suggested, in the state of scientific knowledge, but rather in the structure of private property rights which underlie the market system. In the context of environmental assets, either they are *owned* (for example a forest, a particular stretch of river) in which case the proprietor alone possesses rights over them, or they are ownerless (the air, the ozone layer) in which case they may be overused. Moreover, in the absence of a private property right, there is no market by which a value can be ascribed. Environmental assets such as rivers and forests which can be owned are valued primarily in terms of their benefit to their proprietor. For example, if I wish to sell my forest to a company intent upon its devastation, the loss to the community at large which such a transfer of property might occasion does not tend to find its way into negotiations over price. Because the surrounding community has no property right in the forest, any value it might set upon it is likely to be discounted (absent conservation-conscious public regulation governing the transaction). The system of property rights defines which values count and which do not. Similarly, if a company chooses to set up a factory on the banks of a river which it intends to pollute, the riparian owners have rights in relation to the river but the rest of the community may not (subject to limited benefits of planning regulations). Thus, in making cost/benefit calculations about the potential productivity of the factory, the company need only take account of the potential infringement of the property rights of downstream riparian owners. The social cost to the community, *at least so far as private law is concerned*, is not part of the equation. So viewed, the system of property ownership contributes to the problem of pollution by ensuring that certain values are discounted for purposes of decisions about the use of resources. Private property ensures that we get our sums wrong. Private law, with its emphasis on the protection of proprietary interests, compounds the problem and market-based strategies, which presuppose private property rights, generally reinforce it. It is no accident that until now we have grossly underestimated the environment. The destruction of the environment is directly attributable to the system of private property.

It follows that it is only when we cease to see the environment as a commodity, as something which can be owned, bought, sold and consumed at a price, that we can begin to repair and restore the world around us. Likewise, it is only when we begin to question the prevailing perception of humanity's relationship with nature (as dominant and exploitative) that we can move forward. The main challenge to this 'dominant world-view' comes from the philosophy of deep ecology

(Devall and Sessions, 1985, pp. 42–8, 65–76). 'Deep green' perspectives conceive of the relationship between human and nature in terms of harmony and coexistence rather than dominance and exploitation. Moreover, far from seeing the environment as a resource for human consumption, nature is regarded as possessing intrinsic worth with all its species carrying an equal value. Development, understood in terms of current economic and material expectations, is arguably incompatible with such an ecological vision which emphasises the importance of spiritual, non-material growth.

An alternative critical approach to environmental problems may be found in Marxist theory. Notwithstanding the ecological fiasco in Eastern Europe, many Marxist thinkers attribute environmental problems to the operation of capitalism and, consequently, see their solution in terms of radical change in our mode of production (Wilkinson, 1997, pp. 168–74). 'Sustainable development', by positing the possibility of accommodating the demands of capital with the needs of the environment, is regarded with suspicion if not downright hostility; the popularity of the concept is viewed as evidencing its political and environmental impotency:

> The problem for environmentalists who advocate sustainable development is that Western Governments have adopted the phrase without it making the slightest difference to what they do or altering the human and natural environment in any part of the world. (Gibson, 1991, p. 23)

Thus, in so far as the concept of 'sustainable development' reflects the dominant paradigm of exploitation rather than harmony, it is, arguably, of little value in the struggle to save our planet. The environment we live in should not, as economists suggest, be seen as 'capital' which we are free to dispose of or trade. Whether the way forward lies in deep ecology or, alternatively, in dismantling capitalism, the answer to the serious ecological crisis which presently confronts us arguably lies elsewhere than in the chimeric concept of sustainable development.

CONCLUSION

What can we conclude from exploring the potential of nuisance as an environmental protection mechanism? It is obvious that some gains can be made from the instrumental use of private law. Anti-bloodsport organisations can assert property rights to prevent the pursuit of wild deer on their lands (*League Against Cruel Sports* v. *Scott* (1985)). River conservation groups can buy up riparian land and seek to prevent river pollution by exercising their legal rights as riparian owners. Farmers who use environmentally unfriendly cropsprays may be called to account (*Tutton* v. *Walter* (1985)). Sometimes too, private law can provide an additional means of access to public debate. Although such litigation is generally couched in terms of a conflict between public interest and private rights, what is often contested is the meaning of 'public interest' being utilised (*Gillingham BC* v. *Medway (Chatham) Dock Co Ltd* (1992)). It has also been suggested that private law is capable of developing in ways which reflect a broader range of interests in property than those of the legal 'owner', to include collective interests in environmental conservation (McGillivray and Wightman, 1997).

At the same time, an exploration of the instrumental potential of nuisance in this context suggests that the way forward is fraught with difficulties because, aside from the practical problems (particularly in relation to the funding of private claims), both legal doctrine and its modern instrumental applications continue to proceed upon the basis of a set of ideological assumptions about the environment and our relationship to it which arguably bear considerable responsibility for the problem of pollution in the first place. The recent decision of the House of Lords in *Hunter* v. *Canary Wharf* (1997), for example, restating the strict need for a proprietary interest in land in order to sue in nuisance, evidences the continued vitality of this ideology despite its lack of correspondence with modern concerns to protect the environment and to invest in concepts of property a broader range of protectable interests (Wightman, 1998).

Thus, while some gains can and should be made through law, as a strategy for more fundamental change, its strength lies not so much in those gains, but in the occasion they provide for organising, campaigning and coming together to inform and stimulate a wider public debate about the issues they raise.

7
Feminist Perspectives on Tort Law: Remedying Sexual Harassment and Abuse

INTRODUCTION

> Sexual harassment, the event, is not new to women. It is the law of injuries that it is new to. (MacKinnon, 1989, p. 103)

In recent decades, the emergence of feminist critical approaches to law has been highly visible, both in legal literature and in practice. Salient examples include Smart, 1989; Graycar and Morgan, 1990; Fineman and Thomadsen, 1991; Bottomley and Conaghan, 1993; Olsen, 1995; Bottomley, 1996; Bridgeman and Millns, 1998. A dominant theme of such approaches is the contention that law is gendered: that is, that it embodies and reflects viewpoints which are informed by gender stereotypes or which invoke gendered assumptions about the respective roles, capabilities and aspirations of men and women. Moreover, in most cases, the point of reference upon which law is constructed is male – law, it is said, expresses and reinforces a primarily male point of view.[1] So, for example, feminist lawyers and academics have forcefully argued that the criminal defence of provocation, as traditionally conceived, more accurately characterises male rather than female behaviour, requiring women to comply with this standard or suffer the consequences (Nicolson and Sanghvi, 1993, 1995, commenting, in particular, on *R.* v. *Ahluwahlia* (1992) and *R.* v. *Humphries* (1995)). Similarly, before its final recognition in *R.* v. *R.* (1991), feminists campaigned for years for the legal recognition of an offence of rape within marriage, arguing that the denial of an offence in such circumstances reinforced antiquated notions of wives as the property of their husbands (see, for example, Temkin, 1987). In the sphere of employment law, the Equal Opportunities Commission (EOC) has successfully argued that the exclusion of part-time workers from employment rights constitutes sex discrimination, contrary to European law, because the vast majority of part-timers are women (*R.* v. *Secretary of State for Employment ex parte Equal Opportunities Commission* (1994)). The government has since been compelled to change the relevant legislation so that it no longer discriminates against those in part-time work.

In the same vein, it has been contended that tort law is imbued with gendered perspectives which inform both the setting and application of legal standards and rules. It has been asserted that the 'reasonable man' standard reflects male rather than female perceptions of what is and is not reasonable behaviour (Bender, 1988; Martyn, 1994; see further Chapter 3). It has also been argued that the assessment of damages in tort law, by defining people's worth primarily in terms of their earning power, values men more than women and thus reinforces their social and economic dominance (Finley, 1989, p. 898; Graycar, 1985). It has even been suggested that the interests which tort law protects and the array of harms which it effectively remedies are gendered in the sense that the tortious concept of harm does not easily embrace injuries typically associated with women, such as those arising from domestic violence or sexual harassment (Graycar and Morgan, 1990, pp. 284–95, Conaghan, 1996, 1998).[2] Tort law, then, is gendered not just in terms of the standards it invokes, but also in terms of the conduct to which such standards are applied. While some kinds of harm are easily assimilated within the traditional corpus of tort, others do not lend themselves so easily to tortious characterisation. Feminists contend that gender goes some way in explaining this perceived lack of fit.

It is worth testing this contention by exploring the way in which tort law does, in fact, remedy wrongs more typically associated with (although not necessarily exclusively experienced by) women. In the last edition of this book we sought to do this by probing tort's ability to provide a remedy for a common wrong which affects most women at some point in their lives, namely sexual harassment. In the course of this exercise, we trawled through and tested the limits of the 'intentional torts', particularly those comprising 'trespass to the person', whose character and composition are, in some ways, very different from the otherwise ubiquitous tort of negligence. In so doing, we self-consciously relied upon a central method of feminist legal analysis which seeks to critique case law by uncovering and articulating the gendered assumptions which often lie behind the gender-neutral facade of legal categories and rules. We tried to show not only the difficulties which women faced in seeking to make the wrongs comprising sexual harassment 'fit' with existing tortious categories, but also the possibilities which presented themselves within the interstices of the common law for developing a remedy where none (or virtually none) at that time existed.

Since then, however, the civil law governing sexual harassment (and, indeed, harassment in general) has undergone a virtual revolution. In the sphere of discrimination law, the abolition of the damages cap on sex discrimination claims, following the European Court of Justice decision in *Marshall* v. *Southampton & South West*

Hants Area Health Authority (No 2) (1993), and the adoption by EC members of a Recommendation and Code of Conduct addressing the implementation of measures to combat sexual harassment in the workplace (Commission Recommendation 91/131/EEC and Code of Practice on the Protection of the Dignity of Men and Women at Work), has greatly increased the attractiveness of discrimination law as a forum for redress in this context.[3] At the same time, the availability of tort-based relief has expanded dramatically. By a clever marrying of equitable and common law concepts, the courts enlarged the scope of injunctive relief within their inherent jurisdiction (*Khorasandjian* v. *Bush* (1993);[4] *Burris* v. *Azadani* (1995); injunctive relief has also been statutorily extended (see the Family Law Act 1996, Part IV and the Protection from Harassment Act 1997, s. 3) and, with the recent passing of the Protection from Harassment Act 1997 (PHA), a new statutory tort of harassment has been created.

In these circumstances, it might be suggested that there is no longer any point in scrutinising common law categories in order to assess the ability of tort to capture and redress acts of harassment. Clearly, harassment is now a tort (albeit statutorily created) in its own right. However, for a number of reasons, we consider the exercise to be of value. First, as we shall see, the definition of harassment under the new Act is vague and it may well be that common law concepts will still have a significant role to play in the course of statutory interpretation. Moreover, the Act, while broadly drawn, is not as comprehensive as it might at first appear, and from the perspective of harassment victims, the more hooks upon which to hang a wrong, the better. Such an exploration will introduce the reader to a wide range of different torts crossing a spectrum of interests, including the protection of person, property and economic relations, and, at the same time, effectively illustrate the creative potential of tort law and its ability to reinvent itself, given new and entirely different circumstances. Finally, the ideological critique which emerges from this examination of tort categories is powerful and, we hope, is further strengthened by the accompanying consideration of tort law's effectiveness as a remedy in the context of acts of physical and sexual abuse. In considering some of the difficulties which claimants in such cases have encountered, we hope to further highlight the gendered content of tort law and its potential (or otherwise) to overcome its own in-built deficiencies.

SEXUAL HARASSMENT AND TRADITIONAL TORTIOUS REMEDIES

Harassment is variously defined in statutes (see, for example, PHA 1997, s. 1; Protection from Eviction Act 1977, s. (3)(3A)), leaflets, employment contracts and equal opportunities policies. There is no necessary consistency in the definitions invoked and some embrace a much wider range of conduct than others. Definitions of sexual harassment are similarly diffuse, although they share a common focus on conduct which is *unwelcome* and which is either sexually motivated or sexual in character. According to Women Against Sexual Harassment (WASH), sexual harassment may take a variety of forms, including 'comments about appearance/body/clothes; leering and staring at a person's body; abusive, degrading, patronising or belittling remarks or behaviour, sexist remarks or jokes; unwelcomed sexual invitations or pressure; promises or threats concerning employment conditions in exchange for sexual favours; displays of sexually explicit material; touching, caressing, hugging, even sexual assault or rape' (WASH, *Sexual Harassment in the Workplace: Don't put up with it!*). Although this provides a very wide definition of sexual harassment, not only does it thereby offer a range of conduct whose tortious or non-tortious character can be tested and explored, but, in encompassing serious acts of abuse within the general rubric of harassment, it enables us to consider abuse and harassment issues side-by-side.

1. Trespass to Person

Some acts constituting sexual harassment may be redressable through recourse to the traditional torts comprising trespass to the person.

Battery

According to *Winfield & Jolowicz*, a battery is the intentional and direct application of force to another person (Rogers, 1994, p. 58). 'Force' in this context is usually taken to mean causing contact to the person of another without her consent (Trindade, 1982, p. 216). Thus, 'traditional' affronts to a woman's bodily integrity, including rape and other forms of unwanted sexual assault, are actionable batteries. Until recently, women rarely invoked tortious remedies to redress such wrongs. This is partly because an award of compensation is of little value where the defendant is in no position to pay: liability insurance is not generally available to cover such acts as rape and assault. Additionally, victims of crime may receive compensation from other sources, for example, the Criminal Injuries Compensation Scheme (currently governed by the Criminal Injuries Compensation Act 1995).[5] Recent changes to that scheme, however, resulting in awards which are generally lower than tort damages (Conaghan, 1998, pp. 155–6), combined with a growing consciousness by victims of sexual and physical assault of the remedial possibilities offered by tort claims, are generating an increasing number of (not always successful) civil suits against the perpetrators of harassment and abuse (see, for example, *Church* v. *Church* (1983) – battery suit by wife against estranged husband in context of domestic violence; *Stubbings* v. *Webb* (1993) – suit by adult survivor of childhood sexual abuse against stepfather and stepbrother who abused her; *Pereira* v. *Kelman* (1996) – suit by three daughters against sexually abusive father; see also the recent award of £14,000 to a woman who was raped by her husband, heralded as the first civil suit by a wife against her husband for rape within a subsisting marriage, *The Times*, 10 September 1997).

The essence of the wrong in the tort of battery is the *impermissibility of bodily contact*. It follows that a battery need not produce actual physical harm. As a species of trespass, it is actionable *per se*. Thus, impermissible contact which takes the form of an insult, for example, a spit, constitutes a battery (*R.* v. *Cotesworth* (1704)). As Fleming observes: 'The action serves the dual purpose of affording protection to the individual not only against bodily harm but also against any interference with his person which is offensive to a reasonable sense of honour and dignity' (Fleming, 1987, p. 23). To kiss a woman without her consent, or to touch her in any way sexually without her permission is certainly offensive to a reasonable sense of honour and dignity. It is also a battery. Any act of sexual harassment which involves unwanted contact – a 'friendly' pat or slap, an uninvited caress, the touching of any part of a woman's body in a sexual manner – can amount to battery in tort.

However, the prohibition of unwanted contact which the tort of battery implies, is subject to a number of qualifications. First, the contact must result from a 'direct' and 'positive' act of the defendant (as opposed to being merely 'consequential' upon the defendant's conduct, Heuston and Buckley, 1996, pp. 5–6). Second, case law suggests that certain kinds of bodily contact must be tolerated as 'generally acceptable in the ordinary conduct of daily life' (*Collins* v. *Wilcock* (1984) *per* Robert Goff LJs at 378). Thus, the inevitable 'jostling' in the underground at rush hour, or in a shop on the first day of the sales, is to be regarded as part and parcel of daily life, not as something which should be the subject of legal complaint. While such casual bodily contacts may offend our dignity, they are the inevitable consequences of social life, the price to be paid for the benefits of living in a community.

But, in considering what constitutes contact 'generally acceptable in the ordinary conduct of human life', the behaviour which characterises sexual harassment becomes problematic. Simply put, there is no general consensus as to whether and to what extent a friendly 'slap and tickle' constitutes acceptable or unacceptable behaviour. In particular, there tends to be a divergence in male and female perceptions of such behaviour. What men may see as a compliment, women often experience as an insult; what men offer as a gesture of intimacy and friendship, women may perceive as an invasion of privacy. Both men and women tend to regard certain forms of sexual expression as inappropriate to particular situations, but there is little consensus between them as to where the line should be drawn. In particular, although the operation of a series of sexual norms about women's accessibility, through marriage, relationships or prostitution, tends to influence most men's sexual behaviour up to a point, many see no harm in the occasional sexual gesture of a 'minor' nature which, in their view, should offend no one. It breaks no proscription, threatens no relationship and, it is argued, is only the normal response of a 'red-blooded' man to the presence of a woman.

The perception of sexual harassment as a 'normal' expression of maleness inevitably problematises Robert Goff LJ's notion of 'generally acceptable conduct'. The feminist challenge to this perception, based on the insistence that women experience such behaviour as neither normal nor acceptable, questions both the male perception of what is acceptable conduct and the assumption that there is a consensus about it which the law can reflect. General open-ended standards such as 'acceptable conduct' and 'reasonableness' are particularly vulnerable to the feminist charge of bias in this respect. By embodying male perceptions under a guise of neutrality, they thereby preclude recognition of women's experiences and their divergence from those of men (see further, Chapter 3).

The prevalence of a primarily male point of view, both in the judiciary (in which profession women continue to make few gains – McGlynn, forthcoming) and in legal doctrine, inevitably makes difficult the classification of sexually offensive behaviour as wrongful and legally redressible. A woman who pursues a battery claim in circumstances which involve a 'minor' touching, for example, a slap on the bottom, may be viewed as petty and vindictive. Far from asserting her 'constitutional rights' (Weir, 1996, p. 333), she is more likely to be regarded as wasting the court's time. Possibly, her claim may be thrown out on *de minimus* grounds. The technical presence of a battery is not likely to dispose the court well towards her, and an award of nominal damages will simply convey the court's view that no real harm has been done. Of course, the 'technical' battery may have taken place in the context of an increasingly difficult and stressful situation of continuous verbal harassment, involving sexual innuendos, intimate remarks and other offensive comments which the woman has found insulting and upsetting. However, these are not wrongs which the tort of battery redresses. By focusing on the act of touching as the legally redressable wrong, the law both denies the harm inflicted by non-physical forms of sexual harassment and, at the same time, diminishes the harm engendered by the physical act, by considering it in relative isolation from the surrounding circumstances.[6]

Other aspects of the tort of battery also sit uncomfortably with social perceptions of sexual harassment. In 1704, Holt CJ asserted that 'the least touching of another in anger is a battery' (*Cole v. Turner*

(1704)). In 1987, Croom-Johnson LJ relied on this assertion as authority for the view that battery required 'a hostile touching' (*Wilson* v. *Pringle* (1987) at 253). At first glance, Croom-Johnson LJ's statement seems inconsistent with the traditional view that motive is irrelevant so long as the act of contact is intended. Thus, the fact that the contact was the result of a practical joke (*Williams* v. *Humphrey* (1975)) or an expression of affection is irrelevant, if, in fact, the contact took place without consent: 'an unwanted kiss may be a battery although the defendant's intention may be most amiable' (*per* Lord Denning in *R.* v. *Chief Constable of Devon and Cornwall, ex parte CEGB* (1982) at 471, quoting Heuston, 1977, p. 120).

A closer scrutiny of Croom-Johnson LJ's judgment suggests that he is not employing the concept of hostility in its commonly understood sense (Hepple and Matthews, 1991, p. 580), although what exactly he *does* mean is open to question. As Winfield and Jolowicz remark, it appears to mean 'little more than that the defendant wilfully interferes with the plaintiff in a way to which he is known to object' (Rogers, 1994, p. 60). In a subsequent House of Lords decision, *F* v. *West Berkshire Health Authority* (1989), Lord Goff doubted, *obiter*, the correctness of Croom-Johnson LJ's requirement. Thus, the weight of authority is against a requirement of hostility or anger as a necessary ingredient of battery. However, it continues to cast its shadow over existing case law, having the potential to rematerialise. The perception, whether judicially correct or not, that battery involves a hostile touching, accompanied by the common assumption that sexual harassment is not motivated by hostility and, indeed, is often the product of affection or appreciation, makes such behaviour even less likely to appear wrongful in the eyes of the law.

Of course, from the point of view of women, sexual harassment generally is hostile. The assumption of sexual accessibility which such behaviour implies is insulting. It is, therefore, unacceptable for men to say that their motive for acting was friendly and lacked ill-will. To treat a woman as a sexual object is to devalue, undermine and deny her. It is also to assert power over her. This is hostile behaviour whether those who engage in it expressly acknowledge it or not. However, as social attitudes stand, the woman who responds unfavourably to a wolf-whistle or a 'complimentary' remark is considered at best ungracious and at worst ungrateful. Her sense of insult and embarrassment are discounted as 'over-reaction', precisely because the original act is perceived as benign. It does not take a great leap of imagination to envisage the presence of similar attitudes in judges in the context of tortious litigation involving sexual harassment, particularly while the insidious requirement of hostility continues to lurk in the vicinity of the tort of battery.

A crucial component of the tort of battery is the absence of consent and this, too, poses potential problems for those seeking to use tort law to redress acts of sexual harassment. Consensual sexual touching is obviously not a battery: it is absence of consent that renders the act unlawful. However, although a mistaken belief that consent has been given, when in fact it has not, does not, by itself, excuse the act in tort, a *reasonably held* belief that the plaintiff, based on her conduct, has consented will be sufficient to excuse the defendant (*O'Brien* v. *Cunard Steamship Co* (1891)). The plaintiff, by her conduct, will be deemed to have impliedly consented to the act. As Fleming remarks: 'A girl who is silent to an amorous proposal cannot afterwards capriciously complain of assault' (Fleming, 1987, p. 73).

In what circumstance might a court deem a woman to have impliedly consented to sexually harassing behaviour? Can she be said to have consented if she makes no complaint when sexual remarks are made, if she fails to protest when her bottom is slapped, if she smiles politely or even attempts to enter into the humour of the occasion? While the law answers in the affirmative, sexual harassment commonly takes place in situations where the harasser has some power over his victim, especially at work. In such circumstances, a woman may not feel that an immediate protest – or, indeed, any protest – is worth while. In an effort not to jeopardise her employment position, she may attempt to deal with the situation in ways which do not involve confrontation with the offender, for example by making light of it, ignoring it or talking to someone else at the workplace. She may feel that she has little option but to tolerate the behaviour because the chances of resolving the matter satisfactorily, or to her advantage, are minimal. In these circumstances, the harasser is free to harass. By her conduct a woman consents to his offensive behaviour. Thus, the law places the burden squarely on the woman to take action against the harasser, rather than demanding that the harasser should act in a sensitive, respectful and inoffensive way in the first place. Moreover, the law is unlikely to take much account of the social situation in which the harassment occurs. This is because battery, like tort law in general, utilises a concept of consent which is based on the idea that individuals are responsible for their acts. Thus, a failure to protest signals consent even if it is reluctantly given. This is well illustrated in the nineteenth-century case of *Latter* v. *Braddell* (1880), involving the examination of a housemaid by a doctor on the instructions of her mistress, who thought (mistakenly) that she was pregnant. The plaintiff housemaid submitted to the doctor's examination but protested and sobbed throughout. The court found that in the absence of any actual threat of violence, the housemaid must be deemed to have consented to the doctor's action. The view of the majority was that 'reluctant obedience' (*per* Lindley J) was distinguishable from lack of consent and the court expressly refused to take account of the social and economic pressures which forced a woman to submit to a painful and humiliating medical examination against her will. Although the relatively modern decision of *Freeman* v. *Home Office* (1984) potentially offers a more flexible approach to the question of when consent may be freely given in the context of a relationship of power or coercion (*Freeman* involved the administration of medication to a prisoner), the outcome of that decision evidences the difficulties which plaintiffs have in overcoming a presumption of consent, even in a physically oppressive situation.

Sexual harassment is behaviour which generally takes place in situations where there is some disparity of power between the parties. Whether it be an employment relationship, a teacher/student situation or even a situation where the formal status of the parties is the same, sexual harassment almost invariably involves some abuse of power, sexual, social or economic. However, traditionally, in law, the only abuse of power which will vitiate the 'apparent' consent of the victim in a battery situation is the threat of physical violence. The perception of social activity in terms of interacting individuals whose circumstances are largely irrelevant for purposes of determining liability is of little practical use in combating the insidious wrong of sexual harassment. To deny the relevance of certain aspects of the relationship between the plaintiff and the defendant, to abstract them from their social and economic context, as tort law commonly does, is to ignore a fundamental dimension of the wrong inherent in many acts of sexual misconduct – the violation or abuse of a position of trust and/or authority.

A further factor relevant to a determination of whether a woman has consented to sexual contact is her mode of dress. In the context of sex discrimination cases, evidence that a woman has dressed in a sexually provocative fashion has been considered relevant in determining whether or not the defendant sexually discriminated against her by engaging in sexually harassing behaviour (*Wileman* v. *Minnilec Engineering* (1988)). The reason for regarding mode of dress as a relevant consideration appears to lie in the assumption that a woman provokes, and intends to provoke, sexual advances by what she wears. Thus, the man who advances is not sexually discriminating on grounds of sex but merely responding to an invitation. Similarly, for purposes of battery, provocative dress may contribute to a 'reasonable' belief on the part of the defendant that bodily contact was consented to.

The idea that a man can reasonably assume that a woman's dress offers an invitation to him to make sexual advances rests on the assumption that women dress for men when they dress in a 'sexually provocative' fashion. Apart from the fact that the definition of what constitutes 'provocative' derives from male perceptions of the essentially sexual nature of a woman's body, the notion that women are inviting indiscriminate sexual advances by virtue of what they wear is as ridiculous as assuming that a woman, when she kisses a particular man, is inviting him into her bed (another common but equally absurd assumption). But, it is further asserted, some modes of dress send out signals of availability, regardless of the absence of intention on the part of the woman so dressed to transmit such signals. Certain clothes signal sexual availability. That is their social meaning and men are entitled to assume that such a meaning is intended. Why? Why should a man assume, first, that an invitation is being made (when women often dress with no such invitation in mind) and, second, that the invitation, if present, is directed at him? Why should men assume what women expressly deny? The continued relevance of dress in legal issues revolving around the presence or absence of consent to sexual acts merely serves to illustrate how male stereotypical assumptions about women's behaviour become the primary interpretation which a court is prepared to accept or act upon.

Assault

Assault, according to *Winfield & Jolowicz*, is 'an act of the defendant which causes to the plaintiff reasonable apprehension of the infliction of a battery on him by the defendant' (Rogers, 1994, p. 58). Thus, unlike battery, the wrong lies, not in any actual physical invasion or contact, but in the mental anxiety produced by anticipating such bodily invasion or contact. Assault, then, is rare in providing a remedy for the inducement of purely emotional as opposed to physical harm. Of course, in practice, assault and battery usually occur together. The immediate anticipation of a battery (assault) will almost always be followed by one, although it is possible for the assailant to stop before actual bodily contact occurs, in which case only an assault will have been committed. Likewise, a battery can occur without an assault (for example, by unconsented bodily contact while the victim is asleep). Thus, assault and battery do address and redress technically separable harms, even if they commonly operate as a team.

Why should the law provide a remedy for non-physical harm in this instance and not in many others? Why should anxiety, created by an apprehension of imminent bodily contact, generate a recognised legal wrong when other forms of anxiety and distress, created perhaps by verbal insults or threats falling short of assault (for example, on the telephone), are traditionally non-remediable? Commonly, such a question is answered by pointing to the history of the tort of trespass and its essentially criminal origins: assault, it is said, became a remediable wrong because it posed a potential breach of the peace (Brazier, 1993, p. 28). In particular, it was feared that the absence of legal redress would lead to unlawful retaliatory action (Fleming, 1987, p. 24). Thus, the remedy provided by the tort of assault is a widely acknowledged historical accident. It hardly seems a rational and coherent basis for distinguishing between different types of emotional harm today.

The limits of the tort of assault lie in the requirements of directness (of threat), reasonableness (of apprehension) and imminence (of anticipated bodily harm). The requirement of directness usually necessitates a threat involving more than words alone. Words must be accompanied by a physically intimidating gesture, for example, a clenched fist or a raised weapon (Trindade, 1982, p. 231). However, *Winfield & Jolowicz* observe that there is no binding authority (as opposed to *dicta*) for the proposition that words alone cannot amount to an assault (Rogers, 1994, p. 62), and it seems obvious that the menacing command of the highwayman to 'stand and deliver' poses a direct threat whether or not he raises his pistol at the same time (Fleming, 1987, p. 25). Highwaymen aside, the real gist of the emphasis on gestures rather than words lies in the judicial concern to distinguish a mere insult (for which there is generally no legal remedy) from a serious and immediate threat. Freedom of speech demands that, to a considerable extent, we should put up with words which offend, but the interest in public order is said to justify the inhibition of free expression where a direct and immediate threat is being made. Thus, the requirement of directness and judicial reluctance to recognise an assault in words alone, operate to strike a balance between the conflicting interests of free speech and public order.

It follows that the harasser who makes obscene remarks, 'amorous' proposals or embarrassing and intimate comments is not significantly inhibited by the tort of assault from doing so. There is, after all, no harm in asking (Magruder, 1936, p. 1035). Even continued solicitation, hints, references and comments of a sexual nature are likely to be non-actionable as assaults (regardless of how a woman actually experiences them) unless they create a reasonable apprehension of imminent bodily contact or harm in the victim. The requirement that the apprehension of imminent bodily harm be *reasonable* is designed to deter claims in situations where no real threat is present or intended. But, in the context of sexual harassment, views might differ as to what is and is not reasonable in the circumstances. Suppose that a woman enters a lift with a male colleague at work. He sidles up to her, standing very close (but not touching) and whispers 'sweet nothings' (of a sexually intimate nature) in her ear. They are alone in the lift. Is there an assault? Is it reasonable to apprehend that uninvited bodily contact is about to take place? Suppose the woman takes the situation in hand and knees her colleague in the groin. Is this an actionable battery? Or is it excusable on grounds of self-defence? Is it a *reasonable* exercise of force? The invocation of the reasonable person here may not serve to validate the woman's assessment of, and reaction to, the situation. After all, the words whispered to her were not threatening violence as such; there was insufficient indication that the words would be followed by any immediate physical action; and what is a stolen kiss to a knee in the groin? Surely, she used force 'disproportionate to the nature of the evil sought to be avoided' (Brazier, 1993, p. 86). A very reasonable analysis – from the point of view of the man involved. The point is that, invariably, such situations are assessed from such a male standpoint, not just because judges tend to be men but also because society tends to place a higher value on protecting the man's interest in the avoidance of physical pain than the woman's interest in the avoidance of unwanted sexual intrusion. On this basis, the behaviour of the woman may seem unreasonable. The fact that, from the woman's point of view, violent defensive action is preferable to the violation which she anticipates is about to occur, is less likely to be recognised or taken into account.

An assault also requires apprehension of *imminent* bodily harm. Threats, however violent or intimidating, are not necessarily assaults unless they pose an imminent danger. So, for example, an obscene telephone call is unlikely to constitute an assault. More generally, sexually harassing behaviour, unless it creates a reasonable apprehension of imminent bodily contact – that is unless the harasser behaves in such a way as to make it obvious that a physical intrusion is about to occur – does not amount to assault. Sexually intimidating behaviour is only an assault where it is accompanied by an intention to create a reasonable apprehension of imminent bodily contact. The harasser who stops short of this but sets out deliberately to inflict severe emotional harm on a woman by his behaviour commits no trespass.

False Imprisonment

According to *Collins* v. *Wilcock* (1984), false imprisonment involves the 'unlawful imposition of constraint on another's freedom of movement from a particular place' (*per* Robert Goff LJ at 377). Thus, its essential ingredients are a *constraint* (whether physical or by force of law, for example, submitting to an arrest) on the ability to move *from a particular place*. In this sense, the constraint must be complete. For example, if a person is prevented from progressing on the highway, but is still free to turn back the way she came, this is *not* false imprisonment. Likewise, intimidation or emotional pressure designed to induce a person to remain in a particular place is unlikely to constitute false imprisonment. However, although constraints on freedom of movement short of complete constraint are not actionable as false imprisonment, they may constitute another tort, for example, assault or battery and, possibly, intimidation (see further below).

Examples of false imprisonment will include tying someone up, locking them in a room or making an unlawful arrest. Because of the strict doctrinal restrictions on its application, particularly the need for complete physical or legal constraint, false imprisonment is unlikely to be of much practical use to a victim of sexual harassment or abuse except in the most serious cases.[7] However, although most instances of sexual harassment do not involve this kind of constraint, there is no doubt that the liberty of the individual to express herself – by her mode of dress, her choice of occupation or lifestyle – is threatened and imperilled by the widespread social practice of sexual harassment.

2. The Principle in *Wilkinson* v. *Downton*

Trespass to the person involves harm inflicted intentionally and directly. But if trespass is confined to the intentional infliction of *direct* harm, is there any means of redressing harm which has been intentionally but *indirectly* inflicted? In *Wilkinson* v. *Downton* (1897), the plaintiff was subjected to a practical joke whereby the defendant falsely informed her that her husband had suffered an accident, sustaining serious injuries. Consequentially, the plaintiff became ill resulting in vomiting, serious mental disturbance, physical incapacity and medical expenses. Clearly, the plaintiff had sustained harm (in the form of nervous shock) *in consequence* of the wilfully deliberate behaviour of the defendant but, equally clearly, such harm was not direct for purposes of the tort of trespass. The court nevertheless held that a cause of action existed:

> The defendant has ... wilfully done an act calculated to cause physical harm to the plaintiff, that is to say, to infringe her legal right to personal safety, and has in fact thereby caused physical harm to her. That proposition without more, appears to me to state a good cause of action. (*per* Wright J at 58–59)

In *Janvier* v. *Sweeney* (1919), the Court of Appeal, in not dissimilar circumstances, upheld the decision in *Wilkinson* v. *Downton* but, strangely, for the next 60 years, the case barely surfaced in English tortious litigation. Yet, *Wilkinson* v. *Downton* is remarkable for a number of reasons. First, it unproblematically classified intentionally inflicted nervous shock as 'physical' harm and actionable at a time when, in the context of negligence, a cause of action was still systematically denied.[8] Second, considered literally, the principle articulated by Lord Wright is capable of swallowing whole the torts comprising trespass to the person as mere instances of the more general wrong of wilfully engaging in an act 'calculated to cause physical harm'.

How far does *Wilkinson* v. *Downton* take us from the well-established map of wrongs and remedies carved out by traditional trespass? As far as English law is concerned, no distance at all. *Wilkinson*, although still authoritative, has been, for the most part, ignored by British courts.

However, elsewhere, particularly in the United States, the *Wilkinson* principle has been significantly developed, forming the basis in many states of a distinct cause of action.

Intentional Infliction of Emotional Distress
According to s. 46 of the American Law Institute's Restatement (Second) of Torts (1966):

> (1) One who by extreme and outrageous conduct intentionally or recklessly causes severe emotional distress to another is subject to liability for such emotional distress and if bodily harm to the other results from it, for such bodily harm.

The Restatement's recognition of the existence of a tort of intentional infliction of emotional distress constitutes both an acknowledgement of the weight of existing precedent in its favour and its espousal as a matter of principle. The tort's authority can be traced to *Wilkinson* v. *Downton* (1897) which, in contrast to English law, exercised a firm grip on American tort litigation from early in the twentieth century.[9]

The early cases confined themselves to conduct causing physical harm, in line with the original decision in *Wilkinson*, but in 1952, the Californian Supreme Court in *State Rubbish Collectors* v. *Siliznoff* recognised a 'right to be free from serious, intentional and unprivileged invasions of mental and emotional tranquillity' (*per* Traynor J, cited in Prosser et al., 1988, p. 52), and held that a cause of action might lie where the plaintiff suffered purely emotional harm, whether or not it resulted in physical injury. While different states diverge on this point, the growing tendency to acknowledge such a right entailing legal protection is reflected in the Restatement 2nd, s. 46.

However, the cause of action is subject to a number of limitations. First, most jurisdictions insist that actionable conduct must be 'extreme and outrageous':

> Liability has been founded only where the conduct has been so outrageous in character, and so extreme in degree as to go *beyond all possible bounds of decency, and to be regarded as atrocious and utterly intolerable in a civilised community* ... generally, the case is one in which the recitation of the facts to an *average member of the community* would arouse his resentment against the actor, and lead him to exclaim, 'Outrageous!' (Restatement 2nd, Comment d; our emphasis)

The tort does not, then, render actionable all insults, threat and jibes or all cruel and insensitive practical jokes, even where severe emotional distress results: 'There must still be freedom to express an unflattering opinion, and some safety valve must be left through which irascible tempers may blow off relatively harmless steam' (Restatement 2nd, Comment d). The question of whether particular conduct is extreme and outrageous is for the court to decide on a case by case basis, taking into account a number of factors, including the relationship between the parties, the personality of the plaintiff and the setting in which the conduct took place (*Harris* v. *Jones* (1977)). In addition, common carriers and other public utilities are under a special obligation of courtesy to their patrons rendering them liable for 'gross insults which reasonably offend' (Restatement 2nd, s. 48).

A second limitation on the scope of the tort is need to show that the resulting emotional distress is severe. In *Harris* v. *Jones* (1977), for example, a Maryland Court of Appeals denied recovery to a plaintiff who suffered from a speech impediment and was constantly ridiculed by a supervisor at work, on the grounds that 'the humiliation suffered, was not, as a matter of law, so intense as to constitute ... "severe" emotional distress' (*per* Murphy CJ, cited in Prosser et al., 1988, p. 60). Thus, whether or not persistent ridiculing of a person's disability constitutes 'extreme and outrageous conduct' (see *Bullock* v. *Austaco Inc.* (1997) where a Texas Appeal Court held that persistent bullying of the plaintiff, who suffered from Downs Syndrome, by her co-employees, was sufficient to support a finding of 'extreme and outrageous conduct'), it will found no cause of action unless it produces more than just the normal 'humiliation' and distress which disabled people are expected to put up with for the sport of the more able-bodied.[10]

Existing case law points to patterns in the configuration of fact situations resulting in litigation. A number of cases have involved the harassment of debtors and their families by creditors and debt-collecting agencies (for example, *George* v. *Jordan Marsh Co* (1971)). Another common pattern has arisen from disputes over insurance claims where plaintiffs have suffered emotional distress as a result of the refusal by insurance companies to pay out on policies (*Eckenrode* v. *Life of America Insurance Co* (1972); *Roper* v. *State Farm Mutual Insurance Co* (1998)). A further crop of cases has arisen in connection with the handling of dead bodies by funeral parlours and mortuaries (*Goldsten* v. *Lincoln Cemetery Inc* (1978)), where the courts have shown particular sensitivity to the emotional vulnerability of the bereaved. Other common targets of such claims include police officers, government bodies, doctors and hospitals and, of course, employers, where, increasingly, the tort is being invoked to remedy harassment and discriminatory treatment (see, for example, *Harris* v. *Jones* (1977) involving disability discrimination; *Alcorn* v. *Anbro Engineering Inc* (1970) concerning racial insults in the course of an altercation at work).

Sexually offensive behaviour may be sufficient to ground a claim but only where it passes the necessary threshold of indecency and/or atrocity. A sexual proposal, without more, will not be actionable

(Prosser et al., 1988, p. 60), but repeated, persistent and unwanted advances in circumstances which clearly upset and distress may well be. For example, in *Samms* v. *Eccles* (1961), the defendant made a series of sexually oppressive phone calls to 'a respectable married woman' over a seven-month period and, in addition, came to her home and indecently exposed himself. The court found that the 'aggravated circumstances' surrounding the defendant's sexual solicitation in this instance were sufficient to ground a claim. Likewise, in *Young* v. *Stensrude* (1984), the court held that the showing of a pornographic movie and persistent obscene remarks during a business meeting attended by a woman could ground a cause of action. In *Ford* v. *Revlon Inc* (1987), a woman who was subjected to intensely unpleasant, threatening, abusive and prolonged sexual harassment by her supervisor, succeeded in holding her employer (Revlon) directly (as opposed to vicariously) liable for intentional infliction of emotional distress on the grounds that their conduct, in failing to address the plaintiff's repeated complaints of harassment, was outrageous in displaying a reckless disregard for the emotional distress it produced. Thus, in this instance, not only did the conduct of the harasser constitute an actionable assault and battery, but the conduct of an employer in failing adequately to respond to the employee's situation, was also actionable.

It must be emphasised that the way in which Revlon management conducted themselves in relation to Ms Ford so evidently displayed a full and reckless disregard for her circumstances (as opposed to being the result of sheer incompetence) as to make a finding of outrageous conduct relatively easy to establish. However, the limitations which attach to the scope of intentional infliction of emotional distress make its applicability to harassment more difficult in some contexts than others and the still prevailing tendency to regard sexual harassment as, up to a point, normal (if not always desirable) behaviour makes an insistence on 'extreme and outrageous conduct' problematic, when opinions differ greatly as to what that involves. In the workplace context, there is no doubt that social attitudes have undergone a change which is reflected in the seriousness with which sexual harassment litigation is pursued and won. Sexual harassment on the job is now a classic instance of intentional infliction of emotional distress (*Johnson* v. *Cox* (1997); *Kanzler* v. *Renner* (1997)). Beyond the workplace, however, the tort is less easily invoked. Even in the context of serious and/or prolonged domestic violence, courts do not always accept that the ingredients of the tort have been made out. In *Hakila* v. *Hakila* (1991), for example, a New Mexico court ruled that a husband's conduct towards his wife, which included assault, battery, demeaning remarks, screaming and other actions, was not sufficiently outrageous to found an independent cause of action; by contrast, in *Henrikson* v. *Cameron* (1993), a court held that a husband's emotional and verbal abuse of his wife *was* sufficiently outrageous to state a claim.

The difficulties which the requirement of extreme and outrageous conduct poses for women seeking a tortious remedy for harassment or abuse are, perhaps, nowhere better illustrated than in the recent disturbing decision of the Wyoming Supreme Court in *Garcia* v. *Lawson* (1996). Ms Garcia had the misfortune to be kidnapped by her estranged boyfriend and held captive for two days, during which time she was repeatedly raped and abused by him. Eventually escaping her dire situation, Ms Garcia contacted the Cheyenne police department. Officer Roger Lawson, dispatched to investigate the crime, not only failed adequately to do so (for example, by refusing to have a 'rape kit' (a set of tests for evidence of rape) performed on Ms Garcia and telling her that the police department could do nothing about the matter as it was 'a boyfriend/girlfriend situation') but managed, in the course of his interview with the traumatised Ms Garcia, to comment on the size of a mutual friend's breasts and ask Ms Garcia if she wanted to go for a beer. Lawson was eventually disciplined for his behaviour, but his failure to gather evidence of the crime meant that no charges could be brought against Ms Garcia's abuser. Garcia's claim against Lawson for intentional infliction of emotional distress was dismissed by the District Court. In granting summary judgment in favour of the defendant, the judge effectively found, *as a matter of law*, that the facts did not support the claim alleged. On appeal, the issue was whether or not the judge had acted correctly or whether he should have allowed the jury to consider the evidence. (In the US, juries commonly hear tort claims.) The Supreme Court of Wyoming, reviewing the facts, held that the judge had acted correctly: 'Although Lawson could certainly have been more considerate in his dealings with Garcia, his conduct was, at most annoying, insulting and insensitive' (*per* Macy J at 1167). There was, therefore, no evidence of extreme and outrageous conduct which the jury could consider. Dissenting, Golden J, joined by Lehman J, pointed to the fact that Lawson was in a position of authority and trust and observed that the plaintiff, by virtue of her experience, was particularly susceptible to emotional harm, both factors which previous courts had considered relevant to the question of whether conduct was sufficiently outrageous to be actionable. Golden J concluded that 'reasonable persons could differ in their conclusion as to whether Officer Lawson's conduct was extreme and outrageous'. Therefore, the decision should have been left to 'an impartial jury' (at 1168–1169).

What is remarkable about *Garcia* is that the Wyoming Supreme Court should not only characterise Officer Lawson's appalling conduct (in the face of strong *prima facie* evidence that a serious crime had been committed) as merely 'annoying' but also confidently assume that no reasonable person would consider it otherwise. Just who is the 'average member of the community' (Restatement 2nd, s. 46, Comment d, cited above) they have in mind? More importantly, who does it exclude? While opinions might differ as to the degree of outrage perpetrated by Officer Lawson on Ms Garcia, the Supreme Court seemed blithely indifferent to the fact that its perspective on what has occurred is not generally shared by all. Once again, *Garcia* dramatically illustrates the way in which reasonableness standards in tort law frequently operate both to deny the validity of women's experience (including their experience of harm) and to legitimate the perspective of those whose lack of empathy and understanding precludes them from recognising their own glaring limitations.

Finally, just as the requirement of extreme and outrageous conduct poses particular problems in the context of sexual harassment and abuse because of a significant lack of consensus as to where the threshold lies, the need to show that the emotional distress suffered is severe is also an obstacle. This requirement has both an objective and subjective dimension: the plaintiff must not only show that the distress was, in fact, severe but also that it would, in the circumstances, be experienced by a reasonable person 'of ordinary sensibilities' (Dobbs et al., 1984, p. 63). How much must the reasonable person be expected to tolerate? If a person with a speech impediment is expected to put up with cruel and malicious ridicule from his supervisor (*Harris* v. *Jones* (1977)), then, presumably, women are required to tolerate a certain level of sexual harassment. While it may be that such a restriction on recovery is necessary in order to deter frivolous claims, the still pervasive perception that some kinds of sexual attention are 'normal' expressions of maleness which should provoke no real distress, will, inevitably, tend to inform judicial assessments of how a victim should react.[11] The issue is not whether or not broadly defined causes of action such as the American tort of intentional infliction of emotional distress should be subject to restrictions; of course, they should. However, from a feminist point of view, the concern is that those restrictions, particularly when couched in terms of abstract and indeterminate standards, operate within a social context facilitating the application of personal prejudices, including those derived from gendered assumptions about male and female behaviour. Golden J sums up this difficulty very well, describing the operation of such meaningless standards in the following terms: 'The Court embarks upon ... an endless wandering over factual circumstances, meandering this way and that, blown about by bias and inclination, and guided by nothing steadier than the personal preference of the helmsman' (at 1169).

The Re-emergence of Wilkinson *v.* Downton *in the English Courts*
To date, UK law can boast nothing so elaborate or indeterminate as a tort of intentional infliction of emotional distress There are, however, some signs of a revival of judicial interest in the principle in *Wilkinson v. Downton*. In 1986, the Court of Appeal, on the authority of *Wilkinson*, upheld the granting of an injunction to restrain harassment taking the form of persistent telephone calls (*Burnett* v. *George* (1992)). Remarkably, this resurrection of *Wilkinson* from its untimely burial went virtually unnoticed and, indeed, *Burnett* was not reported until 1992. However, the Court of Appeal's decision in *Khorasandjian* v. *Bush* (1993), on very similar facts, attracted much more attention. Although the focus of much of this attention was on the controversial invocation of private nuisance by a plaintiff who possessed no proprietary right over the land affected (see below and Chapter 6), it is *Khorasandjian's* simultaneous reliance on the *Wilkinson* principle which arguably offers the potential for genuinely radical doctrinal development.

Khorasandjian involved an appeal by a defendant against the imposition of an interlocutory injunction by the County Court restraining his actions in relation to the plaintiff, an 18-year-old girl living with her parents. According to the evidence the defendant, an estranged friend of the plaintiff, had been subjecting her to persistent harassment over a period of time, threatening violence, engaging in aggressive and abusive behaviour (including persistent telephone calls) and an alleged assault. Indeed, criminal proceedings had been brought, resulting in his incarceration for a short period. The object of civil proceedings was to prevent the defendant from engaging in further acts of harassment by securing an injunction in the plaintiff's favour. In other words, the plaintiff in *Khorasandjian* was not seeking damages; she was seeking a remedy which (she hoped) would *stop* the harassment. At issue was the scope of the injunction which (*inter alia*) prohibited the defendant from 'harassing, pestering or communicating' with the plaintiff. The defendant argued that these words did not form the basis of any actionable legal wrong. In particular, the question arose as to whether or not the court had any power to stop the defendant from making persistent and abusive telephone calls to the plaintiff's home.

According to traditional tortious principles, an abusive telephone call does *not* constitute an assault because it lacks the necessary quality of imminence.[12] Did it involve the commission of any other tort, or was the plaintiff to be denied a remedy in the face of such clearly unacceptable and anti-social conduct? In a path-breaking and innovative decision, the Court of Appeal, by a majority, upheld the imposition of the injunction. Speaking for the majority, Dillon LJ considered that the acts in question might give rise to (at least) two potential claims. First, he suggested that persistent and unwelcome telephone calls might constitute the tort of nuisance (see below). Second, even if an action in nuisance did not lie, the plaintiff, he argued, could rely on the principle in *Wilkinson* v. *Downton*. The only difficulty here was the absence of evidence of *actual physical harm* which is expressly stated as a prerequisite of the *Wilkinson* principle (although, as we have already observed, many American states have dispensed with this requirement in the context of a *Wilkinson* claim). Dillon LJ acknowledged that no evidence of actual physical harm (in the form of stress-induced illness)[13] had been offered but he was nevertheless willing to uphold the injunction on a *quia timet* basis, that is to *prevent* the apprehended legal wrong. Clearly, he argued, there was an 'obvious risk that the cumulative effect of continued and unrestrained further harassment ... would cause ... illness'.[14]

Peter Gibson LJ, who dissented from the majority decision, was more cautious. Although prepared to accept the application of the *Wilkinson* principle, he would have preferred to amend the injunction in *Khorasandjian* to include the qualifying words: 'by doing acts calculated to cause the respondent harm'. In other words, he insisted that actual physical harm remained a prerequisite of *Wilkinson* liability. The decision of the majority, on the other hand, pointed the way towards the application of *Wilkinson* to situations where the primary or even exclusive harm alleged is emotional.

Of course, it must be emphasised that *Khorasandjian* involved a dispute over the application of an interlocutory injunction. In order for such a (temporary) injunction to be issued, the plaintiff need not establish her case on its merits; she need only show that there is a 'serious question' to be tried (*American Cyanamid* v. *Ethicon Ltd* (1975)). Strictly speaking, therefore, the court did not hold that an actionable legal wrong had been committed and *Khorasandjian* is not conclusive authority as to the existence of a cause of action in these circumstances. Nevertheless, it is the view of some commentators, for example, Bridgeman and Jones, 1994, that, in 'practical reality' (p. 196) *Khorasandjian* does lay the basis for a cause of action for pure emotional distress. The House of Lords in *Hunter* v. *Canary Wharf* (1997), on the other hand, appear to suggest that any common law development presaged by *Khorasandjian* should be halted in the wake of the passing of the Protection from Harassment Act 1997 (see, for example the judgment of Lord Hoffman at 452). In fact, *Khorasandjian* comes in for some staunch judicial criticism in *Hunter*, leading some commentators to conclude that any gains made there have since been lost. However, reading the decision carefully, it is clear that their Lordships' primary and direct concern is with the scope of the tort of nuisance, not with the application of the *Wilkinson* principle – Lord Goff, for example, purports to overrule *Khorasandjian* only 'in so far as it holds that a mere licensee can sue in private nuisance' (at 441). It remains to be seen whether or not *Wilkinson* will continue to be invoked in the wake of the new statutory tort but American experience suggests that it might – the contours of the American tort of intentional infliction of emotional distress are by no means the same as those envisaged by the 1997 Act and *Wilkinson* may still have a residual role to play in providing a remedy in those circumstances where the 1997 Act does not apply (see further below).

3. Other Torts

A number of other torts might be invoked to remedy some kinds of sexually harassing or abusive behaviour. In the United States, in particular, the courts have proved quite inventive in adapting tort law to claims of sexual harassment. The 'economic' tort of interference with contractual relationships has been employed in situations where a supervisor interferes with the plaintiff's contractual relationship with her employer (for example, by recommending her dismissal or demotion because she has refused to accept his sexual advances – *Kyriazi* v. *Western Electric Co* (1978); Conaghan, 1996, pp. 424–6). Likewise, the distinctly American torts of 'intentional infliction of emotional distress' (above) and 'invasion of privacy' have been successfully applied in the context of sexual harassment (*Phillips* v. *Smalley Maintenance Services* (1983)).[15] The English courts have, on the whole, been less inventive in this respect, although the decisions in *Khorasandjian* and *Burris* are, perhaps, suggestive of hitherto hidden promise. The decision of the House of Lords in *Hunter*, on the other hand, with its insistence on a strict proprietary interest as a prerequisite to the right to sue in private nuisance, is more typical of the conservative instincts of the English judiciary. Not only does *Hunter* weaken the potential of nuisance as a remedy in the context of environmental wrongs (Chapter 6), but it ensures that, except in those cases where the alleged conduct can be characterised as an interference with the use and enjoyment of property, nuisance is also unlikely to provide a remedy for acts of harassment. Nevertheless, an attempt to invoke nuisance against a stalker has recently been made. In *Perharic* v. *Hennessey* (1997), the Court of Appeal upheld an injunction and award of £5000 to a plaintiff who had been the subject of an intense campaign of harassment by her lover's former wife, including persistent and obscene telephones calls (many of which came from men who, through the mischievous intervention of the defendant, mistakenly believed that the plaintiff was a prostitute). It was the defendant's contention (*inter alia*) that the plaintiff could no longer rely on nuisance after *Hunter* to remedy what was, effectively, pure emotional distress. In making this argument, she relied heavily on *obiter* comments of Lord Lloyd (discussed in Chapter 6; see, in particular, note 2), although it can also be argued that the whole tenor of the *Hunter* decision, with its emphasis on a close nexus between the harm alleged and a property entitlement, is, indeed, supportive of such a general position. The Court of Appeal, however, did not think so and, emphasising that the campaign of harassment to which the plaintiff had been subjected could not fail to interfere with her use and enjoyment of property, upheld the claim in nuisance. The decision highlights the continued division of opinion amongst senior judges as to the scope and nature of private nuisance. What is more puzzling is why the claim was framed in terms of nuisance in the first place. The bizarre behaviour of the defendant, designed, as it was, to intimidate and distress the plaintiff, seems an almost classic instance of *Wilkinson* v. *Downton*. Yet no such cause of action appears to have been alleged. As in *Khorasandjian*, one wonders why it is necessary to court judicial controversy through contentious nuisance claims when the application of the *Wilkinson* principle would more readily address and redress the wrong.

The marked reluctance of the House of Lords to extend the boundaries of nuisance in *Hunter* in order to remedy very real interferences with domestic life contrasts starkly with their capacity for inventiveness when confronted with behaviour of which they seriously disapprove. A notorious example of such inventiveness is the decision in *Rookes* v. *Barnard* (1964). *Rookes* involved a challenge to the legality of a threat by trade union officials to call a strike unless an employer dismissed the plaintiff (an employee who had resigned from the union). The House of Lords, with few scruples, resurrected the ancient tort of 'intimidation', which had traditionally been confined to threats of violence, in order to provide the plaintiff with a remedy. Their Lordships held that an *unlawful threat* made by A (the trade union officials) to B (BOAC) with a view to *inducing him* to act or refrain from acting to the *detriment* of C (the plaintiff) constituted the tort of intimidation. The threat to strike (and thereby induce a breach of the union members' contracts of employment) was considered an unlawful means for this purpose, in the same way as threats of physical violence had traditionally sufficed.

Might this reinvented tort of intimidation be successfully invoked in the context of sexual harassment or physical or emotional abuse? The Court of Appeal decision in *Godwin* v. *Uzoigwe* (1993) suggests just such a possibility. *Godwin* involved the domestic exploitation of a young Nigerian girl who had entered the UK when she was 16 under the protection of the Uzoigwe family – a doctor, his wife and children. Mr Uzoigwe (falsely) claimed that the plaintiff was his niece and that he wished her to stay in the UK in order to undergo some domestic training at a local college. In fact, she remained with the Uzoigwes for two and a half years, acting as the household drudge; she worked long hours without pay and with inadequate food; she was beaten, forbidden to have any social life or to mix with anyone outside the home; she was not even provided with a bed. She lived in constant fear of her 'employers' and did not receive the training promised by Mr Uzoigwe. It was only while the family were away on holiday leaving the plaintiff alone with inadequate food, that the authorities were apprised of the situation. The plaintiff entered a women's refuge and eventually sued the Uzoigwes alleging breach of contract, assault and intimidation.

Before Judge Fricker at first instance, her claims succeeded. In the Court of Appeal, the question arose as to whether or not, on the facts, the tort of intimidation had been made out. Judge Fricker had held that the defendants had engaged in deliberate conduct to control and coerce the plaintiff and had unlawfully abused their position in relation to her as persons *in loco parentis*. He pointed to a number of the defendants' acts, including beatings, inadequate food and poor conditions, the absence of leisure, the constant fear which they induced in the plaintiff in order to compel her to work for them and the failure to provide the promised domestic training, as ample for purposes of establishing the necessary element of unlawfulness. This decision was upheld by the Court of Appeal, Dillon LJ emphasising that intimidation could be made out *either* by unlawful threats or unlawful conduct, of which both were well in evidence in this case. Although the Court of Appeal reduced the original award of damages (from £25,000 to £20,000) as too excessive, the decision still constituted a considerable victory by the plaintiff against her abusers.

What is interesting about *Godwin* is the difficulty the plaintiff faced in making out a substantial complaint in the absence of the tort of intimidation. Breach of contract, for example, hardly captures the nature of the suffering she endured. The tort of battery would have been difficult to make out in the absence of corroborating evidence such as bruises or independent witnesses, and assault, by itself, is rather a meagre offering in circumstances as harrowing as these. Nor could the tort of false imprisonment be made out because of the absence of *complete constraint* – the plaintiff was not physically prevented from leaving the Uzoigwe home and, indeed, at the time of her discovery by the authorities was there on her own. But, of course, to say she was not completely constrained is to ignore the very real coercion, emotional and physical, which was deployed to keep her under control. The importance of the decision lies in the way in which the judiciary were prepared to apply the tort of intimidation to circumstances outside the arena of industrial conflict to provide a remedy where otherwise none might lie, certainly in relation to many of the acts of which the plaintiff was rightly complaining. That is not, however, to deny that real problems with the application of intimidation to acts of harassment or abuse remain. One problem lies in the requirement of unlawful means. It might not always be possible to identify independent unlawful means in a harasser's behaviour. Nor is it clear what kind of harm the tort of intimidation seeks to redress. It certainly covers economic harm, as *Rookes* v. *Barnard* (1964) makes clear, but traditional doctrine also suggests that emotional harm, at least where it derives from threats of violence, is also remediable. What, if any, degree of harm must be demonstrated for these purposes? While the recent 'redeployment' of intimidation from economic to physical and emotional harm leaves many of these questions unanswered (for the moment), *Godwin* is generally illustrative of the fluidity and dynamism of tort and its instrumental potential to redress harms not traditionally recognised by law.

Three final points relating to tort law's ability to remedy acts of harassment and abuse require brief consideration. First, where the harassment occurs in the workplace or is work-related, it may be possible to hold an employer vicariously liable for the tortious acts of his employees. An additional action against an employer will obviously be advantageous to the plaintiff, particularly where, as is often the case, the perpetrator of the wrongful acts is without means. However, the need to demonstrate that the alleged tort(s) took place *in the course of employment* is an obvious doctrinal obstacle to success against an employer, particularly where the wrongful acts are of a serious nature. Unless the plaintiff can show that the acts took place to further the employer's business (which, in most cases, is unlikely), then the conduct may well be held to be outside the course of employment (Rose, 1977, and see recently *Trotman* v. *North Yorkshire County Council* (1998) where the Court of Appeal held that a local authority was not vicariously liable for the sexual abuse of a pupil by a teacher while on a school trip). However, in the recent decision of *Jones* v. *Tower Boot Co Ltd* (1997), a case involving serious racial harassment in the workplace, the Court of Appeal distinguished the doctrine of vicarious liability at common law from the liability of employers under s. 32 of the Race Relations Act 1976, holding that the latter provision was not to be construed in the same strict terms as compelled by the common law interpretation of 'course of employment'. This relaxation of the 'course of employment' requirement in discrimination law tilts the balance even further in favour of discrimination claims in the context of harassment at work.

Issues of vicarious liability lead to a more general consideration of the viability of suits against third parties for acts of harassment or abuse. If, as has already been observed, the perpetrator is unlikely to possess the means to remedy the wrong in financial terms, there is sense in seeking a deeper pocket upon whom to pin the blame, if, indeed, blame can be attached. Thus, a number of claims have been made against local authorities (*X* v. *Bedfordshire* (1995)), the police (*Osman* v. *Ferguson* (1993)) and health authorities (*Clunis* v. *Camden & Islington Health Authority* (1998)), alleging either negligence or breach of statutory duty in failing to prevent the harm from occurring or in failing to stop it. By and large, as we have seen (Chapter 2), these claims have not been successful (see, exceptionally, *W* v. *Essex CC* (1998)), not least because they generally involve suits against public authorities in relation to whom special considerations increasingly apply. This is not likely, however, to halt the upsurge in litigation which seems set to continue for the foreseeable future (Conaghan, 1998) spurred on, no doubt, by high-profile cases such as the recent successful claim in Ireland against a health authority which resulted in a damages award of £1 million. The claim was initiated by a family of abused children whose doctor had colluded in covering up years of abuse by their father.

Finally, some allusion must also be made to the particular difficulties which some claimants face when bringing civil claims relating to events which occurred some considerable time prior to filing suit. This is most commonly the case, for example, where adult survivors of child abuse seek to bring their abusers to account many years after the abuse has occurred. Because of the trauma which childhood abuse, in particular, inflicts, many of those affected fail to recognise the nature or degree of the harm done to them until well into adulthood, commonly after a period of therapy or counselling. When full realisation occurs and the plaintiff seeks to pursue a civil claim, she is confronted by limitation rules which lay down specific periods in which a claim must be made. Stated briefly, and based upon the decision of the House of Lords in *Stubbings* v. *Webb* (1993), an abuse victim (certainly where the cause of action is in trespass) must bring her claim within six years of the occurrence of the alleged wrong or, where the abuse occurred in childhood, within six years of attaining her majority (18). Unfortunately, as innumerable cases attest, many victims of childhood abuse simply do not come to a full realisation of the harm they have sustained until well into adulthood (Mullis, 1997). Indeed, some may have repressed all memory of its occurrence. Despite contrary developments in the US and Canada, English law has not yet taken any steps to remedy this situation although it has recently been acknowledged to be unfair by the Law Commission, which recommends a more flexible limitation regime (Law Commission CP No 151, 1998).[16] The European Court of Human Rights, while finding against the plaintiff in *Stubbings and Others* v. *UK* (1997), has also indicated that limitation periods present particular difficulties to victims of abuse. However, until further action is taken, limitation rules remain a significant obstacle to recovery for many abuse victims.

4. Protection from Harassment Act 1997

The 1997 Act was presented by its initiators as a response to a perceived public concern about harassment and, in particular, stalking.[17] The primary focus of the Act is the creation of a new criminal offence of harassment[18] but, in s. 3, the Act also introduces a civil remedy for harassment, which includes the right to damages for 'anxiety' and 'any financial loss resulting from the harassment' (s. 3(2)). Injunctive relief is also available accompanied by strong criminal sanctions in the event of a defendant's non-compliance with its terms (s. 3(3)–(9)).

The 1997 Act does not define harassment with any precision. It is described as 'a course of conduct' (s. 1(1)) which 'must involve conduct on at least two occasions' (s. 7(3)), so 'one-off' acts, such as the 'practical joke' perpetrated by the defendant in *Wilkinson* v. *Downton* (1897) remain outside its scope. The conduct may include 'alarming the person or causing [them] distress' (s. 7(2)) and must also be such that the alleged harasser 'knows or ought to know [that it] amounts to harassment of another' (s. 1(1)(b)). In determining what ought to be known, the court will consider what 'a reasonable person in possession of the same information' as the alleged harasser would know to be harassment (s. 1(2)). In other words, whether or not the conduct under scrutiny amounts to harassment for purposes of the Act will depend upon how it would be perceived by the reasonable person in the position of the harasser. Such a formulation is problematic, to say the least. First, the assumption that a reasonable person would know whether or not a course of conduct amounts to harassment assumes a degree of consensus which we doubt, in fact, exists. Many people might disagree, for example, as to when and whether a supervisor's persistent criticisms constitute harassment at work; as to the precise point when a rejected lover's attempts to patch up a relationship are transformed into criminal behaviour; as to exactly when a photographer or journalist's honest efforts to secure a 'scoop' involve 'stalking'. Although it may be perfectly obvious in most cases that the behaviour under scrutiny is unacceptable, the reasonable person standard is a singularly inappropriate technique for distinguishing between legitimate and illegitimate activity in an area so dogged by controversy and disagreement. Additionally, the adoption of the perspective of a 'reasonable harasser' is puzzling, given that what makes the behaviour unacceptable is, primarily, its *effect* upon the person to whom it is directed. The 'reasonable harasser' perspective precludes any direct consideration of how the behaviour would be experienced by the 'reasonable harassee'. The victim's perspective is, in other words, irrelevant, except in so far as the 'reasonable harasser's' knowledge of it (which may be limited) is relevant to his assessment of whether his conduct constitutes harassment. Furthermore, the focus on the perspective of the perpetrator incorporates an inevitable gender dimension into the standard applied.[19] While such a perpetrator focus may be defensible, up to a point, in the context of criminal behaviour, in relation to a civil claim, doctrinal tradition is as likely to derive a claim from the nature of the harm (private nuisance) as from an evaluation of the conduct of the actor (negligence). By marrying civil and criminal remedies for harassment in the same legislative initiative, the 1997 Act introduces as a statutory tort a wrong which has been largely constructed within discourse about criminal behaviour.

Not only, then, does the indeterminacy of the reasonableness standard in the 1997 Act provide a poor framework within which to ascertain whether or not the conduct in question is actionable, it is also ideologically loaded, privileging the perspective of the perpetrator over that of the victim. The difficulties are compounded by a series of exceptions listed in s. 1(3) which exclude certain conduct from the definition of harassment in s. 1(2). Thus, where a course of conduct is pursued for the purpose of preventing or detecting a crime, or under any enactment of a rule of law, or, curiously, where the pursuit of that course of conduct is 'in the particular circumstances ... reasonable' (s. 1(3)(c)), it will not amount to a harassment. In other words, even where a reasonable person in the position of the harasser knows or should know that the course of conduct in which they are engaging amounts to harassment, if it is reasonable to pursue that course of conduct, it does *not* amount to harassment! Put bluntly, there may be situations where it is reasonable to harass other people but the Act gives us no clues whatsoever as to what kinds of situation it has in mind. (It is thought to address the activities of 'journalists, salespeople, religious activists, debt collectors and others carrying out legitimate activities' (*Equal Opportunities Review*, 1997, 32).) Moreover, there is a certain inelegance in invoking reasonableness to determine that a course of conduct amounts to harassment only to invoke it again to say that it does not. One might conclude that the serious lack of legislative guidance as to exactly what kind of conduct will or will not fall under such a broad and imprecise definition, may well lead the courts back to drawing upon existing common law categories in order to aid their interpretation of the Act or flesh out what kinds of conduct are likely to attract liability. In this context, the Act leaves a host of questions unanswered: for example, how relevant is a victim's consent to the harassing behaviour and how is consent to be determined in this context; to what extent will or should the courts take account of the social situation in which the alleged harassment occurs – are they more likely to find in favour of the plaintiff where a relationship of trust or power has been abused or will they adopt an approach which focuses on the behaviour in relative isolation from its social setting? To what extent does the Act as currently drafted conflict with civil rights to freedom of speech and movement, rights which are soon to be legally and constitutionally enshrined in English law with the passing of the Human Rights Bill? Finally, assuming a wide judicial interpretation of harassment (which, while by no means ensured, may be difficult to avoid given the rather skeletal proscriptions embodied in the Act), do the common law torts still have a role to play in remedying acts of harassment and/or abuse?

Obviously, as has already been mentioned, the common law torts, particularly *Wilkinson* v. *Downton,* will still remain relevant to situations where the conduct complained of is 'one-off'. In this context, the willingness of the courts to develop the *Wilkinson* principle and resolve the various doubts about its scope and application becomes crucial.[20] Similarly, trespass to person is likely to remain the primary cause of action in the context of serious abuse, including rape or unlawful killing. It is possible, too, that cases like *Godwin* will still have a role to play; in a sense, the wrong in *Godwin* is much more effectively caught by the concept of intimidation than harassment. What is most troubling about what happened to Ms Godwin was the coercion and exploitation to which she was subjected; this is a very different kind of wrong from that perpetrated by the stalker in *Khorasandjian* or *Perharic*. Finally, depending upon the lines which the courts choose to draw round the cause of action under the 1997 Act, the common law will, inevitably, be invoked to plug the gaps. For example, conduct which does not strike a reasonable person in the position of the harasser as harassment, or which, while doing so, nevertheless appears to be a reasonable course of conduct, might still constitute an unreasonable *interference* with the use or enjoyment of another's property for purposes of the tort of nuisance. Similarly, a course of conduct might be deemed to lack the necessary qualities to constitute harassment, but still amount to some kind of intentional infliction of harm, giving rise to an action under *Wilkinson*. In fact, it is likely that the presence of a statutory tort of harassment will direct *Wilkinson* arguments towards emotional distress claims which lack an element of harassment, but which nevertheless involve shocking and stress inducing conduct. The recent, albeit unsuccessful, invocation of *Wilkinson* in the context of alleged dishonesty on the part of medical practitioners (*Powell* v. *Boldaz* (1998), see note 20 above) and social services (*W* v. *Essex CC* (1998)) are, perhaps, indicative of this trend. However, for the moment, this is all speculation.

CONCLUSION

It is clear that since the first edition of *The Wrongs of Tort* in 1993, the range of civil remedies available to combat sexual harassment and abuse have expanded considerably. The same period has also witnessed a sea change in social attitudes to sexual harassment, particularly in the workplace. No longer is it viewed as a normal expression of male/female relations but rather as a taboo so sacred that its alleged violation is enough to compromise the integrity and credibility of the most powerful man in the world. In fact, it might be suggested that sexual harassment victims, far from being deprived of the opportunity to seek redress through law, are spoilt for choice when it comes to the selection of legal remedies.

In one sense this is true as is evidenced by the continued increase in the volume and range of sexual harassment litigation. It is also true that sexual harassment allegations may be used, on occasion, against those who are, in fact, its victims rather than its perpetrators (as, for example, where a female student's accusation of sexual harassment against her male lecturer formed part of a broader campaign of harassment directed against him – *Fine* v. *McLardy* (1996)). But the visibility of sexual harassment as a modern taboo should not lead us to forget the continued struggle which many women still have, both inside and outside the workplace, to combat the insidiousness of a pervasive set of gendered assumptions about their capability and self-worth. Sexual harassment in the police force, for example, is still endemic and often extreme (similar examples of serious sexual harassment have been attributed to the armed forces – see the *Guardian*, 22 February 1997). Officers who complain encounter serious difficulties in gathering the necessary evidence (for example, witness testimony) to support their claims. Moreover, women are still the victims of widespread sexual and physical attacks at the hands of their partners and other family members. Even in the absence of explicit sexual harassment, gendered assumptions still inform women's everyday experience of work and social life in a world in which only the chosen few achieve the unenviable status of Demi Moore in the movie *Disclosure*, as one who abuses rather than is abused by the exercise of power.

Thus, despite the rhetoric and reality of social change in this context, sexual harassment remains a problem which largely affects women and affects them significantly. The difficulty with tortious remedies (whether arising from statute or from the common law) is that this gender dimension is largely lost: sexual harassment becomes reconceptualised as a wrong practised by one individual upon another. As MacKinnon observes: 'tort is conceptually inadequate to the concept of sexual harassment to the extent that it rips injuries to women's sexuality out of the context of women's social circumstances as a whole' (MacKinnon, 1979, p. 171). By focusing on a *particular* man as the *individual* cause and perpetrator of the harm done, the sense in which his behaviour is part of an overall culture of sexually oppressive behaviour, for which neither he nor the woman in question is *personally* responsible, is lost. Indeed, viewed as a problem between two individuals, it makes little sense to talk about sexual harassment as a wrong against women as such. Sexual harassment becomes a gender-neutral wrong. Not only is this, in a very real sense, a misrepresentation of the problem, it inevitably affects tort law's capacity to redress it. While it may be that the cry of sexual harassment has considerably stronger weight against the backdrop of a legal regime which recognises it as wrongful, the failure to properly identify the *nature* of the wrong, that is, as an expression of sexually oppressive social relations, means that law does not so much remedy as redefine it, and, in so doing, further contributes to the maintenance of a legal culture in which the gender dimension is neither acknowledged nor properly understood.

This comes out in the practice of law in a number of ways. First, as the above analysis suggests, the open-endedness of tort standards provides a vehicle for the application of often problematic gendered assumptions within an apparently gender-neutral framework; the preferences and prejudices of those who have traditionally exercised power continue to inform even where the harm which is addressed is, in part, a product of those preferences and prejudices. Second, and relatedly, it remains the case that tort law protects some interests (for example, the economic interests or the protection of reputation) much more effectively than others, reflecting a continuing preoccupation with injuries more likely to be suffered by men.[21] If one were to redesign the tort system in terms of the harms commonly suffered by women, one would not be surprised to find that wrongs such as rape, domestic violence and sexual harassment and abuse would be much more central and more easily remedied. In other words, the concept of harm which tort law reflects is gendered, tailored to meet the needs and preoccupations of men rather than women.

Thus, while feminists, like other progressive lawyers, must not desist from efforts to make the law more sympathetic and responsive to the wrongs which women (or other particular groups) suffer, real effort must also be directed towards changing a social and legal culture which views such wrongs as separate and isolated events in the first place. In the context of sexual harm, it is doubtful whether such change can be brought about without an accompanying transformation in sexual relations as currently constructed and expressed in our society.

8
Concluding Thoughts

In the five years since the first edition of this book, a change of government, a number of far-reaching and authoritative judicial decisions, and a plethora of new texts in tort might be thought to have fundamentally changed any radical reappraisal of the tort system. Are the utopian aspirations expressed in our concluding chapter of five years ago as far as ever from realisation or, indeed, have they proved to be mere phantasms which are best exorcised? While readers' answers to this question will probably, ultimately, depend upon their ideological perceptions, we make no apology for suggesting, once again, that while a revolutionary change in the attitudes prevailing in society towards the needs of its individual members is not imminent, it remains both possible and *crucial* to envisage a community whose members do not suffer as do those in need in our society. The tort system is but one small aspect of a society which chooses to allow most provision, beyond the minimal, for those in need, to be left largely to individual chance or misfortune. Most, but not all (because, as we have seen, privileged tort victims are fortunate to receive financial awards intended to alleviate the consequences of their injuries) will be held responsible for events over which they have little or no control, whether stemming from congenital illness, misadventure (including misconduct by others not attracting tortious liability) or merely limited intelligence.

The realisation that tort is only a small, if integral, part of the system which defines how individual need is to be met is at once disabling, yet it must also *enable* if it is to precipitate change. It is disabling because many of the most immediately attractive solutions to the concerns raised by a needs-based perspective (for example, the introduction of a no-fault accident compensation scheme, whether public or private) suddenly appear not only limited, but scarcely more rational than our present system of privileging some sorts of causes of need over others. The moment one asserts that society's response to individual misfortune should be determined not by fault or cause, but by the needs which such misfortune occasions, a whole new set of consistency problems arises:

> Our society may revere medicine and sympathise with the sick, but it holds no view that could explain distinctions between persons

totally unable to work according to whether their condition results from an illness or, on the other hand, from limited natural abilities, decades of racism or sexism, homosexuality, family burdens, technological change, a broken home or national fiscal policy. (Liebman, 1976, p. 864)

As Jane Stapleton comments:

Until there is a re-evaluation of such fundamental issues as why, if at all, the disabled should be treated preferentially over victims of other misfortunes, there will not be much gained from formulating detailed designs for schemes of benefits. The daunting lesson to be learned ... is that the 'compensation debate' is fundamentally and disturbingly more complex than we have generally assumed. (Stapleton, 1986, p. 183)[1]

If, then, we are to advocate a move away from a focus upon the cause of need to a consideration of the need itself, we will still require criteria to distinguish different sorts of need, assuming a hierarchy which determines which needs ought to be met and to what extent. The fact that this is so difficult is itself instructive because it forces us to confront the reality that it is our own ideolog(ies) which will define any hierarchy. The enthusiasm with which many students embrace no-fault accident compensation is often tempered severely by the prospect of the ill or the financially or emotionally unfortunate being similarly compensated. Such considerations lead one to ask whether a compassionate society, a society which recognises and takes responsibility for individual suffering, is possible or, indeed, desirable.[2]

While a needs-based focus brings its own inherent problems, it is nevertheless (at least potentially) enabling in forcing us to confront again the wrongs of tort. In this context, it might be argued either that the vagaries and injustices of the current system may be ameliorated from within the tortious realm of individual rights and responsibilities, or that change must come from without, for example, through the establishment of a system of redress based on a conception of social justice wherein the risks of each are borne, at least to some degree, by all. Clearly, each approach has its difficulties – the former in terms of coherence, equity and compassion, the latter in terms of political reality and alleged cost. How, then, do we choose which strategy to adopt? Indeed, need we choose or can both approaches be pursued simultaneously?

Before such questions can properly be answered, it is useful to ask: what is tort law for? What are its goals and purposes, if any? It must immediately be acknowledged that to ask this question is, in itself, to adopt an ideological position because it assumes, implicitly, that law can and should be viewed as an instrument of social engineering and change; that is, as a means to a chosen end. For example, consideration of tort law as part of a general social response to the needs arising from accidents assumes, first, that society should respond to the needs of accident victims and, second, that tort law either is or is not an effective mechanism for the achievement of that purpose. Similarly, a re-evaluation of the land torts in terms of their environmental impact proceeds upon the basis that environmental protection is a goal to be pursued and that tort law can (or cannot) be adapted to secure that objective.

It cannot be denied that such instrumentalist approaches express their aims and purposes quite explicitly and, in articulating particular goals and assessing legal doctrine in terms of its ability to realise them, present themselves as overtly political. Indeed, 'law in context', an idea which pioneered modern instrumentalist reinterpretations of law in Britain (Chapter 5), is generally associated with 'left' or progressive tendencies in legal education (Thomson, 1987); its politics are easily identifiable. Yet, it is not just self-consciously instrumentalist approaches to tort law which house a political agenda (whether more or less contentious). One of the points we have sought to make throughout this book is that even approaches to law which are not self-consciously political – and which, indeed, articulate a position which asserts the general separation of law and politics – are, nevertheless, just as ideologically grounded. To this end, we have argued that the emergence of tort as a separate legal discipline and, in particular, the growth in scope and influence of the fault principle within the corpus of tort law as a whole, can be attributed, to a considerable extent, to the process of industrialisation. Additionally, we have sought to demonstrate how the shape and content of the legal rules and principles which emerged, reflected and reinforced the values and assumptions which characterised the period (Chapter 4).

In other words, tort law did not emerge in a vacuum. It grew out of and expressed a particular set of views about the role of the state, the responsibility of the individual and the pre-eminence of choice and individual freedom. Over the years, popular views on these issues have shifted and changed,[3] as too have views and perceptions of the tort system, particularly in relation to the role of negligence in the compensation of personal injury. It has, on occasion, been asserted that tort law performs the function of promoting economic efficiency (Calabresi, 1961; Posner, 1972), that its role is to give effect to principles of corrective justice (Epstein, 1973) or to facilitate loss-spreading (Nolan and Ursin, 1995). There are also those who take issue with the idea that tort law performs any or all of these functions. Ernest Weinrib, for example, has argued that 'the purpose of private law is to be private law' (Weinrib, 1995, p. 5); that, far from being a multi-purposed instrument, tort law (as private law) constitutes 'a normatively distinct mode of interaction' possessing its own internal structure and ordering, which cannot be explained externally (that is, through its ability to serve socially desirable purposes) but can only properly be understood from within.

A consideration of the literature thus reveals that all or most of the assertions which have been made about tort law's role or function are contentious, not least because of the politics they express. At the same time, it must be recognised that the original values which informed the development of the law of tort, and which remain imbued within the fault principle, carry, by virtue of legal tradition, a considerably stronger ideological sway than is at first apparent. In this sense, although our modern tort system expresses and accommodates a number of different viewpoints, some are more privileged than others by virtue of the discourse within which they are played out. While tort law may appear multi-purposed – and, indeed, is often treated as such – it possesses inherent limitations which give some weight to Weinrib's articulation of a 'special morality of private law', while, at the same time, undermining its claim to political neutrality.

Bearing in mind such considerations, how should the critical lawyer approach the question of tort law reform? Should she vigorously pursue litigation strategies with a view to reinforcing the instrumental effectiveness of tort law, as, for example, a mechanism to combat discrimination, pollution or other social problems? Or should she eschew tort in favour of non-litigatory alternatives?

In this context, we have sought to identify a competing tension between, on the one hand, the aspiration to escape the ideological restrictions of tort law which undermine (often fatally) its effectiveness as an instrument for social change and, on the other hand, the tendency to approach tort law creatively in order to exploit its doctrinal gaps and uncertainties in pursuit of a particular purpose or goal. Such a tension might suggest the incompatibility of strategies which compete. Surely, one cannot adopt a theoretical position which is both for and against the tort system at the same time? However, in our view, questions of theory and strategy are inseparable. The value of a theory lies in its ability to inform the moment, and theory must, in turn, be informed by the concrete reality which it addresses. A critical approach need not eschew tort law but it must call for a very careful consideration of its strategic costs and benefits. Indeed, to a large extent, this is what this book has been addressing. While we have focused on different areas – accident compensation, pollution, sexual harassment – we have not sought to reach any universal conclusions about the instrumental and strategic merits of the tort system.

This can be illustrated by exploring the problems the radical lawyer confronts in the context of accident compensation reform. Clearly, in attempting to highlight the political nature of tort, we have also engaged in politics. Indeed, the point of unmasking the politics of negligence has been to seek to return questions of loss distribution and compensation to the political agenda where they belong. To go further, however, is no easy task as the limited effects of Atiyah's seminal work (Cane, 1993) and the Pearson Royal Commission (Pearson, 1978) demonstrate (see generally Mansell, 1997). It is, therefore, tempting to suggest that the lack of progress in securing, for example, some form of no-fault compensation scheme in Britain to mitigate the harms people suffer through accidents and/or other vicissitudes of life can be related, at least in part, to an ideology which tort law expresses and sustains (albeit reflecting values and assumptions which also find expression elsewhere). The twin concepts of fault and individual responsibility, the ideological bedrock of negligence, come to inform the way in which we talk – indeed the way in which we know and understand problems – making it difficult for us to find arguments which escape their constraints. The very premises upon which a capitalist society depends – growth, competition, individualism – might be seen to be antithetical to more collective ways of perceiving and talking about things. So pervasive is the ideology and methodology of individualism in our knowledge and understanding of the world, we find it difficult not to view the world as an aggregate of individuals who have, at best, been granted *rights*. This in turn predisposes us to fear the usurpation of these rights in a recurring and apparently inescapable conflict between our own entitlements and the needs of others. The economic and political freedoms of the individual become viewed as the central freedoms upon which all others depend.

This realisation provides the radical critic with a major dilemma. Desirable though it might be to begin with a *tabula rasa*, we are faced with the reality of what exists. Yet the dilemma is that improvements which merely ameliorate the worst features of the existing system might well have the effect of hardening our perception and drawing new but equally arbitrary distinctions between varieties of human need, ranging from accidental injury to congenital disability, illness and poverty. Thus, an old difficulty appears to arise in deciding whether to 'accept reality' and argue for goals which might be realisable or to propose solutions which are 'revolutionary' in their implications and unlikely to be achieved until a crisis or collapse of the system makes dramatic change inevitable.

One problem with even considering the possibility of radical change in societal protection and provision for sufferers of misfortune is that such goals are too often dismissed as utopian. So clearly does common sense inhibit our perception of what might be, and so decisively have the economic and political imperatives of capitalism and liberal democracy triumphed over other forms of economic and social organisation, that Mrs Thatcher's famous declaration that 'there is no alternative' tends to prevail (even in the policies of 'New Labour'). Moreover, the internationalisation of capital, the immense power of multinational corporations and the consequent decline in national economic sovereignty, make any substantial reorganisation of the way in which the disadvantaged could be enabled subject to considerations of international competitiveness. Community goals become hostages to 'economic reality' in the shape of globalisation.

At the same time, the constant effort to imagine radical alternatives, even if not immediately realisable, plays an important part in identifying the existing constraints on effective reforms of a more limited nature. Thus, the pursuit of the ideal and the real at the same time are not incompatible but complementary goals. The effort to secure modest reform is not misguided if informed by a wider understanding of the limits of such a strategy and its role within the broader endeavour to secure a just and humane society.[4]

In this context, it is pertinent to consider a recent proposal for significant change in the tort system, coming from none other than Professor Patrick Atiyah (Atiyah, 1997).[5] His new book is a sustained, relentless and highly accessible examination of the problems which beset personal injury litigation, exposing the system as indefensible (both rhetorically and legally), unjustifiably expensive and producing a fundamentally unfair distribution of the 'compensation cake'. Emphasising the good fortune of those whose injuries may be remediable in tort compared with those whose injuries are attributable to a cause not likely to attract a tortious remedy, Atiyah isolates the elements which, in his view, sustain and aggravate such privileging. Many disparate factors, he argues, combine to produce what Lord Steyn calls 'the expansionist tendencies of our wasteful modern tort system' – a system whose error is being compounded by its inherently 'plaintiff sympathetic' approach. Thus, Atiyah's criticisms are directed both to the system in general and to its particular tendency to recognise more causes of action for more types of harm.

His central argument is that the present method of awarding damages for personal injury is 'as unjust and inefficient as could be', leading to many of the wrong people getting compensated in circumstances where 'they get too much and the wrong people pay for it – in fact the public pays for it, but not in fair shares' (p. 2). Many of these criticisms coincide with our own, but Atiyah also devotes considerable attention to the role of insurance companies, arguing that they are wrongly perceived as being able to pay damages without cost, whereas, in fact, the cost of the damages they pay falls upon each of us through the payment of insurance premiums, taxes and higher prices (pp. 111–13). Similarly, he expresses immense dissatisfaction with the system of third party insurance whereby a first party, for example, a car owner, effectively insures everyone but herself. While each of us must be insured against causing the most catastrophic harm, or even harm which is unpredictably expensive, to anyone else, third party insurance does not protect the only person whose needs can be calculated by the insurer in advance – the assured herself! At the same time, it accords to wealthy accident victims greater value from their insurance than to the poor, since in each case the victims' costs will, at least theoretically, be met in full (pp. 122–4).

However, more significantly, Atiyah argues that the expansion of negligence liability in recent decades has severely exacerbated pre-existing inequities. The law, he contends, has been systematically 'stretched' so that not only are claimants recovering for injuries resulting from conduct which would not, hitherto, have been deemed negligent, either because of the absence of fault (as traditionally conceived) or because of an inability, on the part of the plaintiff, to establish causation (pp. 32–52), but claimants are also recovering for *types* of harm which tort law has not typically or enthusiastically remedied, for example, psychiatric harm and economic loss (pp. 52–65). As a result, more plaintiffs are receiving more damages (in real terms) but in circumstances where the overall distribution of who gets what becomes even more indefensible.

Atiyah further urges us, fairly it must be acknowledged, to view the present system of personal injury compensation as one of insurance, in which context its defects become all too clear. In relation to road accidents, for example (where compulsory liability insurance has long been prevalent), current coverage is quite good except in relation to injuries to the person(s) responsible for the accident. Overall, however, the position is (as we confirm) little less than tragic. Atiyah estimates that road accidents aside, where a person suffers accidental disablement the chance of tort compensation is one in ten, and where the cause is something else such as disease or congenital in origin, it is probably no more than one or two in a hundred (p. 178). Moreover, most of the obvious ways of increasing the level of protection afforded are not regarded as viable, either for practical political reasons or for ideological ones. Thus, the idea that all those suffering personal injuries or disability should receive tort level compensation, for example, through a universal compensation scheme, is clearly financially prohibitive – according to Atiyah it would cost about £75 billion annually, necessitating a tax rise well beyond the bounds of current political acceptability (p. 179). Even increasing the level of social security benefits available to those not currently covered by the tort system, in order to achieve some kind of parity, is rejected as simply not in keeping with the prevailing tendency of governments to reduce rather than expand welfare coverage (p. 180). In the same vein, more limited state compensation schemes (not offering tort level damages), whether confined to accidents, such as the New Zealand scheme, or offering more comprehensive coverage (to include, for example, congenital disability and illness 'naturally' arising), are also considered and rejected despite their 'visionary and courageous' qualities (p. 185). Given Atiyah's own involvement with the devising of such schemes some 25 years ago, his rejection of them is inevitably hedged and ambivalent. Describing them as utopian, Atiyah argues that experience has revealed their substantial limitations, not just in terms of cost but also because of the necessary and generally inefficient bureaucracy involved.[6] However, his criticisms do not stop with an indictment of their practical operation. Atiyah reveals a singular distaste for systems which, in his view, encourage people to malinger while others pay the bill. He also expresses enthusiasm for 'flexible' market solutions in preference to the 'rigidity' which he attributes to state-based systems. There remains, too, the insoluble problem of where and how to draw the line in relation to the vicissitudes of life which are to be compensated.

What reform then does Atiyah advocate? Perhaps surprisingly, given his earlier allegiance to collective solutions,[7] Atiyah's proposals remain firmly within the world of individual rights and responsibilities. Much of what was seen as desirable in schemes such as the New Zealand one, Atiyah now locates within what he characterises as the 'blame culture' of the 1960s and 1970s which, in his view at least, 'certainly encourage[d] the public to think that it is someone else's responsibility to pick up the pieces after a misfortune has occurred' (p. 184). Even more strongly, in a passage which has the doubtful merit of making his own ideology clear, he states that:

... it is highly desirable to shift the law away from the strongly paternalist ideology which has influenced it for some decades. As we have seen, paternalism underlies much of the blame culture; it encourages people to see others as responsible for taking precautions against accidents and injuries, and also as responsible for protecting them by insurance or other means when misfortune does strike. The messages sent by this sort of paternalist ideology are little short of disastrous, and are closely linked to the culture of the welfare state in its heyday – the idea that the state would be responsible for caring for its citizens 'from the cradle to the grave'. It may well be, in fact, that it is the gradual collapse of this welfare state ideal which is driving so much of the litigation process today. People who have grown up believing that the state would always look after them, no matter what misfortune should strike, are now driven to find someone to sue, when they discover that the state will not and cannot deliver on this expectation. (p. 176)

The sentiments expressed in this quite revelatory passage are accompanied by other allusions, by no means approving, to the decades of the 1960s and 1970s, when, he asserts, it was common to blame the government for most of the social ills the country suffered from (pp. 140–1). While it is probably fair to say that his historical appreciation of this period is based more on prejudice than any sustained and critical examination, it does nevertheless reflect the dominant perspective of the present in which a welfare state is widely perceived as paternalistic, stultifying and repressive of individual effort. Indeed, as presented by Atiyah, both the welfare state and the tort system have (at least) one thing in common: they both encourage people to foist responsibility on to others rather than assume it themselves.

From this, Atiyah's solutions are easily anticipated. In keeping with the times, he seeks to enhance individual responsibility, to make it real rather than the illusion which tort law peddles today. To this end, he suggests that individuals be encouraged to take out (first party) insurance to protect themselves. In the context of road accidents he argues that the future should lie in a no-fault scheme run by the private insurance industry, with compulsory first party insurance replacing third party insurance and coverage made universal by providing that passengers and pedestrians, if not covered by their own policies, be covered by the insurance policy of the vehicle involved in the accident (pp. 185–8). The negotiation of first party policies would, of course, allow bargaining, depending upon the financial and personal circumstances of the insured. Actions in negligence would disappear (or, preferably, be abolished).

While accepting the need for legal compulsion in relation to road accident insurance, he advocates the abolition of the tort actions for personal injury in relation to other accidents, injuries and disabilities, in favour of a free market in first party insurance policies. Thus, each would be responsible for assessing and insuring against risks to herself and her family, allowing people 'the free choice to make their own decisions as to what kind of insurance they want' (p. 190). Through education we might all be encouraged to insure even against congenital disabilities which might affect our babies, or diseases which might strike family members.

It is possible that, given certain circumstances (such as a highly developed welfare state), these proposals might bring about some improvement in the 'damages lottery' of the current tort system. However, in no way can they be considered, even on the most generous interpretation, to represent a real panacea: their full implementation would still produce as arbitrary a distribution of loss as currently exists and, possibly, even greater unfairness. The assertion that individuals must be educated to insure against real risks makes sense only for those who have sufficient income for insurance choices to be anything other than theoretical. Regrettably, such people are often not those most at risk of accident or illness; indeed, the very people most at risk will have the least disposable income to allocate to protect against dangers which, for most people, will never materialise. In orthodox economic terms, it is, probably, simply an inefficient allocation of scarce resources for low income earners to take out insurance, but it does not mean that where the risks do materialise they will not be devastating.

Atiyah is aware of this problem but it is alluded to only in his penultimate paragraph where he suggests that the savings brought about by a first party insurance system would allow almost everyone to save more money than they would need to pay for such insurance. This seems doubtful. Although it may be that a first party insurance system would bring some improvements, it would clearly generate problems of its own. In particular, as the risks one insures against are of suffering rather than causing an accident, no-claims bonuses would scarcely be relevant. And because Atiyah envisages that pedestrians and passengers will be covered by first party vehicle insurance, the same difficulty with the differential cost of maiming or killing the rich as opposed to the poor, would remain. Furthermore, those most at risk of giving birth to congenitally disabled children or even suffering disablement through illness (very often the poor) would be asked for the highest premiums. Finally, and perhaps most obviously, the system would perpetuate an enormous injustice in enabling the rich to protect themselves quite comprehensively while leaving the poor, by virtue of their poverty, to 'choose' to assume risks, relatively, if not completely, unprotected.

Atiyah acknowledges this, observing that 'some state social security safety net will still be needed for those who are not otherwise covered' (p. 193). We think, however, that this point deserves considerably more attention than Atiyah gives it. Indeed, it is arguable that it is the degree of safety provided by the state which ultimately determines the fairness and viability of his arguments. In a society where basic needs (broadly defined to include, for example, health care, education and employment) are adequately met, there is nothing wrong with asking the rich to pay an additional premium to protect their wealthy status. In a society where basic needs are barely met, or not at all, the idea that wealth should dictate who is and who is not protected from the vicissitudes of life, including those which result from the wanton carelessness of others, is as chilling as it is unjust. Yet Atiyah suggests that we eschew developed welfare programmes because they encourage people to blame others for their misfortunes rather than to assume responsibility for themselves. While 'the blame culture' remains a popular rhetorical device invoked by those who seek to reduce, if not abolish, welfare spending, its implications flow not from welfare provision as such but from the misplaced assumption that a social response to individual need is a denial of personal responsibility. We do not accept, however, that assuming responsibility for others is necessarily incompatible with taking responsibility for ourselves. The mistake is to assume that our responsibilities should be defined in individualistic terms in the first place. Likewise, the idea that we should look to the community to aid us in misfortune can only be perceived as 'blame' where the framework invoked is one which assumes precisely what social responsibility explicitly challenges: that people 'own' their own problems and should take care of them themselves.

To us, therefore, Atiyah has not solved the problem of the damages lottery, but has simply substituted one system of arbitrary and fortuitous distribution for another. After all, in what sense is it more justifiable for protection from injury or illness to depend on ability to pay rather than on what causes the injury or illness in question? It is only if one accepts that the distribution of wealth is itself just (rather than the random product of a socio-economic system where there is, too often, little correspondence between individual merit and financial reward) that its outcomes appear defensible. And it appears that Atiyah *does* accept this when he remarks that the variations in coverage likely to flow from a free market approach are justifiable because they reflect the free choice of individuals (p. 190).

At this point one confronts more clearly the problems of possibility in the capitalist system. It is because Atiyah's proposals fit so easily within existing economic ideology that they seem so attractive. But their inherent limitations arise from that same fact and, in the process, ideas of community responsibility such as those which informed the Woodhouse Report in 1967 (presaging the introduction of the New Zealand no-fault scheme) continue to slip further from our grasp, no longer even occupying the realm of our imagination. Yet, in a world of increasing social inequality, these ideas still hold their appeal. Unfortunately, as we observed at the beginning of this chapter, the problem does not stop here. While it may be possible for some to accept the need to reallocate risk in the context of congenital or other illnesses, the question of how to distinguish such misfortunes as these from others such as unemployment and poverty remains both pertinent and, apparently, insoluble. The need to do so seems politically inevitable because to compensate even illness would require a significant redistribution of wealth as previously allocated, no matter how such a scheme were financed. Indeed, such a decision would be no more compatible with the Labour government's insistence upon personal financial responsibility than with the worst excesses of Conservative government, both parties having internalised the need for low cost, 'efficient' industry in an economically non-interventionist state. Because of the continuing and ever increasing need to compete with industries in other states and because of the freedom of capital and multinational enterprises to flee where they will – to homes of low taxation and de-regulation – additional costs in terms of taxation are anathema to governments committed to international 'competitiveness'.

We are, then, in the position of considering changes which for the moment seem politically unacceptable. The fact is that the government – each government – has named the price it is prepared to pay for those who suffer. Individual responsibility and the fault principle then become the rhetoric by which that price, inadequate as it is, is defended. Moreover, this is a rhetoric whose effects extend well beyond the tort system. Although official ideology does not *generally* hold the individual who is unemployed or dependent upon social security responsible, there is little doubt that the (not so hidden) message of the system is that those who fail, fail because of their individual inadequacy. And the idea that the unemployed could or should be rewarded with remuneration comparable to those in work might give rise to apoplexy. Thus, the dilemma for the would-be compensation reformer is that changes which appear necessary if a significant number of citizens are to have any chance of a fulfilling life, seem to be politically unrealisable.

And yet, if they cannot be immediately realised, they must nevertheless continue to be envisioned and re-envisioned, fashioned and refashioned: 'By unfreezing the world as it now appears, new possibilities for meaningful and innovative social interaction can be imagined or grasped' (Hutchinson, 1988, p. 295). To this effect, Hutchinson continues to argue for 'deconstructive criticism' even in a climate where the opportunities for practical legal reform are limited. In exploring the debate between 'faulters' (defenders of the tort system) and 'no-faulters' (proponents of variants of no-fault schemes), Hutchinson argues that both points of view are basically informed by the same set of ideological presuppositions. He maintains that both 'conservatives' and 'welfarists' pose the issue of compensation in essentially the same way, that is, in terms of the relationship between the state and the individual. While the two sides may hold different views about when it is legitimate for the state to coerce the individual into taking responsibility for others, they continue to view the issue in terms of individual responsibility and, therefore, in terms which 'resist acceptance of our basic sociability' (Hutchinson, 1988, p. 301). Moreover, Hutchinson further challenges the traditional welfarist approach to compensation by highlighting the relationship of state dependency which it nourishes and promulgates. His solution is to advocate a radical and participatory democracy whereby people are empowered at all levels to take an active part in decisions which affect their lives as part of a broad communitarian strategy towards achieving a more just, equal and compassionate society (Hutchinson, 1988, pp. 213–20).

Hutchinson's arguments reflect both a general disillusionment with the welfare state and, at the same time, compel an immediate reassessment of the more limited welfarist strategies which characterise current reform. By focusing on the need to empower *people* rather than the state, Hutchinson escapes the traditional conservative accusation that social responsibility restricts freedom where freedom is understood in terms of the individual's power to decide what is in her own best interests. Hutchinson's argument is that individual empowerment is dependent on social collaboration: the hallmark of modern 'democratic' society is precisely the powerlessness which people experience in the face of eventualities which confront them – job loss, illness, accident or disability are all circumstances about which they can do little or nothing despite the liberal promise of freedom which the current system seeks to assure. In this sense, Hutchinson's prescriptions avoid the line-drawing dilemma of the traditional compensation agenda. While community responsibility acknowledges our basic sociability, it does not necessarily require us to hierarchise needs but rather to participate in the development of a system in which they are no longer perceived as such.

If this is accepted, it becomes easier to see that an injury to one is indeed an injury to all. Every individual who is prevented (or disabled) from participating fully in society (which implies the possibility of individual fulfilment) is deprived of contributing to that society as she might have, to the detriment of all. We have become so used to the arguments about the limits to resources available for compensation that we forget the colossal waste in perpetuating people in a state of poverty and dependence in which they are able to contribute nothing regardless of their potential. The tragedy of social need and unemployment is not that it is expensive but that it fails to utilise the talents of many of society's members. Yet, paradoxically, while we have high unemployment, we still have a plethora of socially necessary tasks being ignored, from the building of houses for the homeless, to the improvement of public services, to the expansion of education – education not necessarily for a competitive vocation but to improve the quality of life, political participation and our comprehension of the world in which we live. It is the meanness of vision of liberal capitalism which is most depressing. Yet it is precisely because of its myopic goals – and, in particular, of its dominant goal of material wealth – that it is possible to dimly perceive that the world might be other than as it is, while, at the same time, the true costs of the economic growth goals we have tolerated for so long begin to become more apparent. Whether the costs appear in the form of irreversible environmental damage, the use of weapons we have so aggressively sold, the potential collapse of an economic system threatened by the irresponsible and unconscionable loans made to the poorest countries, or pressures for migration by those whose lives have been made impossible, it seems clear that fundamental economic reorganisation cannot be for ever delayed in any country.

All this may seem far removed from reforming the tort system. It is not. Until we fundamentally reassess what we perceive as injury and how we should respond to it and until we recognise that all must be integrated as full members of communities, we are in no position to view compensation as anything other than payment to enable victims to avoid participation. In this sense, Hutchinson may be right in seeking to direct us away from a focus on compensation (howsoever distributed) towards the key issue of democratic empowerment.

Thus, it seems apparent that the problems tort law seeks to address and redress are not amenable to quick or easy solutions. For the radical lawyer, critical tort law involves grappling with strategies of reform both short term and long, while at the same time endeavouring to forge and fashion new visions of social organisation which are more responsive to the needs of all citizens. Whether the problem is disability, sexism or environmental pollution, the critical lawyer will not long be bound by the rigid and narrow confines which tort categories impose. While an excursus through the myriad of doctrines, practices and processes which make up the tort system is necessary fare for any critical lawyer, it is a journey which, when once undertaken, is likely to take the traveller into territory never likely to occupy the pages of *Winfield & Jolowicz on Tort.*

Notes

CHAPTER 1: INTRODUCING A CRITICAL PERSPECTIVE

1. An earlier version of this chapter appears in Grigg-Spall and Ireland, 1992, pp. 83–90.

2. 'Policy' tends to operate as a 'catch-all' phrase, used by judges and commentators alike, to describe judicial considerations which are 'non-legal', that is not based on a recognised legal principle or an established precedent. Additionally, a policy consideration usually involves a consideration which goes beyond the facts of the case at hand and focuses on the wider social, economic and political impact of a decision. Some policy considerations are recurrent in judicial decision-making and their introduction is generally non-controversial, for example, the traditional 'floodgates' concern that the extension of liability in a particular case will generate more litigation than the system can effectively take. Other policy concerns, for example, in relation to the effect of insurance on liability rules, may be more controversial and their applicability to judicial decision-making is questioned.

   The notion of 'policy' as used by judges and commentators is, however, highly ideological; first, because it implies that there is an ascertainable and limited set of non-legal arguments which judges can rightly introduce into the decision-making process; and second, because their characterisation as 'non-legal' suggests that 'legal' arguments are separate from and not dependent on policy. As we shall see this is a fiction, which even the judges themselves find hard to maintain. An equally unconvincing pretence is the idea that 'policy' in judicial decision-making as distinct from 'politics', is an essentially neutral and impartial concept (bolstered by common judicial references to 'public policy'). A final observation relates to the role of policy in judicial decision-making. While not uncommonly invoked to *deny* liability (as in *X* v. *Bedfordshire CC* (1995) it is rarely tolerated as a ground for *imposing* liability, the courts in this context being much more willing to defer to the power of Parliament to impose liability if it chooses (see, for example, Lord Goff's judgment in *Cambridge Water Co Ltd* v. *Eastern Counties Leather plc* (1994) at 76 (discussed in Chapter 6).

CHAPTER 2: THE DUTY OF CARE IN NEGLIGENCE

1. Winfield defines the tort of negligence as 'the breach of a legal duty to take care which results in damage, undesired by the defendant, to the

plaintiff' (Rogers, 1994, p. 78). Traditional texts usually break this down into three basic requirements – duty, breach and consequence – which are taken to make up the tort of negligence. To what extent these requirements form distinct and separate enquiries is of course another matter, as the text will reveal.

2. In *Anns* v. *Merton LBC* (1978), the plaintiffs sought compensation from (*inter alia*) the local authority for its failure to satisfactorily carry out a building inspection during the construction of their dwellings, resulting in structural damage to the property. The problematic nature of the harm at issue (see above) gave rise to the more general question of duty which Lord Wilberforce addressed.

3. See also *Governors of the Peabody Donation Fund* v. *Sir Lindsay Parkinson and Co* (1985) *per* Lord Keith at 240; *Leigh & Sillivan* v. *Aliakmon Shipping Co Ltd* (1986) *per* Lord Brandon at 153; *Curran* v. *Northern Ireland Co-ownership Housing Association* (1987) *per* Lord Bridge at 17 for further examples of judicial disapproval.

4. In the context of the facts in *Yuen Kun-yeu* v. *Attorney General of Hong Kong* (1987), Lord Keith considered that the absence of a 'close and direct relationship' between the parties, the fact that the Commissioner had not, in any sense assumed responsibility for the plaintiffs' investment, accompanied by a finding that it was unreasonable of the plaintiffs to rely on the Commissioner's register as a guarantee of soundness, were all factors pointing to the absence of a relationship of proximity, despite the foreseeability of harm (712–714).

5. 'Foreseeability of harm is a necessary ingredient of such a relationship [of proximity], but it is not the only one. Otherwise there would be liability in negligence on the part of one who sees another about to walk over a cliff with his head in the air, and forbears to shout a warning' (*per* Lord Keith at 710).

6. See note 4 above. The question as to whether Lord Keith's concept of proximity absorbed in full factors such as policy, which would ordinarily fall to be considered separately under the *Anns* formulation, was left open by his Lordship. However, in *Hill* v. *CC of West Yorkshire* (1989), the House of Lords suggested that even where a relationship was established as 'proximate' in the sense alluded to by Lord Keith, there might still be good policy reasons for refusing to recognise a duty of care (*per* Lord Keith at 60–63). See also *Osman* v. *Ferguson* (1993).

7. See in particular *Simaan General Contracting Co* v. *Pilkington Glass Ltd (No. 2)* (1988); *Caparo* v. *Dickman* (1989, CA); *Van Oppen* v. *Clerk to the Bedford Charity Trustees* (1989).

8. In *Caparo*, the plaintiffs sued the defendant auditors in the context of a takeover bid, made in reliance of a negligent audit of the target company's accounts carried out by the defendants. The question at issue was whether or not a duty of care was owed.

9. The suggestion that judges make 'subjective' decisions does not necessarily carry the implication that judges can and should make 'objective' decisions, that is, that there is some 'true' or 'correct' answer which they deliberately evade or conceal for their own particular interests.

Indeed, as we point out in Chapter 1, we reject the possibility of articulating an impartial, disinterested or neutral perspective. Our focus on judicial subjectivity seeks rather to highlight the ideological use which the language of law makes of concepts of objectivity, rationality and truth. These tools, which judges, among others, employ, facilitate a process of mystification. They are 'discursive and significatory mechanisms that may occlude, legitimate, naturalise or universalise' or otherwise misrepresent (Barrett, 1991, p. 167). Thus, our focus is as much on the *process* as on the content of judicial decision-making. Moreover, our concept of the judicial 'subject' employs the notion of the private person with particular perspectives and experiences but not the notion of the pre-social individual with an identity which can be recognised and understood separate from social context. In this sense, the social context which shapes and moulds the perspectives of many of those who attain judicial status is such as to create a certain continuity of content in the subjectivity which judges articulate as law.

10. This is particularly well illustrated in the House of Lords decision in *X* v. *Bedfordshire CC* (1995) where their Lordships, having already acknowledged that the facts express issues which are 'justiciable', i.e. appropriately the subject of a civil claim, nevertheless decline to recognise a duty on the grounds that it is 'not just and reasonable to do so' (at 371). The express invocation of policy considerations to deny liability is legitimated by their reconceptualisation in terms of justice and reasonableness. On *Bedfordshire* generally, see Cane, 1996; Brodie, 1998.

11. As Lord MacMillan observed in *Donoghue*: 'The categories of negligence are never closed' (at 619).

12. *Murphy* v. *Brentwood DC* (1990) involved a suit by an occupier against a local authority in relation to the negligent approval of defective foundations which the plaintiff alleged (*inter alia*) constituted an imminent danger to himself and his family (although in fact he had sold the house on discovery of the defect). The House of Lords held that the local authority owed him no duty of care and expressly overruled *Anns* on this point. Whether or not a suit lies against a builder and in what circumstances is unclear but see the comments of Lords Keith and Bridge to this effect at 916 and 928–929, respectively.

13. For an excellent account and critique of Hayek's jurisprudence, see Thomson, 1991. The essential thrust of Hayek's arguments, namely that the development of the common law is a neutral, facilitative and non-ideological process whereby judges 'discover' standards which are already accepted in practice by society is, of course, fundamentally challenged by this text.

14. *Junior Books* v. *Veitchi* (1982), for example, which represents the highpoint of judicial liberality in relation to economic loss recovery, allowing a claim against a sub-contractor for the economic consequences of a defectively laid floor, has never been expressly overruled and therefore remains an uncertain authority in favour of economic loss recovery although it has frequently been judicially observed that it has a very narrow and limited application – see *Muirhead* v. *Industrial Tank Specialities*

(1985); *Candlewood Navigation Corporation Ltd* v. *Mitsui OSK Lines Ltd* (1985). Indeed, in *Simaan* v. *Pilkington Glass* (1988) the Court of Appeal (*per* Dillon J) went so far as to say 'I find it difficult to see that future citation from *Junior Books* can ever serve any useful purpose' (805). The denial of a duty of care in *Pacific Associates* v. *Baxter* (1989) on facts very similar to *Junior Books* is a testament to the skill of the judges in avoiding the application of a precedent without actually overruling it. It is also indicative of how little constrained the judges feel by cases they do not like.

15. Evidence of a tradition in tort doctrine which distinguishes between words and acts for purposes of liability is patchy not least because the distinction itself is by no means easy to draw. For example, carelessness will often involve a combination of acts and words as where a negligent building inspection is followed by an inadequate report. The problems of line-drawing inherent in the distinction discredit its overall coherence. Unsurprisingly, and notwithstanding Lord Atkin's reference to 'acts and omissions' in *Donoghue* (above), the court in *Clayton* v. *Woodman* (1962) recognised that careless words causing personal injury were just as actionable as careless acts.

16. Lord Keith describes the decision in *Anns* v *Merton London Borough Council* (1978) as 'unprincipled' and 'calculated to put the law of negligence into a state of confusion, defying rational analysis' (922–923). Lord Oliver is equally troubled by what he sees as a departure from principle in *Anns* over the question of economic loss (932).

17. One final irony has to be observed. The judicial opprobrium which was heaped upon *Anns* before and after *Murphy* is impressive and one might infer that if ever a decision has proved to be incorrect, *Anns* is it. Yet, perhaps surprisingly, given the weight of judicial antipathy, the conclusion in *Anns* (that a local authority did, in such circumstances, owe a duty of care to inspect plans and buildings carefully, and that if they did not, loss would be recoverable in tort by those adversely affected) remains good law in several Commonwealth jurisdictions where not only have its errors not been accepted but the reasoning in *Murphy* has been rejected. In particular, in *Invercargill City Council* v. *Hamlin* (1996), the Privy Council, which included Lord Keith as one of its four Law Lords, accepted that the New Zealand courts were free to reject *Murphy*, which they did unanimously. Although it was stressed in that decision that the different conclusion reached by the New Zealand Court of Appeal resulted from different community standards and expectations in relation to local authorities, Lord Lloyd was frank enough to suggest that whether 'circumstances are in fact so very different in England and New Zealand may not matter greatly. What matters is the perception' (at 767). Even in Australia, which had anticipated *Murphy* v. *Brentwood* (1990) in *Sutherland Shire Council* v. *Heyman* (1985), an extensive passage from which was quoted with approval by Lord Keith in *Murphy*, the court has since held a negligent builder liable for economic loss to a subsequent purchaser in *Bryan* v. *Maloney* (1995). Similar developments have also occurred in Canada – see generally Stychin, 1996.

18. The torts comprising the law of defamation are not the subject of coverage in this book; they are, however, generally well covered in the standard texts. See in particular Stanton, 1994, Chapter 24 and Howarth, 1995, Chapter 12 as well as the recently enacted Defamation Act 1996.

19. A subtext of the *McLoughlin* decision involved judicial consideration of the appropriateness of invoking policy considerations to limit recovery. Couched very much in terms of Lord Wilberforce's approach to the determination of duty in *Anns*, the House of Lords reflected upon whether or not policy should operate explicitly to limit liability for reasonably foreseeable harm. Lord Wilberforce thought that it should, as did Lord Edmund Davies (although the latter did not consider the policy concerns in this context sufficiently compelling to displace the test of reasonable foreseeability). By contrast, Lord Scarman argued strongly that principle must prevail over policy so that, where psychiatric harm was foreseeable, it should be recoverable (subject to the fulfilment of general principles of liability). If it was considered that policy *should* restrict liability in such circumstances, any restrictions should come from the legislature not the judiciary. With Lord Russell of Killowen accepting that policy did sometimes fall to a court to decide and Lord Bridge deciding that the dividing line between successful and unsuccessful actions depended upon the good sense of the judge on a case by case basis, it is obvious that the House of Lords, while unanimous that Mrs McLoughlin should succeed, were far from being in agreement as to the reason why. The case, as a whole, is illustrative of the constant dilemma which the courts face, not merely in deciding such a case but rather in making it appear 'objective' and 'correct'. Although most of their Lordships in *McLoughlin* demonstrated a remarkable willingness to accept the relevance of policy considerations, in terms of doctrinal coherence, the case rendered no clear principle or rule by which future courts might be guided. Once the judges 'come clean' about what they are doing, the uncertain and subjective nature of the exercise they are engaged in is all too apparent.

20. The 'shock' requirement was first expressly articulated in *Alcock* (see, in particular, the judgment of Lord Ackner at 916–918) in the context of judicial efforts to draw limits on recovery where claimants had not perceived the trauma-causing event unaided but had learned of it, for example, by watching television or listening to the radio. However, although *Alcock* was clearly concerned with secondary victims, that is, with those who are not directly involved in the accident causing injury to another, subsequent decisions suggest that the shock requirement (or something like it) extends to at least some categories of primary victims, for example, rescuers and/or employees (*Frost* v. *Chief Constable of the South Yorkshire Police* (1997) *per* Henry LJ at 556; see also *Hegarty* v. *EE Caledonia Ltd* (1997) *per* Brooke LJ at 266). The fairness of the requirement has rightly been questioned. In *Sion* v. *Hampstead Health Authority* (1994), a father who sat at his child's hospital bedside for 14 days and watched him die, while gradually becoming beware that the hospital were negligent in the treatment they provided, was denied recovery on the grounds that he failed the 'shock' test – a harsh and arbitrary result which

seriously challenges the assumption that the current law is rational. See generally Law Commission, No 249, 1998, paras 2.61–2.65.

21. *Vernon* v. *Bosley (No 1)* (1997) is of interest in this context and is also a wonderful illustration of the uncertainties and vagaries of the tort system. In *Vernon*, the plaintiff eventually recovered for 'pathological grief disorder', a type of grief which is so severe as to fall into a recognised category of psychiatric illness. When the case was before the High Court, much of the debate turned on whether the plaintiff was suffering from post-traumatic stress disorder or pathological grief disorder, Sedley J considering that only the first, defined in terms of the nervous shock of witnessing an accident or its immediate aftermath, could lead to a remedy. The Court of Appeal held that a secondary victim could recover for either condition so long as the *Alcock* limitations governing secondary victims (see below) were met. Interestingly, in *Vernon* v. *Bosley (No 2)* (1997) (a case in which the cynicism sometimes expressed about psychiatric harm appears to be boosted), the Court of Appeal, before making a final order on damages, was made aware of a County Court judgment relating to family proceedings between the plaintiff and his wife in which the plaintiff had presented medical evidence (diametrically opposed to the evidence he had led in his action for damages) to show that his psychiatric health was markedly improved and that he was substantially, if not fully, recovered. Yet better evidence of the games which plaintiffs must play if they are to win 'the damages lottery' (Atiyah, 1997).

22. A similar doubt hovers over the status of 'professional rescuers' such as the police or firefighters: are they required to exercise greater, equal or, indeed, any 'reasonable phlegm', as compared to members of the general public? In *Frost*, it was strongly urged by the defendants that professional rescuers, because of their experience and expertise, could be expected to remain untraumatised by distressing events; they should not, therefore, recover damages when they (unexpectedly) *were* traumatised by events in which they participated as professionals. Rose LJ, however, insisted that professional rescuers were subject to the same 'reasonable phlegm' requirement as non-professionals: 'The only difference between professional and non-professional rescuers is that the former are more hardened and therefore it may be more difficult to foresee psychiatric injury to them, but that does not change the scope of the duty owed' (at 546).

23. The House of Lords approach gives rise to a host of problems here. While the emphasis on proximity suggests giving certain relationships a presumptive status – it is reasonably foreseeable to the negligent defendant that parents and spouses will be distressed by injury to their loved ones – by permitting other relationships to acquire the necessary status by demonstrating, on a case by case basis, closeness in terms of love and affection, their Lordships render the defendant liable for losses which he could not possibly reasonably have foreseen, having no particular knowledge of the relationship at issue. Yet, to deny compensation in such circumstances would inevitably lead to arbitrary

results in which access to compensation would depend upon the plaintiff's formal relationship with the primary victim rather than the degree of harm she has, in fact, sustained. The Law Commission's solution to these difficulties is a legislative 'fixed list' – see Law Commission, No 249, 1998, paras 6.24–6.35.

24. The facts of *McLoughlin* require elaboration. Mrs McLoughlin, the plaintiff, was summoned to hospital an hour after an accident involving her husband and three of her children. When she arrived she was told that her three-year-old daughter was dead; she then saw other members of her family in considerable distress, suffering injuries ranging from bruising and shock to severe head injuries, fractures and abrasions. This extraordinarily traumatic event caused the plaintiff to suffer severe shock, organic depression and a change of personality. The question which eventually came before the House of Lords was whether an action for damages should lie when the plaintiff had neither witnessed the injury-causing accident nor its immediate aftermath (understood in prior cases to mean coming upon the *scene* of accident within *minutes* of its occurrence – *Benson* v. *Lee* (1972)). Their Lordships unanimously held that the harm suffered by Mrs McLoughlin was both foreseeable and recoverable, effectively extending the concept of 'immediate aftermath' by some way and allowing compassionate courts to make similarly generous decisions in favour of bereft parents in *Hevican* v. *Ruane* (1991) and *Ravenscroft* v. *Rederiaktiebolaget Transatlantic* (1991) (the trial court decision here was later overturned by the Court of Appeal in 1992). What was most problematic about *Alcock* was that the courts, faced with the possibility of literally hundreds of nervous shock claims arising from the same event, could no longer afford to indulge in such compassionate case by case resolution of individual tragedies. The lines which had been steadily eroded in *McLoughlin*, *Ravenscroft* and *Hevican* threatened to open the feared 'floodgates' unless redrawn.

25. Ironically though, Lord Lloyd did not achieve what he set out to do because, by insisting that no distinction should be made, for purposes of recovery, between physical and psychiatric harm when the plaintiff was within the range of physical injury, he ensured that foreseeability of *physical* injury remained the plaintiff's ticket to avoidance of the *Alcock* criteria – Law Commission, No 249, 1998, para. 5.47.

26. The 6 plaintiffs were representative of 18 other police officers who had undertaken similar roles with similar effects at Hillsborough. The defence admitted liability in the case of a further 14 officers who were most intimately involved with the tragedy.

27. *Clunis* and *Palmer* both involve horrific facts. In the former, Clunis, a mental patient with a history of serious violence, attacked and killed Jonathan Zito, a complete stranger, at Finsbury Park tube station. After being convicted of manslaughter on grounds of diminished responsibility, Clunis sued his local authority for failing to act to treat or restrain him (and thereby prevent his act on Mr Zito), although knowing of his condition. His claim was rejected by the Court of Appeal on grounds of public policy (in particular, the maxim *ex turpi causa non oritur actio* –

no cause of action arises out of a wrongful act). *Palmer* involved the murder of a four-year-old child by a homicidal maniac residing in the same district. The mother's claim against a local authority for failing to warn her of the risk posed by the close vicinity of so dangerous a person was rejected on grounds of lack of proximity (there were no special factors which placed the mother/child at risk over other members of the public). Incidentally, the mother also lost a nervous shock claim on the grounds that she did not actually see her daughter's mutilated body until three days after being told of the child's death.

28. The legal position here is quite complicated. *Stovin* involved a road accident at a junction which resulted in a claim by an injured motor cyclist against a driver who had emerged from the junction. The cyclist's view of the junction was obscured by an earth bank on railway land adjacent to the road. The driver therefore joined the highway authority to the action as a joint tortfeasor, claiming that the authority should share responsibility for failing to have the bank removed, particularly as, it turned out, not only did they know the bank was dangerous but they had actually sought an estimate as to the cost of removing it but, for reasons unknown, had proceeded no further. Under s. 79 of the Highways Act 1980, highway authorities have the *power* to remove potential sources of danger from the highway, including obstructions to the view of road users, but they have no statutory duty to do so. The question was whether a duty to act existed at common law. The majority of the House of Lords held that no such duty arose.

29. Lord Hoffman in *Stovin* offers a comprehensive articulation of the reasons militating against the imposition of liability for omissions:

> There are sound reasons why omissions require differential treatment from positive conduct. It is one thing for the law to say that a person who undertakes some activity shall take reasonable care not to cause damage to others. It is another thing for the law to require that a person who is doing nothing in particular shall take steps to prevent another from suffering harm ... One can put the matter in political, moral or economic terms. In political terms it is less an invasion of an individual's freedom for the law to require him to consider the safety of others in his actions than impose upon him a duty to rescue or protect. A moral version of this argument may be called the 'why pick on me?' argument. A duty to prevent harm to others to render assistance to a person in distress may apply to a large and indeterminate class of people ... Why should one be held liable rather than another? In economic terms the efficient allocation of resources usually requires that an activity should bear its own costs ... so liability to pay compensation for loss caused by negligent conduct acts as a deterrent against increasing the cost of the activity to the community and reduces externalities. But there is no similar justification for requiring a person who is not doing anything to spend money on behalf of someone else. (at 819)

For a comprehensive critique of most of these arguments, see Cane, 1993, pp. 63–7.

30. The notion of responsibility underpinning judicial discomfort in this context is, in fact, highly problematic, resting as it does on a number of contentious assumptions. For example, in what sense is the health authority who carelessly releases a dangerous psychopath into the community, less responsible for the harm which results than the psychopath himself? The temporal and spatial relationship with the victim may be less direct but why should that be the exclusive or even primary determinant of responsibility? One might argue that, in terms of moral culpability, the health authority is *more* responsible than the psychopath. In part, this depends upon one's construction of the psychopath: is he an autonomous individual who deliberately makes bad choices or is he a vulnerable individual who is himself in need of protection (compare the arguments in *Clunis* and *Palmer* in this context). The point is that the question of responsibility in cases where liability is sought to be imposed upon a 'third party' (itself a troubling and leading allusion to the limited nature of the party's involvement) is permeated with problematic assumptions whose validity will vary depending on the particular circumstances at hand.

31. It is worth noting that, in both the *Bedfordshire* and *Osman* cases, claims have been lodged with the European Court of Human Rights alleging, *inter alia*, that the plaintiffs were denied a right to a fair hearing under Article 6 of the European Convention. A similar claim has been lodged on behalf of the plaintiffs in *M* v. *Newham Borough Council* (1995) which was decided alongside *Bedfordshire*. The outcome of these decisions could have significant implications for tort law, particularly in the context of determining duty. See Wright, 1998, for a full discussion of the human rights implications of the *Bedfordshire* and *Newham* cases.

CHAPTER 3: CARELESSNESS, CAUSE AND CONSEQUENCE

1. Interestingly, the imposition of an allegedly objective standard taking little or no account of individual human frailty collides head on with claims that the fault principle corresponds with notions of morality-based justice. What is moral about holding someone liable for an accident which, by virtue of their particular weakness, was unavoidable but which *could* be avoided by the non-existent reasonable man?

2. The idea that men and women apply different analytical approaches to their assessment of situations of conflict and/or moral dilemmas is usually attributed to Gilligan, 1982, whose empirical work suggested that while men approach problem-solving from a 'rights-based' perspective, that is, by the invocation of abstract principles, women are more attentive to context and more likely to seek a compromise which preserves the integrity of any relationships under threat. Gilligan's work has proved controversial not least because it is unclear whether the gender differences she identifies can be attributed to society or biology (Auerbach et al., 1985; Kerber et al., 1986), but it has nevertheless sig-

nificantly informed much of the feminist critique of the reasonableness standard in tort, particularly as developed by Bender, 1988, 1990a, 1990b.

3. In the US, a number of courts have applied a 'reasonable woman' standard to the question of whether conduct was sufficiently offensive to constitute sexual harassment. See, for example, *Ellison* v. *Brady* (1991), *Robinson* v. *Jacksonville Shipyards* (1991). In *Harris* v. *Forklift Systems Inc* (1993), the US Supreme Court declined the opportunity to either expressly endorse or repudiate the standard, thus continuing to leave room for manoeuvre in the lower courts. See generally, Conaghan, 1996, pp. 58–61.

4. The fact that the club did pay damages and costs to Miss Stone and did everything they could to see that she did not suffer financially is interesting (*Law Quarterly Review*, 1951, p. 3). Despite the allegedly moral basis of the fault principle, the defendants felt uncomfortable with its outcome.

5. Although the determination of whether or not a duty of care has been breached is generally characterised as a question of fact, *Bolton* v. *Stone* purports to raise a question of law, namely, what test should be applied to establish the standard of care to be met in a particular instance. See Cane, 1993, pp. 28–31.

6. The House of Lords denied the suggestion made by Lord Denning in the Court of Appeal that a clinical error of judgment could not be negligent but reasserted the proposition that such an error was not *necessarily* negligent, *per* Lord Fraser at 281.

7. The *Bolam* test has also been criticised by feminists on the grounds that, despite its neutral exposition, it is highly gendered and has a disproportionate effect upon men and women – Sheldon, 1998.

8. Only Lord Scarman argued that the doctrine of informed consent should be part of English law. Their Lordships *did* acknowledge the ultimate right of the courts to define the extent of a doctor's obligation to disclose regardless of medical practice, but only in circumstances where prevailing medical practice denied information to a patient where it was obviously necessary to an informed choice (see, in particular, the judgment of Lord Bridge at 505). Margaret Brazier has argued that despite their Lordships' retention of a right to intervene, the overall effect of the *Sidaway* decision is to reinforce the power of doctors to decide what to tell their patients, Brazier, 1992, p. 85; see also Deakin and Markesinis, 1994, pp. 258–9. This seems confirmed by subsequent decisions including *Gold* v. *Haringey Health Authority* (1988) and *Blyth* v. *Bloomsbury Health Authority* (1987), although there is evidence of a recent reversal of the trend – see, for example, *Smith* v. *Tunbridge Wells HA* (1994) where Morland J. held a doctor liable for failure to disclose a risk despite the fact that evidence showed he acted in accordance with accepted practice; see also *Bolitho* v. *City and Hackney Health Authority* (1997), discussed above.

9. By contrast, the Australian courts have subsequently embraced the 'prudent patient' test of disclosure in *Rogers* v. *Whitaker* (1992).

10. The fact that the American healthcare system is largely privately funded is not without significance in explaining doctrinal differences between the two countries.

11. A 'no-fault' scheme differs from a standard of strict liability. Under the latter the plaintiff must still engage in litigation against an individual defendant to establish, however faultlessly, that the defendant caused the injury. A no-fault scheme, however, is not concerned with liability. The injured victim claims for her injury from either a public compensatory body (in the case of a public no-fault scheme) or from private insurance (in the case of a private no-fault scheme). However, even under no-fault schemes, formidable problems may still block access to compensation. For example, in the context of proposals for a no-fault scheme governing medical accidents, there may still be a need to show that some 'medical misadventure' took place as opposed to 'mere medical misfortune' thus importing many of the causation problems which characterise the tort system into non-tort alternatives – see below and Vennell, 1989.

12. There is a strange contradiction in taking account of social utility here. Either the conflict is one between two individuals, in which case, surely, social considerations are irrelevant; or the conflict is a social issue in which case why do the judges and the texts insist so adamantly that it is resolvable by application of the principle of individual responsibility? See *Watt* v. *Hertfordshire County Council* (1954) which is illustrative of the absurd results which flow from this judicial schizophrenia.

13. As where two independent but simultaneous causes concur to bring about the same event in circumstances where either one of them, operating alone, would have been sufficient to cause the same result, *Anderson* v. *Minneapolis, St Paul & Sault Ste Marie Railway Co* (1920), see also Hepple and Matthews, 1991, pp. 311–12.

14. In *McGhee* v. *National Coal Board* (1973), a worker contracted dermatitis while working amidst clouds of abrasive coal dust. He alleged that his employers' failure to provide washing facilities, compelling him to travel home unwashed, multiplied his chances of contracting the disease. He was thus arguing not that the absence of washing facilities had necessarily caused the disease but rather that it had *materially increased* his chances of getting it. The House of Lords accepted that the facts were sufficient to establish liability.

15. By contrast, in the United States, there are a number of examples of authorities reversing the burden of proof in difficult questions of causation. See, for example *Summers* v. *Tice* (1948) (reversing the burden of proof in the context of simultaneous causes); *Ybarra* v. *Spangard* (1944) (applying the doctrine of *res ipsa loquitor* ('the thing speaks for itself') to medical negligence; and *Sindell* v. *Abbot Laboratories* (1980) (applying 'market share liability' to DES litigation). But see *Snell* v. *Farrell* (1990) where the Canadian Supreme Court declined to formally reverse the burden of proof in a complex medical case.

16. Contemporary difficulties with causation in medical cases are further illustrated in the context of the current litigation concerning the

misreading of cervical smear tests at the Kent and Canterbury Hospital. Indications are that, for at least five years, somewhere between 20 per cent and 50 per cent of abnormal smears were wrongly read as normal (*The Times*, 21 May 1997). Nevertheless, even the best laboratories may misread 10 per cent and so the testing is not an exact science. The result of the national screening programme has, however, been to reduce over a ten-year period the number of cervical cancer deaths by one-third, to some 1500 per year. In Kent, it is clear and accepted that a number of women developed cervical cancer which an adequate screening system would have avoided. The difficulty in legal terms is to prove on the balance of probabilities in any particular case that, but for the negligent misreading, early treatment would have been given which would have prevented the onset of the disease, at least in its invasive stage. As the Health Authority has elected to dispute liability in many cases and because of changes in legal aid provision, many women who are already ill are having to take truly agonising decisions about whether to take the chance of litigation at the possible cost of whatever resources they may have. Because of the very expensive nature of pretrial legal work in such cases and because the probability of success is not high, it is unrealistic to expect them to proceed on a 'no win, no fee' basis. See further below and Chapter 5.

17. One way of avoiding the all-or-nothing approach implicit in *Wilsher* was suggested by the trial court in *Hotson* v. *East Berkshire AHA* (1987). The plaintiff suffered injury to his hip in a fall producing a 75 per cent chance of permanent disability. It was alleged that negligent medical diagnosis eliminated the 25 per cent chance of recovery, as a result of which the trial judge awarded the plaintiff damages totalling 25 per cent of the full cost of the disability, effectively damages for loss of a chance. The decision was upheld by the Court of Appeal but reversed by the House of Lords who, while not entirely ruling out the possibility of litigation for loss of a chance in all circumstances, affirmed that the plaintiff must prove that the defendant's negligent diagnosis had, on the balance of probabilities, caused his injuries. See Jones, 1996, pp. 183–90 for a comprehensive discussion of loss of chance litigation including *Allied Maples Group Ltd* v. *Simmons & Simmons* (1995) where the possibility of recovery for loss of chance was approved by the Court of Appeal in a commercial context.

18. In *Ward* v. *Cannock Chase* (1985), a council was held liable for some but not all of the damage inflicted on the plaintiff's property by vandals. In *King* v. *Liverpool City Council* (1986), a court denied that the council owed a duty of care in relation to vandalised property. Likewise, in *Smith* v. *Littlewoods Organisation Ltd* (1987), the House of Lords absolved the defendant property owner from liability for damage caused by vandals. Although the cases tend to deny liability, they do not generally do so on the same grounds. For example, in *Ward* the question was viewed primarily in terms of remoteness, while in *King* and *Smith* the primary focus was on whether or not a duty of care arose. Clearly, however, the issue in all the cases (including *Lamb*) is substantially the same, thus

clearly demonstrating the way in which the supposedly separate components of negligence encompass essentially the same enquiries.

19. Judicial reluctance to impose liability in this context is particularly marked where the 'deep pocket' contains public funds. Thus, for example, in suits against the police *(Osman* v. *Ferguson* (1993)) and against local authorities *(X* v. *Bedfordshire CC* (1995)) in relation to unlawful/criminal acts committed by third parties, liability has been denied on grounds of public policy, even where the defendants have been shamefully neglectful and/or careless. For further discussion of this line of cases, see Conaghan, 1998, pp. 150–5.

20. The only real exception is when the court (or some member of it) expressly admits to making a 'pragmatic' or 'policy' decision; this often elicits disapproval or a sense of discomfort from lawyers and scholars alike precisely because it *does* render less certain (and therefore less authoritative) the decision reached.

21. In fact, because property damage is more likely to be covered by first party insurance (i.e. insurance taken out by the property owner to cover the loss), it tends to generate fewer tort claims, so much so that it has been suggested that 'no hardship would probably be caused by total abolition of the tort action for damage to property', Cane, 1993, p. 424.

22. The recovery of compensation from 'collateral sources' (for example, sickness and disability schemes, first party insurance) in addition to tort may lead to over-compensation in some instances. According to Richard Lewis, some US studies suggest that because of collateral sources, the average plaintiff injured in a road accident receives $1.40 for each $1.00 of pecuniary loss (Lewis, 1998). This raises the question of whether and in what circumstances such benefits should be deducted from damages awards. The relevant law, which currently comprises an amalgam of complex common law and statutory provisions, has recently been considered by a Law Commission Consultation Paper which tends towards increasing the degree to which such benefits are deducted from damages awards – Law Commission No 147, 'Damages for Personal Injury: Collateral Benefits' (1997). For a full discussion of the range of policy issues involved, see Lewis, 1998. On the problems of *under*-compensation, particularly in the context of medical uncertainty about the future health prospects of a plaintiff, see below.

23. The Oxford study looked only at those who, as a result of an accident, were unable to carry on normal activities for two weeks or longer – Harris et al., 1984. By contrast, the Pearson figures include all those injuries requiring an absence from work of four days or more (or the equivalent), Pearson, 1978.

24. This is not to suggest that Woolf is being implemented to the letter. Many of the proposals made in the Report have undergone some considerable transformation since. For example, the Lord Chancellor intends to increase the small claims limit to £5000, not £3000 as Woolf originally suggested. Similarly, the 'Fast Track' limit has been raised from £10,000 to £15,000. See generally 'Implementing Civil Justice Reform: Progress Report', http://www.open.gov.uk/lcd/civil/progrep.htm.

25. Conditional fee arrangements were first introduced in the UK under the auspices of s. 58 of the Courts and Legal Services Act 1990 and represented a half-hearted attempt to secure some of the benefits of the American 'contingency fee' system (whereby claimants can secure legal representation in return for a percentage of their 'winnings'). These include increased access to justice without additional pressure on the public purse. However, because in the UK losing clients remain liable for their opponents' costs (under the US system the parties take responsibility for their own costs), significant financial risks remain, although these can be reduced or even eliminated by the purchase of appropriate legal insurance. The Law Society has also imposed strict controls on the ability of solicitors to charge a 'mark-up' where conditional fee agreements operate. Unlike in the US, it is not a straightforward percentage arrangement. Solicitors must charge normal prices for their services although they *can* include a 'success fee' of no more than 25 per cent of the damages received by the plaintiff (after deductions). This means that they currently have little incentive to make conditional fee arrangements unless damages are likely to be large and/or legal costs are likely to be low. It is, therefore, highly questionable whether or not such arrangements will contribute to solving the financial problems associated with personal injury litigation. Despite these difficulties, the current government is set to expand the use of conditional fee arrangements by proposing to withdraw legal aid entitlement from virtually all personal injury claims (see Lord Chancellor's Department, 'Consultation Paper on Access to Justice with Conditional Fees' (March, 1998). The outcome of the current consultation process will be a government White Paper expected in late 1998. Broader ethical and social questions about the desirability of contingency or conditional fee arrangements remain, see Atiyah, 1997, pp. 27–30.

26. It is worth noting that the costs rule does not apply to the small claims procedure where each side is generally expected to bear its own costs. On the more general question of financing of civil claims, the Court of Appeal has recently addressed a potential glitch in conditional fee arrangements which arose in the context of mass litigation by lung cancer victims against tobacco companies. In *John Barrie Hodgeson and Others* v. *Imperial Tobacco Limited and Others*, the Court of Appeal (12 February 1998) ruled (*inter alia*) that solicitors representing clients on a conditional fee basis are not at any greater risk of having costs orders made against them personally than where the litigation is legally aided or privately funded. For an excellent analysis of the trials and tribulations of tobacco litigation in the US, see Givelber, 1998.

27. The Pearson Commission recommended the introduction of periodical payments for future pecuniary loss (Pearson, 1978, Vol. 1, paras 555–73) but it was not until recently, under s. 2 of the Damages Act 1996, that the court was empowered to award damages, with the consent of the parties 'wholly or partly ... [in] the form of periodic payments' (s. 2(1)). It is at present too early to assess the impact of this provision. More significant is the growing trend in recent years towards 'structured

settlements' whereby, instead of paying damages to the plaintiff in the form of a lump sum, an annuity is purchased by the (defendant) insurer for the benefit of the plaintiff. In this way, the plaintiff receives compensation in the form of a periodic payment and, at the same time, gains the benefit of favourable tax arrangements and significant protection from inflation. The practice has recently received statutory recognition and approval in the Damages Act 1996, ss. 4 and 5. However, structured settlements still require the assessment of a lump sum at the outset and, therefore, all the difficulties attendant upon predictions of future events remain. See further Markesinis and Deakin, 1994, pp. 705–8 and Lewis, 1993, 1994.

28. The Pearson Commission recommended that damages for non-economic loss should not be awarded for the first three months after an accident (Pearson, 1978, Vol. 1, paras 382–8). They also recommended that damages for non-economic loss should no longer be recoverable for permanent unconsciousness (a proposal with which Weir is in agreement). Despite criticisms from Lord Reid (dissenting), the House of Lords in *West H. & Son Ltd* v. *Shephard* (1964) held that the comatose plaintiff should recover for her loss of amenities (although not for pain and suffering, *Wise* v. *Kaye* (1962)). See generally Law Commission No. 140, *Damages for Personal Injury: Non-Pecuniary Loss* (1996) which addresses a number of issues relating to compensation for non-pecuniary loss while taking the general view that such loss should remain compensatable.

CHAPTER 4: HISTORICAL PERSPECTIVES ON NEGLIGENCE

1. The idea that judges 'discover' rather than create legal rules is a traditional characteristic of 'classical common law thought' sometimes described as the 'declaratory' theory of law. See Cotterrell, 1989, pp. 25–30.
2. Notice, for example, the different weight attached to Lord Wilberforce's formulation of duty in *Anns* v. *Merton LBC* (1978) by *Junior Books* v. *Veitchi* (1982) on the one hand, and *Murphy* v. *Brentwood DC* (1990) on the other (see Chapter 2). See also David Howarth who observes that 'the fundamental unit of law is not the rule but the argument' (Howarth, 1995, p. v). Surprisingly, however, Howarth's prize-winning and undoubtedly fine text does not, in our view, fully acknowledge the vital importance of an historical understanding of law in the construction of successful legal arguments.
3. Conventional presentations of tort law may be described as 'imperialistic' in that they conquer and suppress other ways of knowing and understanding negligence, while at the same time posing as the only possible way of knowing and understanding these phenomena.
4. For a good general account of the emergence of 'law-in-context' approaches to legal education, see Thomson, 1987, pp. 185–6; see also Chapter 5.
5. The debates with which Winfield and his contemporaries engaged reveal a preoccupation with the *form* of tort, i.e. with its anatomy and structure,

a preoccupation which is less prevalent in most modern accounts of tort which tend to be functionalist in outlook (i.e. they look at tort primarily in terms of what it can do or what can be done with it) – see, for example, Stanton, 1994; Cane, 1993; Nolan and Ursin, 1995. However, it may be that formalistic approaches are regaining their appeal – Ernest Weinrib, for example, has recently argued that tort law cannot properly be understood except in terms of its own internal form, structure and rationality (Weinrib, 1995). Weinrib criticises analyses of tort which are 'external'; which assess it in terms of the goals or purposes it serves or might serve. The political implications of Weinrib's analysis are significant as he is essentially arguing for a non-political understanding of tort law. See further, Chapter 8. See also Cane, 1997, for a distinctive analysis of the 'anatomy' of tort.

6. The writ of trespass was originally confined to acts carried out *vi et armis*, that is, with the direct and immediate application of force. The action on the case is thought to have emerged during the middle of the fourteenth century to provide a remedy in situations where injury was not caused *vi et armis* (Fifoot, 1949). The distinction between the two writs in terms of the direct or indirect nature of the injury inflicted is usually accredited to the judgment of Fortescue J in *Reynolds* v. *Clarke* (1725): 'If a man throws a log into the highway and in that act it hits me I may maintain trespass because it is an immediate wrong; but if, as it lies there, I tumble over it and receive an injury, I must bring an action upon the case' (636). But the case of *Scott* v. *Shepherd* (1773) suggests that even in the late eighteenth century the boundaries between the two forms of action were far from clear. The trend towards identifying trespass with intentional acts (see Chapter 7) is of later origin, emerging during the course of the nineteenth century (*Williams* v. *Holland* (1833); *Brown* v. *Kendall* (1850); see also *Letang* v. *Cooper* (1964) *per* Lord Denning at 931–932). As the focus shifted more towards the unintentional character of an act rather than on whether it was directly or indirectly inflicted, negligence emerged as the dominant form of action on the case.

7. *Williams* v. *Holland* (1833) held that an action on the case might lie for injuries inflicted *directly* but unintentionally. There were also other advantages to proceeding by way of case – for example, a more favourable limitation period. Moreover, the doctrine of vicarious liability, holding a principal liable for the acts of his agent and a master liable for the acts of his servant, was not available in trespass (Cornish and Clark, 1989, p. 488).

8. A teleological view of history basically assumes that events can be understood in terms of some ultimate purpose which directs and determines the course of things.

9. Consider, in the same vein, the remarks of American torts scholar William Prosser in a casebook note: 'The early common law strict liability of the type of *Weaver* v. *Ward* has *persisted most stubbornly* in connection with trespass to real property and has been *exorcised* only in recent times' (Prosser et al., 1988, p. 15, our emphasis). Strict liability is

presented as a stubborn vestige of ancient times, an evil which requires for its elimination the process of exorcism no less.

10. Nevertheless, some writers, such as Gary Schwartz, are unwilling to accept claims that negligence emerged primarily as a product of the industrial age. In a close examination of Californian and New Hampshire case law during the relevant period, he finds evidence to suggest that negligence was in much more widespread operation around 1800 than is contended by writers such as Horwitz, and he consequently claims that the legal 'transformation' which Horwitz purports to identify (see below) is in fact unsupported, certainly in relation to tort law (Schwartz, 1981). The dispute between Horwitz and Schwartz as to what can be gleaned from the case law further evidences the limits of case law alone as a source of historical understanding.

11. Manchester records that during the four-year period 1872–75, 5231 people were killed and 16,944 were injured in railway accidents (Manchester, 1980, p. 283).

12. According to Horwitz,'the conventional wisdom' that trespass and case were subject to different standards of liability before the nineteenth century – that is, to strict liability and negligence standards respectively – is misguided at least so far as American law is concerned. The principle of strict liability, he alleges, governed both procedures (Horwitz, 1977, p. 89).

13. Millner suggests that it may have been of more relevance to the defence, for example through the plea of 'inevitable accident' whereby the defendant, in effect, asserted the absence of carelessness as excusing the wrong (Millner, 1967, p. 203).

14. Unlike Horwitz, Gregory viewed judicial instrumentalism of the period very favourably as an appropriate response to a radically changing society (Gregory, 1951, p. 396). Similarly Lon Green views judicial activity during the period as part of the legitimate pursuit of 'a bounteous new world' expressing the willingness of all 'to pay the price, to share the risks, even more, to sacrifice the individual in order to achieve our ends' (Green, 1958, p. 31; see Rabin, 1969, p. 58).

15. On the doctrine of common employment, see, in particular, *Priestley* v. *Fowler* (1837); *Hutchinson* v. *The York, Newcastle Railway* (1850).

16. Of course, Holmes was not the only scholar working in this area, nor were his views universally accepted (White, 1985, p. 14).

17. A significant difference between the two traditions lies in the American adoption of the 'casebook' approach to legal education in contrast to British reliance on the student text (Sugarman, 1991, pp. 39–40, 61).

18. Dicey regards the mid-nineteenth century period as dominated by a belief in the principle of *laissez-faire*, that is limited state intervention (Dicey, 1914, pp. 126–210). However, it has been pointed out that Dicey's account is somewhat misleading in that conflicting views on the role of the state emerged as the nineteenth century progressed. McLaren identifies a 'cleavage of judicial opinion' on the common law response to industrialisation, which he explains in terms of a broader division in political and philosophical thought between market-based ideas, which

were necessarily abstentionist, and utilitarian ideas which, while individualist, were compatible with legislative intervention if it contributed to the greatest happiness of the greatest number (McLaren, 1983, pp. 190–4). (On the question of whether Britain really did enjoy 'an age of *laissez-faire*', see Taylor, 1972, pp. 53–64.)

CHAPTER 5: NEGLIGENCE AS ACCIDENT COMPENSATION

1. The latter goal has increasingly become almost synonymous with the pursuit of economic efficiency (Calabresi, 1970; Posner, 1977). The object of tort, so viewed, is to ensure that the sum total of accident costs and accident prevention costs are minimised, thus producing wealth maximisation through an efficient allocation of resources (see Cane, 1987, pp. 506–42; Deakin and Markesinis, 1994, pp. 22–34 and Chapter 3, above).

2. This latter approach has recently been powerfully defended by Ernest Weinrib (Weinrib, 1995) who insists that private law can only properly be understood in its own terms, *not* as a means to some 'external' end(s). See Chapter 4, note 5 and Chapter 8 for further consideration of his arguments.

3. Stanton, 1994, which is mainly organised around the *interests* tort law protects (protection from personal injury, economic and property interests) rather than the different torts it comprises represents a refreshing and often insightful attempt to break away from the traditional structure of student texts. (Regrettably, such departures from tradition are not always welcomed by students who tend to prefer the safety of traditional categories.) Peter Cane has also questioned the utility of traditional tortious categories by focusing on the interests tort protects and the techniques which it deploys to do so. See Cane, 1995, 1997.

4. Atiyah was at Yale during 1968 and was clearly influenced by contemporary legal debate, particularly in relation to proposed no-fault auto accident schemes (above).

5. A 'Restatement' in American law is a codified statement of legal principles, derived from case law and drafted (usually) by a joint team of lawyers, judges and academics. It carries persuasive but not binding authority in American courts who may reject the Restatement's articulation of legal doctrine if they choose, or rely upon it to support their decision in a particular instance. The Second Restatement of Torts was drafted in the early 1960s by the American Law Institute Committee, chaired by William Prosser. It is now being replaced by a Third Restatement which devotes significantly more space to products liability but is widely regarded as narrowing the scope of recovery – American Law Institute, *Restatement (Third) of Torts: Products Liability* (1998).

6. Strict products liability was not introduced in the United Kingdom until 1987 (Consumer Protection Act 1987, Part 1) implementing the EC Directive on Product Liability (85/374/EEC), adopted in 1985. It increases rather than replaces existing private law remedies and it still remains possible to sue the manufacturer of a defective product in ordinary

negligence. Many commentators have argued that the standard of liability under the 1987 Act does not differ significantly from the old fault standard represented in negligence. Moreover, limitations in the *scope* of the action created by the 1987 Act, for example, in relation to limitation periods (s. 6(6) and Schedule 1, amending the Limitation Act 1980) and the recovery of property damage (s. 5), suggest that the negligence action will remain significant as a source of liability for damage caused by defective products. To date, little UK case law has emerged, a fact which speaks volumes about the practical significance of the legislation in the context of consumer protection. See generally Stapleton, 1994.

7. American scholars, Nolan and Ursin, 1995, argue that Calabresi's intervention fundamentally undermined Traynor's loss-spreading rationale. In their view, the political effect of economic analysis on tort theory was to eclipse compensation and loss-spreading arguments (what they describe as 'enterprise liability theory') by providing an alternative rationale for strict liability. This, in turn, generated analyses of tort which were not compensation-led but, in competition with the utilitarian tone of efficiency arguments, focused on philosophical-oriented approaches based on individual rights and corrective justice, in which context the fault principle re-emerged, significantly rehabilitated. See, for example, Weinrib, 1995, pp. 145–203.

8. To date in the UK, road accidents remain governed by negligence law. However, since the mid-1960s, arguments have been made in favour of adopting some form of no-fault scheme, whether public or private. A private no-fault scheme, broadly speaking, involves an arrangement between individual motorists and their insurers whereby the insurers pay the insured a sum representing compensation in the event of an accident. Thus, instead of pursuing the person allegedly at fault (or more accurately his insurers), the insured simply makes a claim on her own insurance policy. A public no-fault scheme involves the state acting as insurer (social insurance) to those injured in road accidents in the form of a compensation fund (funded by general taxation or, perhaps, a road or car tax). The latter has the advantage of covering all those who are injured in road accidents and not just those who are privately insured (although private insurance systems can still make some provision for the uninsured – see, for example, the operation of the Motor Insurance Bureau, Hepple and Matthews, 1991, pp. 898–903). The Pearson Report recommended the adoption of a public no-fault road accident scheme (funded by a levy on petrol), modelled along the lines of the existing industrial injuries scheme and thus not precluding a separate claim in tort (Pearson, 1978, Vol. 1, paras 1004–57, 1068). The proposal stimulated further discussion (Lewis, 1981; Trindade, 1980) but was never implemented and for a decade the issue was all but buried. In 1988, the Civil Justice Review recommended that the Lord Chancellor consider the feasibility of a no-fault motor insurance scheme in consultation with the insurance industry. This was followed in May 1991 with the publication by the Lord Chancellor's Department of a consultative document

proposing the adoption of a private no-fault scheme, run by the insurance industry and funded by higher motor insurance premiums. Although the proposal was never adopted, Atiyah has recently affirmed the desirability of such a scheme (Atiyah, 1997). However, at present, the main focus of legal reform appears to be on improving procedure rather than transforming the substance of legal claims as is exemplified by the current wave of civil justice reforms following from the publication of the Woolf Report on 'Access to Justice: Final Report' (Woolf, 1996) – see further Chapter 3 and above.

9. Although the New Zealand scheme still operates, it has been substantially reformed (and narrowed) by the Accident Rehabilitation and Compensation Insurance Act 1992. General accounts of the original scheme include Ison, 1980; Palmer, 1979. Palmer has also documented recent changes in the scheme – Palmer, 1994. Salient features of the scheme include: (i) it provides compensation for personal injury resulting from accidents but excludes other sources of disability (Stapleton, 1986, pp. 142–58; for changes in the definition of 'accident' post-1992, see Palmer, 1994); (ii) the scheme replaces rather than supplements the tort system which is abolished in relation to accidents covered by it. However, as the scope of the scheme has narrowed, tort has gained back some of its old territory (Oliphant, 1996); (iii) because the object of the scheme is to replace financial loss rather than to provide some minimum standard of living, it is earnings-related; (iv) finally, the scheme is administered by a public body, the Accident Compensation Corporation, and is funded by a number of combined sources including a Motor Vehicle Fund (relying on a levy on motor vehicles), an Employers' Fund, contributions from earners and non-earners and a 'medical misadventure' premium, the general gist of which is to ensure that the funding of the scheme facilitates both the internalisation of injury costs and their deterrence – see, in particular, Palmer, 1994, pp. 252–8.

10. There is no doubt that those engaged in promoting this perspective *did* regard it as novel. Ison comments that 'this book is about tort liability, not in its *familiar context* as a branch of private law, but in its social perspective as one of the media of personal injury compensation' (Ison, 1967, p. ix, our emphasis).

11. Atiyah was also involved in the political campaign for accident compensation reform. For example, in 1969 he authored a memorandum presented to the Lord Chancellor calling for a Royal Commission to consider the question, printed in the *New Law Journal* (Vol. 114, p. 653) and *The Times* (5 July 1969). For a detailed discussion of his most recently expressed (and rather different) views on tort law reform, see Chapter 8.

12. This doubt was removed by the statutory creation of a right to sue in the Congenital Disabilities (Civil Liability) Act 1976. On the common law position, see now *Burton* v. *Islington Health Authority* (1992).

13. For an analysis of the pertussis story, see Harlow and Rawlings, 1984, pp. 398–406. The current operation of the Vaccine Damage Payments Scheme is described in Stanton, 1994, pp. 300–2. The introduction of the scheme did not end the problems of alleged pertussis victims in obtaining

compensation. In particular, for those who chose to pursue their claims in tort, litigation foundered on problems of causation which many claimants faced and failed to overcome – *Loveday* v. *Renton* (1990). Despite a successful claim in the Irish case of *Best* v. *Wellcome Foundation Ltd* (1994) (based in part upon the claim that the defendants had distributed a 'faulty' batch of the vaccine), pertussis litigation since *Loveday* has all but ceased. See generally Goldberg, 1996.

14. The Report is still cited by those who wish to preserve the present system from a no-fault assault. For example, Stephen Dorrell, Conservative Under-Secretary of Health in October 1990 in the course of a debate about the claims of haemophiliacs who had contracted the AIDS virus from NHS-supplied infected blood and were seeking compensation from the government, remarked that the principle of no-fault had been satisfactorily laid to rest by the Pearson Commission some twelve years earlier – this about a Report which expressly asserted its inability to *consider* let alone lay to rest a general no-fault compensation scheme.

15. It is arguable whether Conservative policy in the 1980s in fact followed a non-interventionist policy, particularly in relation to the regulation of trade unions and the exercise of civil liberties – see Thornton, 1989; Gamble, 1988.

16. The first Workmen's Compensation Act was passed in Britain in 1897 imposing a statutory liability on employers in relation to 'accidents arising out of and in the course of employment'. In 1946, after the Beveridge Report (Beveridge, 1942), the liability scheme was abandoned in favour of incorporating industrial accidents into the general framework of social security, at the same time retaining the 'industrial preference' (whereby those suffering from work-related accidents were significantly better compensated than those who sustained injuries or illness otherwise than at work) by the implementation of an industrial injuries scheme (National Insurance Act 1946; National Insurance (Industrial Injuries) Act 1946). The system remained relatively intact until the 1980s when short-term industrial injury benefit was merged with the Statutory Sick Pay Scheme to more or less eliminate the difference between industrial and other disabilities for purposes of short-term benefit entitlement. At the same time, changes in the rules relating to deductions from tort damages (see now Social Security (Recovery of Benefits) Act 1997) have greatly reduced the value of long-term industrial benefits where a tort claim is also pursued. The system (or what's left of it) remains, however, a pertinent example of a no-fault state-funded compensation scheme and continually begs the question as to why the line between fault and no-fault is drawn at this point. See Cane, 1993, pp. 270–96. On changes in the rules relating to deductions from tort damages, see Stanton, 1994, pp. 273–6.

17. This argument, perhaps wrongly, assumes that modern business relations have generated new and more complex situations than the existing legal framework could manage. After all, the facts in *Hedley Byrne* v. *Heller* (1964), for example, could equally well have occurred in the nineteenth

century. Yet, it does seem curious that the period during which the debate about accident compensation was most heated and the fault principle most criticised, also coincided with considerable judicial *extension* of the fault principle into hitherto unchartered areas such as economic loss. Likewise, judicial retreat in this area in the 1980s and early 1990s (see Chapter 2) was as much about *eschewing* the fault principle in favour of a principle of no-liability (in the absence of contract) as reclaiming it. This return to a more contractarian view of business relations echoes the revival of market economics and business 'deregulation' policies which were at the forefront of Conservative economic policy in the 1980s. However, as the subsequent decisions in, for example, *White* v. *Jones* (1995) and *Spring* v. *Guardian Assurance plc* (1994) show, tort law has retained its potential to widen the scope of obligations in contractual situations, suggesting that the shift to contractarianism does not necessarily spell the end of liability extension. See generally Wightman, 1996, pp. 137–42; 145–7 and Chapter 2 above.

18. The story of those infected with the HIV virus after using contaminated NHS blood products is illuminating. Originally, the group of complainants confined itself to 1200 haemophiliacs who had contracted the disease from NHS-infected blood. At the outset, their claims were denied by the (then Conservative) government but early in 1991, it succumbed to public pressure and settled a sum of £42 million on those affected. This was immediately followed by claims from other NHS patients, such as road accident victims, who were also infected by contaminated blood transfusions. The government's initial position was again to deny responsibility for the sufferers and to attempt (with difficulty) to distinguish them from the haemophiliac cases. Indeed Stephen Dorrell, junior Health Minister, at the time admitted that the haemophiliacs had only succeeded in obtaining compensation because 'they were a group who developed a very strong public argument' (*Observer*, 16 June 1991). Despite the government's obstinate stand, the campaign for compensation continued until, in February 1992, the Secretary of State for Health, William Waldegrave, accepted that the haemophiliac compensation scheme should be extended to all those who had contracted the HIV virus from NHS blood transfusions and tissue transfer. The extended scheme was finally signed by the Secretary of State on 24 April 1992 (*Law Society Gazette*, 22 July 1992, Vol. 89, p. 26).

Echoes of this tragedy and the issues that it raises can be found more recently in ongoing litigation against the government alleging negligence in the NHS provision of a growth hormone treatment in the 1970s which is believed to have caused the onset of CJD in its young victims – see *Creutzfeldt-Jacob Disease Litigation Straddlers A & C* v. *Secretary of State for Health* (1998) (a preliminary hearing on matters relating to causation).

19. The Law Commission investigation has produced, *inter alia,* the following consultation papers and reports: Law Commission, No 224, 'Structured Settlements and Interim and Provisional Damages' (1994); Law Commission, No 225, 'Personal Injury Compensation: How Much is Enough?' (1994); Law Commission, No 140, 'Damages for Personal

Injury: Non-Pecuniary Loss' (1996); Law Commission, No 247, 'Aggravated, Exemplary and Restitutionary Damages' (1997); Law Commission, No 147, 'Damages for Personal Injuries: Collateral Benefits' (1997); Law Commission, No 148, 'Claims for Wrongful Death' (1997).

20. Interestingly, such an act of imagination has recently been performed by none other than Patrick Atiyah who, in his most recent book, *The Damages Lottery* (Atiyah, 1997) proposes the abolition and/or phasing out of tort litigation in the context of personal injuries in favour of a system of private (first party) insurance. For our assessment of these proposals, see Chapter 8 and Conaghan and Mansell, 1998.

CHAPTER 6: NUISANCE: THE PALE GREEN TORT

1. Early cases which considered whether or not interference with television signals constituted an actionable nuisance included *Bridlington Relay Ltd* v. *Yorkshire Electricity Board* (1965) and the Canadian case of *Nor-Video Service v. Ontario Hydro* (1978). In the former, Buckley J concluded that interference with television reception could not constitute a nuisance because it affected the enjoyment of a purely recreational activity. *Nor-Video*, on the other hand, recognised the possibility of a claim in nuisance in certain circumstances. In 1997, the House of Lords affirmed that where the interference with TV reception was caused by the mere presence of a building, no cause of action in nuisance would arise (*Hunter* v. *Canary Wharf Ltd/London Docklands Corporation* (1997)). The question of whether or not an interference caused, for example, by the emission of electromagnetic waves (as in *Bridlington Relay*) was left open by their Lordships. See, in particular, the judgments of Lords Goff and Hoffman on this point.

2. In fact, the majority of their Lordships in *Hunter* were fairly strongly of the view that nuisance should not provide a remedy for personal injury. See, for example, Lord Goff at 438, Lord Lloyd at 442 and Lord Hoffman at 453. Lord Goff (at 439) also questions whether or not nuisance should properly cover physical (as opposed to amenity) damage to land, citing Gearty, 1989. For an excellent discussion of these and other aspects of the *Hunter* decision, see Wightman, 1998.

3. More recently, in *Gillingham BC* v. *Medway (Chatham) Dock Co Ltd* (1992), Buckley J held that the granting of planning permission could change the nature of the locality for purposes of establishing a nuisance. Thus, where a council granted planning permission authorising the operation of a commercial port in an area which had hitherto been largely residential, it was held that no action in nuisance arose because, given the nature of the locality after planning permission, the interference complained of (largely traffic noise) was not unreasonable. However, in *Wheeler* v. *Saunders* (1995), the Court of Appeal made it clear that the granting of planning permission did *not* necessarily alter the character of the neighbourhood for purposes of defining locality although it might do so in the context of 'a strategic planning decision affected by considerations of public interest' (*per* Staughton LJ) or 'a major

development altering the character of a neighbourhood with wide consequential effects'(*per* Peter Gibson LJ).

4. In *Bradford* v. *Pickles* (1895) the presence of malice was considered insufficient to establish a nuisance because the act of the defendant (the abstraction of water from a borehole with the deliberate intention of depleting the supply available to his neighbour) violated no legal right of the plaintiff. Similarly, while Lord Cooke in *Hunter* considered that malice might be a relevant factor in the determination of whether or not interference with TV reception could constitute a nuisance (at 465), the assertion of the majority that no claim could arise from an interference caused by the mere presence of a building would suggest that, in line with *Bradford*, the presence of malice in these circumstances is irrelevant (see further Wightman, 1998).

5. The absence of a proprietary interest bars a claim (*Malone* v. *Laskey* (1907); *Oldham* v. *Lawson (No 1)* (1976). In *Khorasandjian* v. *Bush* (1993), Dillon LJ in the Court of Appeal suggested that mere occupation of the property affected might be enough to generate a claim in nuisance. However, this suggestion was firmly repudiated by the majority of the House of Lords in *Hunter* v. *Canary Wharf Ltd* (1997) where it was affirmed that only persons with a right over the land affected (defined by Lord Goff as a right to exclusive possession) could sue in nuisance. Lord Cooke dissented from the majority position, considering that substantial occupation was sufficient to found a cause of action – for further discussion, see Wightman, 1998.

6. *Per* Lord Goff at 72, relying on the Privy Council decision in *The Wagon Mound (No 2)* (1967). On the application of *Cambridge Water* to the scope of a claim under *Rylands* v. *Fletcher*, see further below. Atiyah has observed that the only difference in the scope of liability for negligence and nuisance lies in the focus of the latter on the harm-creating activity itself and not just on how the activity is carried out (Cane, 1987, p. 139). Moreover, where a nuisance is caused by the act of a trespasser (or by a natural hazard), the imposition of liability on the occupier of land from whence the nuisance arises is governed by a standard which is almost synonymous with the duty of care in negligence (*Sedleigh-Denfield* v. *O'Callaghan* (1940); *Goldman* v. *Hargrave* (1966); *Leakey* v. *National Trust* (1980)).

7. After 20 years' continuance, an interference will become lawful by prescription. However, time does not begin to run until the plaintiff is aware of the interference (*Sturges* v. *Bridgman* (1879)). If a nuisance is authorised by statute (statutory authority), it will not be actionable. Whether or not a particular statute authorises a nuisance can be a matter of some doctrinal and factual complexity, but the basic approach appears to be that in the absence of express authority to the contrary, an activity authorised by statute will still attract liability if it is carried out negligently, *Allen* v. *Gulf Oil Refining* (1981). In *Gillingham BC* v. *Medway (Chatham) Dock Co Ltd* (1992), Buckley J drew an analogy between statutory authority and the granting of planning permission, suggesting that the latter operates to 'authorise' a nuisance by changing

the nature of the locality. However, his position has attracted judicial disapproval in the Court of Appeal decision of *Wheeler* v. *Saunders* (1995) which took a much more circumspect approach (above, note 3).

8. The measure of damages in nuisance was a focus of their Lordships' attention in *Hunter* where it was suggested that as the harm addressed by the tort of nuisance was property-based not personal it should generally correspond to the diminution in the value of the property (*per* Lord Lloyd at 441–442) and should not depend upon the number of people resident in the property affected. For a trenchant critique of their Lordships' approach, particularly to the question of the measure of amenity damages, see Wightman, 1998.

9. A relator action is one in which a person or body claiming to be entitled to restrain interference with a public right or to abate a public nuisance must bring such action in the name of the Attorney-General.

10. Even Rogers despairs of the possibility of bringing any kind of coherence to the case law on this point (Rogers, 1994, p. 452), particularly because judicial perceptions of what constitutes a natural or non-natural use of land are highly historically and culturally specific. To give a mere flavour – in 1919, a court held that keeping a car filled with petrol in a garage was a non-natural use (*Musgrove* v. *Pandelis*) but in 1947 the House of Lords suggested that keeping a munitions factory in time of war might be regarded as a *natural* use of land (*Read* v. *Lyons*). To compound things, it is not entirely certain that 'non-natural use' *is* a necessary requirement of the rule in *Rylands* given that it was not part of Blackburn J's original articulation but was, rather, a gloss offered by Lord Cairns in the House of Lords. On the legal standing of the non-natural user requirement after *Cambridge Water*, see note 11 below.

11. Although there is some acknowledgement that 'natural use' might extend to activities which benefit the local community, Lord Goff is extremely vague as to precisely what activities this might include. However, he clearly acknowledges the 'non-natural user' requirement to be a prerequisite of *Rylands* liability, whatever its origins. Moreover, he is undoubtedly seeking to turn away from the wider conceptualisation of natural use reflected in earlier cases such as *Read* v. *Lyons* (1947) which enabled defendants to escape *Rylands* liability so easily. In this sense, *Cambridge Water* may be interpreted as extending rather than restricting the scope of the *Rylands* principle. However, it is important to remember that Lord Goff's comments on this point are strictly *obiter* and, in any case, highly inconclusive. See his judgment at 78–80 and further, below.

12. McLaren's study of nineteenth-century nuisance law bears this out. Highlighting the institutional, procedural and social rather than *doctrinal* obstacles to effective suit, he concludes that the substantive law of nuisance failed to challenge the adverse impact of industrialisation on the environment simply because the common law generally was no match for so relentless and revolutionary an opponent (McLaren, 1983, pp. 194–9, 205–19).

13. For an excellent description of the environmental devastation wrought by industrialisation, see McLaren, 1983, pp. 161–9.
14. On the general problem of establishing causation in nuisance litigation, see McLaren, 1983, pp. 197–9. For a modern parallel in the context of radioactive harm, see *Merlin* v. *British Nuclear Fuels* (1990).
15. A court does not actually have to decide that a tort had been committed in order to grant interlocutory relief. They need only consider whether or not there is a serious issue to be tried and, if so, whether the balance of convenience lies in favour of granting or refusing relief (*American Cyanamid Co* v. *Ethicon Ltd* (1975)). See further Rogers, 1994, pp. 678–80.
16. In fact, after 1976 ECL changed its method of storing PCE and the spillage stopped. The contamination identified in the early 1980s was a consequence of the continued progress of solvent, already spilled, down-catchment to the borehole. It was, as Lord Goff described it, an example of 'historic pollution' (at 77).
17. *Ballard* involved a dispute between two neighbours, both of whom shared the same water source by means of a well on each land which was sunk into a chalk aquifer. The plaintiff pumped water from the well to use in his brewery but the defendant used his to dump sewage, eventually contaminating the plaintiff's water so that it became unusable for brewing purposes. The plaintiff's claim for an injunction and damages initially failed but succeeded at the Court of Appeal. The case is rarely mentioned in standard tort textbooks prior to 1994; even in a specialist book on *Water Pollution Law* it merits only a brief footnote (Howarth, 1988, p. 72, n. 54).
18. 'Statutory nuisance' connotes the statutory classification of certain activities or harms, usually injurious to public health, as criminal nuisances. Statutes often rely upon the common law concept of public nuisance for definitional purposes, though not exhaustively. See Buckley, 1981, Part III.
19. Economic analysis does not always command the pursuit of efficiency. It may be desirable to take decisions which are not efficient but are nevertheless justifiable on other grounds such as equity (Le Grand, 1985, p. 113). At the same time, economic analysis claims it can 'cost' such decisions, thus providing fuller information about their overall impact and effect.
20. Such attempts to bring together the public and private dimensions of environmental regulation are not necessarily welcomed by environmental law scholars. For example, McGillivray and Wightman argue that a 'twin-track' approach to public and private regulation (whereby public and private law do not necessarily deliver the same answers) enhances private law's ability to challenge 'official' definitions of public interest in the context of environmental protection (McGillivray and Wightman, 1997, pp. 180–1).
21. However, a 1994 Command Paper, 'Sustainable Development: The UK Strategy' (DOE, Cm. 2426, 1994), while describing legal liability rules as an 'economic instrument' in the context of environmental protection,

barely discusses them, suggesting a diminishing enthusiasm for private law mechanisms in this context, at least domestically.

22. But note that the attribution of 'market' goals to private law in the context of pollution control has been challenged by some environmental law scholars – see, for example, Steele, 1995, p. 237; McGillivray and Wightman, 1997.

23. 'It is not from the benevolence of the butcher, the brewer, or the baker, that we expect our dinner, but from their regard to their own interest' (Adam Smith, 1910, p. 13).

CHAPTER 7: FEMINIST PERSPECTIVES ON TORT LAW: REMEDYING SEXUAL HARASSMENT AND ABUSE

1. For a discussion of different ways in which the law may be said to be 'male', see Conaghan, 1996, pp. 56–8.

2. Some of these arguments may, potentially, be vulnerable to the claim that they themselves invoke or rely upon stereotypical or oppressive notions of 'male' and 'female' identity: they 'essentialise' gender in a way which belies its socially constucted character. For a discussion of these theoretical difficulties in the context of feminist analyses of sexual abuse, see Conaghan, 1998, pp. 134–5 and, more generally, Jackson, 1993.

3. The Sex Discrimination Act 1975 (SDA) does not address the problem of sexual harassment specifically. However, a line of case law has developed which recognises sexual harassment as 'less favourable treatment on grounds of sex' and, therefore, direct discrimination (SDA 1975, s. 1(1)(a); *Porcelli* v. *Strathclyde Regional Council* (1986)). A woman who has been dismissed or has resigned because of sexual harassment in the workplace may also be able to pursue a claim of unfair dismissal if it can be shown that her employer acted unreasonably in dismissing her or in causing her to resign (*Bracebridge Engineering* v. *Darby* (1990)). In a recent sex discrimination claim against Hereford and Worcester County Council, a female firefighter secured a settlement of £200,000 (in addition to legal costs) after five years of sexual harassment by her male colleagues which had destroyed her personality and self-confidence, shattered her career and left her 'a shadow of her former self', *Equal Opportunities Review* 73: 2 (1997).

For a number of reasons, employment law remedies are generally regarded as preferable to tort as an avenue of redress for complainants of sexual harassment. First, sex discrimination and unfair dismissal claims are heard by Industrial Tribunals, posing a cheaper, quicker and less formidable method of obtaining redress. Second, the SDA can embrace a much wider concept of harassment than traditional tort law. Under the SDA, sexual harassment can be actionable either where a woman is treated unfavourably for refusal to comply with a sexual request ('quid pro quo' harassment, MacKinnon, 1979, pp. 32–40), or where conditions of work are such that persistent sexual remarks, language and conduct create a 'hostile working environment'

(MacKinnon, 1979, pp. 40–7; *Porcelli* v. *Strathclyde Regional Council* (1986)). Moreover, a woman may have a cause of action even though she has not been subject to any physical assault or unwanted bodily contact, and damages can include a sum for emotional distress resulting from the harassing behaviour (some of these advantages also attach to the new tortious remedy provided by the Protection from Harassment Act 1997, discussed below). However, in some instances, advantages may lie in pursuing a tort claim. First, tort law can cover instances of sexual harassment beyond the context of an employment relationship. More significantly, tort does not depend on a concept of comparability to establish the wrong. Under the SDA a woman must show she was treated *less favourably* than a man in order to establish direct discrimination. Thus, in the context of sexual harassment, it is not the harassment as such which is wrongful but the fact that it is *sexually specific*. Presumably, if an employer were to contend that he sexually harassed his employees indiscriminately and regardless of their sex, he would not, technically, be discriminating on grounds of sex and technically would not, therefore, be liable. While in practice this is not likely to be a significant bar to bringing a sexual harassment claim under the 1975 Act, it is still problematic ideologically, suggesting that the wrong lies in the *differential treatment* and not in the *harassing behaviour*. Tort law, where applicable, is directed at the harassment *per se* and does not depend on concepts of comparability or discrimination in order to establish wrongfulness.

4. Aspects of the decision in *Khorasandjian* were overruled by the House of Lords in *Hunter* v. *Canary Wharf Ltd/London Docklands Corporation* (1997) but, as *Khorasandjian*, in effect, relied upon two alternative grounds for injunctive relief (see Conaghan, 1993), only one of which – the nuisance claim – was later the subject of criticism in the *Hunter* decision, it is arguable that *Khorasandjian* still stands as an authority on the scope of liability under *Wilkinson* v. *Downton,* discussed below.

5. Criminal Courts also have the power, in criminal cases involving personal injury or damage to property, to award compensation to the victim but these powers are rarely exercised in serious cases, Cane, 1993, pp. 251–2.

6. A general background of unpleasantness may be relevant evidence as to the degree of insult intended by the act of touching but it nevertheless remains the bodily contact which is the legally wrongful ingredient, not the sexually harassing behaviour as a whole.

7. In 1988, a woman successfully sued the London Fire Brigade after she was subjected to an 'initiation ceremony' in which her fellow employees (firemen) tied her to a ladder, threw water and urine at her, exposed themselves and made obscene suggestions to her. She alleged assault, battery and false imprisonment on the part of the firemen (for which London Fire Brigade were held vicariously liable) and negligence and breach of contract on the part of London Fire Brigade. A settlement of £27,000 was approved by the High Court (IRLIB, 1988, p. 11).

8. *Dulieu* v. *White* (1901) was the first case to take a more relaxed attitude to the problem posed by nervous shock in negligence actions. See generally Chapter 2.

9. See, for example, *Nickerson* v. *Hodges* (1920) involving a cruel practical joke against a mentally infirm lady; *Bielitski* v. *Obadisk* (1922) concerning a false rumour about a son's suicide; and *The Great Atlantic and Pacific Tea Co* v. *Roch* (1931), where a dead rat was offered to the plaintiff instead of a loaf of bread. See also the classic article on the scope and nature of the tort by Magruder, 1936.

10. It should also be noted that the Restatement envisages liability for the infliction of severe emotional distress even where the harm is caused recklessly rather than intentionally. Thus, an action will lie not just where the harm is intended, but also where it is caused by conduct engaged in wilful disregard of the consequences to the plaintiff. In this respect, the scope of the tort is quite wide and a defendant cannot easily avoid liability for cruelly insensitive conduct by pleading that he had no intention to harm.

11. Consider, for example, the English decision in *Wileman* v. *Minilec Engineering* (1988), a sex discrimination claim, in which an Employment Appeal Tribunal upheld the award of a nominal sum (£50) to a woman who had been subjected to sexual harassment by a director in her employer's company for four years but who had not, according to an Industrial Tribunal's findings, been upset by the conduct, which included actual physical contact of a sexual nature. It seems strange that the Tribunal should accept that such advances were unwanted (which they did) and then conclude that the victim was not upset by them. If the advances were unwanted, then it would seem to follow that she was, indeed, upset by them. Is the assumption that unwanted sexual advances are not always truly unwanted implicit in this decision? A Tribunal's conclusion that a woman has not been 'too upset' by behaviour which is clearly upsetting may tell us more about judicial attitudes than about what a woman actually felt and endured.

12. A series of recent decisions in criminal law have held that abusive telephone calls may amount to a *criminal* assault occasioning actual or grievous bodily harm, provided that psychological harm occurs – see the House of Lords decision in harm *R.* v. *Ireland, R.* v. *Burstow* (1997). These decisions are generally viewed as creative judicial responses to the perceived absence of anti-stalking laws, a problem which has since been statutorily addressed by the Protection from Harassment Act 1997, discussed below.

13. In modern parlance, the *Wilkinson* requirement of 'actual physical harm' is similar to the requirement in negligence cases that, for a claim based on purely psychological harm to succeed, it must correspond to a recognised psychological illness. What is distinctive about *Khorasandjian* is that Dillon LJ effectively dispenses with this requirement, at least for purposes of granting an injunction. See further Bridgeman and Jones, 1994, pp. 192–201 and note 8 above.

14. A *quia timet* injunction is 'one which issues to prevent the infringement of the plaintiff's rights where the infringement is threatened but has not yet occurred' (Martin, 1993, p. 72). In *Burris* v. *Azadani* (1995), the Court of Appeal went one step further. Like *Khorasandjian*, *Burris* also

involved a dispute over the scope of an injunction in circumstances where the plaintiff had been subject to a long and distressing campaign of harassment by the defendant, her former martial arts instructor. The terms of the injunction were very similar to those in *Khorasandjian* but also included a requirement which restrained the defendant from coming within 250 yards of the plaintiff's home. The defendant contended that the county court had no jurisdiction to impose an exclusion zone because it involved the restraint of conduct which was not necessarily unlawful or tortious. The Court of Appeal rejected the defendant's appeal and upheld the terms of the injunction, holding that the court had power to restrain conduct which was not necessarily unlawful 'if such an order is reasonably regarded as necessary for the protection of a plaintiff's legitimate interest' (*per* Sir Thomas Bingham MR at 808). Thus, while in *Khorasandjian*, Dillon LJ went to considerable lengths to find a wrong upon which to hang Ms Khorasandjian's claim and thereby grant her relief, the court in *Burris* appear to have dispensed with the need to identify a wrong in the first place. For further discussion of the legal background and implications of the *Burris* decision, see Conaghan, 1996, pp. 420–2.

15. Sexual harassment as a social harm has clear privacy implications: in addition to the violation of a person's emotional and physical integrity, it is an unwelcome assertion of intimacy and an intrusion into the individual's sexual, social and professional identity. However, English common law does not recognise a tort of invasion of privacy as such, although the individual's interest in privacy may be protected to some extent by other torts, for example, defamation, nuisance or the newly emerging tort of breach of confidence (Heuston and Buckley, 1996, pp. 34–5), which is viewed by some as the natural precursor to a right to privacy (see, for example, Clare Dyer's report in the *Guardian*, 17 February 1998 suggesting that 'Senior judges ... have signalled their willingness to develop the law on breach of confidence into a full-fledged privacy law, if the right case comes before them'). A series of government reports have considered the viability of a statutory right to privacy. In particular, in 1990, the 'Report of the Committee on Privacy and Related Matters' (The Calcutt Committee, 1990, Cm. 1102) accepted the possibility of defining a statutory tort of infringement of privacy (para. 12.17), but did not accept that the case for legislation was sufficiently compelling at that time. A further report in 1993 recommended that the government should consider the introduction of a new statutory tort in the wake of the perceived failure of press self-regulation (Calcutt, 1993) and this was swiftly followed by a consultation paper from the Lord Chancellor's Department along similar lines. In fact, events have since been overtaken by the successful legislative campaign to improve the range of legal remedies available to combat harassment, and the PHA 1997 offers some possibility of redress in the context of media intrusion. Similarly, the imminent incorporation of the European Convention of Human Rights into English law (the Human Rights Bill is currently going through Parliament), including a right to privacy under Article 8, is likely further

     to improve existing legal rights. On the Human Rights Bill, see generally Bennion, 1998.

16. The Law Commission's provisional recommendation is that a uniform limitation period of three years should be introduced covering all claims, running from the time when the plaintiff discovers or ought reasonably to discover that she has a legal claim against the defendant. So long as the rules on 'discoverability' are interpreted sympathetically, such a limitation regime is more likely to facilitate claims by victims of abuse. The Commission does *not* recommend special limitation rules attaching to abuse claims, as have been adopted, for example, in some US states, Conaghan, 1998, pp. 143–4.

17. The legislative debate on stalking began with the introduction (by Janet Anderson MP) of a Private Member's Bill in the spring of 1996, seeking to make persistent stalking a criminal offence. The Bill attracted considerable media attention – the *Daily Mirror*, for example, publicly backed it – as did the issue of stalking generally. In the midst of a series of high profile stalking cases, involving, among others, the Princess of Wales, in July 1996 the government published a consultation paper, 'Stalking: the Solutions', following it up with the proposals that formed the basis of the legislation passed in 1997.

18. In fact, such an offence already exists in the Public Order Act 1986 (as amended by the Criminal Justice and Public Order Act 1994). The offence created by the 1997 Act is, however, distinguishable, not least because it does not require any proof of intention on the part of the harasser.

19. Men, of course, may also be the victims of sexual harassment, including harassment of a serious and highly disturbing nature, as in *Fine* v. *McLardy* (1996), involving the persistent stalking of a male university lecturer by a female student. The point is not that the application of a reasonableness test in the context of sexual harassment *necessarily* reinforces a male point of view (although, as a matter of practical reality it tends to) but rather that it assumes the legitimacy of only one point of view in this context.

20. Particular doubts revolve around the degree of intention required to activate *Wilkinson*. For example, it is not clear in English law whether or not the harm (as opposed to the act inducing the harm) must be intended, although it is an arguable interpretation of Lord Wright's remarks that an intention to harm the plaintiff's interests is required (Brazier, 1993, p. 33). In *Powell* v. *Boldaz* (1998), which involved a suit against a group of doctors for, allegedly, deliberately concealing their own misdiagnosis of a child's illness from the child's parents, the Court of Appeal rejected a *Wilkinson* claim on the grounds that there was insufficient evidence of intention to found a claim, but suggested that so long as the act which caused the harm was intended in circumstances where the harm itself was a foreseeable and probable consequence of that act, then an intention to harm could be imputed for purposes of the *Wilkinson* principle.

21. Such a point is most dramatically made by comparing the relative value which tort law places on harms typically suffered by men as opposed to women. For example, in *Meah* v. *McCreamer* (1985), the plaintiff, Meah, was awarded damages of £45,000 in relation to injuries he sustained in a road accident, resulting in brain damage which induced a personality change and allegedly caused him to engage in aggressive and sexually perverted behaviour towards women. When two of Meah's female victims sued him, alleging sexual assault and rape respectively, they received only £6750 and £10,250 leading to a public outcry as to the disparity of damages awarded (*W* v. *Meah, D* v. *Meah* (1986)). The inconsistent and extraordinary values which tort damages reflect are further evidenced in the high awards commonly secured in celebrated libel cases. Loss of reputation is financially perceived to constitute a much greater compensatable harm than violations of bodily integrity. See, for example, *Jeffrey Archer* v. *Star* (1987), £500,000; *Maxwell* v. *Ingrams* (1986), £500,000; *Jason Donovan* v. *The Face* (1992), £100,000; and *Lord Aldington* v. *Tolstoy and Watts* (1989), £1,500,000. Such comparisons suggest that a man's reputation is, in the eyes of the tort system, worth a considerable amount more than a woman's right to physical and emotional integrity. On recent efforts to reduce the excessive level of defamation awards, see Jones, 1996, pp. 431–3.

CHAPTER 8: CONCLUDING THOUGHTS

1. Stapleton's focus on disease in the context of compensation is a good example of the way in which tort concepts direct our understanding of the problems posed by accident compensation in general, particularly the way in which we continue to perceive of 'accidents' (howsoever caused) as a category of harm distinguishable from other misfortunes such as the natural occurrence of disease (Stapleton, 1986). So, for example, the provision of no-fault compensation for *accident* victims in New Zealand reflects a preoccupation with cause which is undoubtedly part of the legacy of the tort system (see further Chapter 5, note 9). In the same way, the assumption that some (or all) of life's misfortunes should attract *compensation* (rather than a range of social responses including prevention, amelioration, social reorganisation, tolerance and/or compassion) is an unfortunate but all too typical by-product of a tort focus on disability and human suffering.

2. Tony Weir is probably of the view that it is not, on the grounds that it encourages dependency and a lack of fortitude in the face of misfortune: 'Gone without trace are both the pagan stoicism of the year dot and the meek Christian acceptance of the slings and arrows of medieval misfortune' (Weir, 1996, p. vi). Patrick Atiyah is similarly dismissive of the view that the good society should be measured by its compassion: 'I entirely accept that sympathy and compassion have their proper place, but that place is in personal relationships' (Atiyah, 1997, p. vii).

3. For example, the idea of a limited state gave way, in the early twentieth century, to the concept of an interventionist state which accepted

responsibility for the welfare of its individual subjects, if not universally, at least to the extent of providing free health care, education and basic social security. In turn, this perception of the state, popularly regarded as 'progressive' in its time, has been abrogated to a degree which was scarcely imaginable in the 1950s and 1960s, in the face of questions both in relation to the cost of universal welfare provision and its effectiveness in achieving the goals of a 'just society'. Similarly, the balance of debate around the perceived conflict arising from the privileging of individual responsibility, on the one hand, and pursuing conceptions of social justice which embrace some notion of collective or community responsibility, on the other, has shifted over time. Indeed, notwithstanding the recent return of a Labour government, the former preoccupation with the centrality of individual responsibility is currently in the ascendant. At the same time, ideas of freedom and consent as the source of political and legal obligation have come under frequent and recently renewed scrutiny in the face of a legal edifice which had, to a considerable extent, abandoned them (see Chapter 5). For a provocative and accessible historical account of western liberal ideas, see Arblaster, 1984.

4. The pursuit of reformist strategies can be far more subversive of the *status quo* than is generally thought. Take, for example, the pursuit of a no-fault medical compensation scheme which may be seen as both attractive *and* (to a limited extent) politically realisable. Although attempts in the early 1990s to pass a Bill implementing such a scheme failed, the public debate it engendered suggests that support for such a scheme is widespread. It offends the common sense of many that a baby suffering severe brain damage at birth through the negligence of hospital employees should, eventually, recover a substantial sum in compensation, while a baby suffering identical trauma as a result of medical treatment where fault *cannot* be established, is entitled only to such benefits as the state may provide. The result seems even more bizarre when one considers that the sum paid in compensation together with legal costs must be met from a limited health budget which may, in turn, require (for budgetary purposes) the closing of a ward treating hundreds of such babies a year.

   The appeal of a scheme which avoids such an arbitrary and irrational distribution of resources is self-evident to many. Yet, at the same time, the radical is rightly wary of such a proposal. Why should the victims of medical accidents be singled out for special treatment? How should the problem of the accountability of negligent doctors be addressed, if not through the mechanism of compensation? Might not advocacy of such a scheme deflect crucial political energy away from more far-reaching solutions such as a New Zealand-type accident compensation scheme or a universal disability scheme?

   Considered in the light of other 'pockets' of 'no-fault' compensation – the industrial injuries scheme, the vaccine damage scheme, the *ex gratia* payments made to those infected with the AIDS virus by contaminated NHS blood supplies – the introduction of a no-fault medical accident scheme becomes attractive to the radical in part because, by its very randomness, it makes the fault principle even harder to sustain and defend. For this reason, a medical compensation scheme may be worth striving for, not so much as an end in itself (although its immediate benefits should not be underestimated), but as a step towards further undermining our compensation system as a whole. In other words, in a political climate where radical change is patently out of the question, more limited reforms may usefully be pursued where their object and effect is to subvert rather than to legitimate the system. So viewed, law reform is not the exclusive province of the 'liberal' but may also be part of a broad, radical and evolutionary strategy. The very inadequacy of the reform in question to solve the problem it seeks to redress becomes a reason to push further, once the reform is in place. For an update on the current fate of no-fault proposals including in the medical context, see Chapter 5.

5. The arguments below are further developed in Conaghan and Mansell, 1998.

6. In fact, Atiyah's arguments in this context are highly questionable. As Ken Oliphant has pointed out (Oliphant, 1996), despite the frequency of reports that the New Zealand scheme has been virtually dismantled (see, for example, Markesinis and Deakin, 1994, p. 5), and the acknowledged re-emergence of tort-based compensation in some contexts, the political will to eschew the scheme altogether is lacking because, despite its alleged flaws, it is still cheaper and more efficient to operate than the system it replaced. Moreover, the social justice arguments for a scheme of this sort remain compelling. Its obvious advantages include the equality of treatment of similarly harmed victims, a considerable increase in the benefits received by the victim of a non-tortious accident, the protection given to a victim who has contributed to the cause of her own injury, and the ability to pay at once a large percentage of lost wages, not as a lump sum but as periodic payments the need for which, and the amount of which, can be regularly reviewed. However, the scheme is no panacea for all those suffering misfortunes in life, confining itself, somewhat problematically, to *accident* compensation (note 1 above). As it is by no means clear why we should wish to redistribute the loss of earnings through accidents at work to other earners and employers, or the losses caused to motor accident victims to other motor vehicle operators, and yet not distribute the loss caused to those who suffer from congenital disabilities or disease to all those who are similarly at risk (that is, everyone), the presence of an accident compensation scheme based, as it generally is, on the principle of social or community responsibility, raises serious questions about society's responsibility for those misfortunes not immediately attributable to 'accident' or the intervention of a human actor. This has led some commentators to conclude that a more radical solution would be to implement some form of *universal* disability scheme which covers and protects in the event of any disabling occurrence (Ison, 1980; Abel, 1982), although not all radical tort scholars are convinced by such

arguments (see, for example, the arguments of Hutchinson, 1988, discussed below).

7.   See, for example, the following observations made by Atiyah in 1970:

> It is difficult to resist the conclusion that the right path for reform is to abolish the tort system so far as personal injuries and disabilities are concerned, and to use the money at present being poured into the tort system to improve the social security benefits and the social services generally. (Atiyah, 1970, p. 611)

References

Abel, R. (1982) 'Torts', in Kairys, D. *The Politics of Law: A Progressive Critique* (New York: Pantheon)

Allen, D. K. (1979) 'Introduction', in Allen, D. K., Bourn, C. J. and Holyoak, J. H. (eds) *Accident Compensation After Pearson*, p. 3 (London: Sweet and Maxwell)

American Insurance Association (AIA) (1968) 'Report of Special Committee to Study and Evaluate the Keeton-O'Connell Basic Protection Plan and Automobile Accident Reparations'

Ames, J. (1874) *A Selection of Cases on the Law of Torts* (out of print)

Anthony, L. and Witt, C. (1993) *A Mind of One's Own: Feminist Essays in Reason and Objectivity* (Boulder: Westview Press)

Arblaster, A. (1984) *The Rise and Decline of Western Liberalism* (Oxford: Basil Blackwell)

Atiyah, P. S. (1970) *Accidents, Compensation and the Law* (London: Weidenfeld and Nicolson)

Atiyah, P. S. (1979a) *The Rise and Fall of Freedom of Contract* (Oxford: Clarendon)

Atiyah, P. S. (1979b) 'What Now?', in Allen, D. K., Bourn, C. J. and Holyoak, J. H. (eds) *Accident Compensation After Pearson*, pp. 227–55 (London: Sweet and Maxwell)

Atiyah, P. S. (1980) *Accidents, Compensation and the Law*, 3rd edn (London: Weidenfeld and Nicolson)

Atiyah, P. S. (1997) *The Damages Lottery* (Oxford: Hart Publishing)

Auerbach, J., Blum, L., Smith, V. and Williams, C. (1985) 'Commentary on Gilligan's *In a Different Voice*', *Feminist Studies*: 11

Bagshaw, R. (forthcoming) 'The Duties of Care of Emergency Care Providers', *Lloyd's Maritime and Commercial Law Quarterly* (forthcoming)

Barrett, M. (1991) *The Politics of Truth* (Cambridge: Polity Press)

Baxter, W. and Altree, L. (1972) 'Legal Aspects of Airport Noise', *Journal of Law and Economics* 15: 1

Bender, L. (1988) 'A Lawyer's Primer on Feminist Theory and Tort', *Journal of Legal Education* 38: 29

Bender, L. (1990a) 'Changing the Values of Tort Law', *Tulsa Law Journal* 25: 759

Bender, L. (1990b) 'Feminist (Re)Torts: Thoughts on the Liability Crisis, Mass Torts, Power and Responsibilities', *Duke Law Journal* 848

Bennion, F. (1998) 'Which Sort of Human Rights Act?' *New Law Journal* 148: 488

Beveridge, W. (1942) 'Social Insurance and Allied Services, Report by Sir William Beveridge', Cmd. 6404 (London: HMSO)

Blackstone, W. (1765–69) *Commentaries on the Laws of England* (Oxford: Clarendon Press)

Bohlen, F. (1911) 'The Rule in *Rylands* v. *Fletcher*', *University of Pennsylvania Law Review* 59: 298

Bottomley, A. (ed.) (1996) *Feminist Perspectives on the Foundational Subjects of Law* (London: Cavendish)

Bottomley, A. and Conaghan, J. (eds) (1993) *Feminist Theory and Legal Strategy* (Oxford: Basil Blackwell)

Brazier, M. (1992) *Medicine, Patients and the Law*, 2nd edn (Harmondsworth: Penguin)

Brazier, M. (1993) *Street on Torts*, 9th edn (London: Butterworths)

Brenner, J. F. (1974) 'Nuisance Law and the Industrial Revolution', *Journal of Legal Studies* 3: 403

Bridgeman, J. and Jones, M. (1994) 'Harassing Conduct and Outrageous Acts: a Cause of Action for Intentionally Inflicted Emotional Distress', *Legal Studies* 14: 180

Bridgeman, J. and Millns, S. (1998) *Feminist Perspectives on Law: Law's Engagement with the Female Body* (London: Sweet & Maxwell)

Brodie, D. (1998) 'Public Authorities – Negligence Actions – Control Devices', *Legal Studies* 18: 1

Buckley, R. A. (1981) *The Law of Nuisance* (London: Butterworths)

Cahn, N. (1992) 'The Looseness of Legal Language: The Reasonable Woman Standard in Theory and Practice', *Cornell Law Review* 77: 1398

Calabresi, G. (1961) 'Some Thoughts on Risk Distribution and the Law of Torts', *Yale Law Journal* 70: 499

Calabresi, G. (1970) *The Cost of Accidents* (New Haven: Yale University Press)

Calabresi, G. and Hirschoff, J. (1972) 'Towards a Test for Strict Liability in Torts', *Yale Law Journal* 81: 1055

Calabresi, G. and Melamed, D. (1972) 'Property Rules, Liability Rules, and Inalienability: One View of the Cathedral', *Harvard Law Review* 85: 1089

Calcutt, Sir D. (1990) 'Report of the Committee on Privacy and Related Matters', Cm. 1102 (London: HMSO)

Calcutt, Sir D. (1993) 'Review of Press Self-Regulation', Cm. 2135 (London: HMSO)

Cane, P. (1982) 'Justice and Justifications for Tort Liability', *Oxford Journal of Legal Studies* 2: 30

Cane, P. (1987) *Atiyah's Accidents, Compensation and the Law*, 4th edn (London: Weidenfeld and Nicolson)

Cane, P. (1993) *Atiyah's Accidents, Compensation and the Law*, 5th edn (London: Butterworths)

Cane, P. (1995) *Tort Law and Economic Interests*, 2nd edn (Oxford: Clarendon Press)

Cane, P. (1996) 'Suing Public Authorities in Tort', *Law Quarterly Review* 112: 113

Cane, P. (1997) *The Anatomy of Tort Law* (Oxford: Hart Publishing)

Civil Justice Review (1988) 'Report of the Review Body on Civil Justice', Cm. 394 (London: HMSO)

Coase, R. (1960) 'The Problem of Social Cost', *Journal of Law and Economics* 3: 1

Collins, H. (1993) *The Law of Contract*, 2nd edn (London: Butterworths)

Conaghan, J. (1993) 'Harassment and the Law of Torts: *Khorasandjian* v. *Bush*', Feminist Legal Studies 1: 189

Conaghan, J. (1996) 'Tort Law and the Feminist Critique of Reason', in Bottomley, A. (ed.) *Feminist Perspectives on the Foundational Subjects of Law*, p. 47 (London: Cavendish)

Conaghan, J. (1997) 'Gendered Harms and the Law of Tort: Remedying (Sexual) Harassment', *Oxford Journal Legal Studies* 16: 407

Conaghan, J. (1998) 'Tort Litigation in the Context of Intra-Familial Abuse', *Modern Law Review* 61: 132

Conaghan, J. and Mansell, W. (1998) 'From the Permissive to the Dismissive Society: Patrick Atiyah's Accidents, Compensation and the Market', *Journal of Law and Society* 25: 284

Cornish, W. R. and Clark, G. (1989) *Law and Society in England: 1750–1950* (London: Sweet and Maxwell)

Cotterrell, R. (1989) *The Politics of Jurisprudence* (London: Butterworths)

Council of Europe (1993) 'Civil Liability for Damage Resulting from Activities Dangerous to the Environment' (the 'Lugano' Convention)

Denning, Lord (1972) 'Freedom of Assocation and the Right to Work', in Vallat, F. (ed.) *An Introduction to the Study of Human Rights* (Europa Publications)

Department of Employment (1986) 'Building Businesses not Barriers', Cmnd. 9794 (London: HMSO)

Department of Environment (1990) 'This Common Inheritance', Cm. 1200 (London: HMSO)

Department of Environment (1994) 'Sustainable Development: the UK Strategy', Cm. 2426 (London: HMSO)

Devall, B. and Sessions, G. (1985) *Deep Ecology* (Salt Lake City: Peregrine Smith Books)

Dias, R. W. M. and Markesinis, B. S. (1989) *Tort Law*, 2nd edn (Oxford: Clarendon Press)

Dicey, A. V. (1914) *Law and Opinion in England* (London: Macmillan)

Dobbs, D., Keeton, R. and Owen, D. (1984) *Prosser and Keeton on Torts* (St Paul, Minnesota: West Publishing)

EC (1993) 'Green Paper on Remedying Environmental Damage' (COM (93)47 final)

EC (1996) 'Progress Report on the Fifth European Community Environmental Action Programme'

Elliot, D. W. and Street, H. (1968) *Road Accidents* (Harmondsworth: Penguin)

Epstein, R. (1973) 'A Theory of Strict Liability', *Journal of Legal Studies* 2: 151

Epstein, R. et al. (1984) *Cases and Materials on Torts*, 4th edn (Boston: Little, Brown)

Fifoot, C. H. S. (1949) *History and Sources of the Common Law, Tort and Contract* (London: Stevens)

Fineman, M. and Thomadsen, N. (1991) *At the Boundaries of Law* (London: Routledge)

Finley, L. (1989) 'A Break in the Silence: Including Women's Issues in a Torts Course', *Yale Journal of Law and Feminism* 1: 41

Fleming, J. G. (1987) *The Law of Torts*, 7th edn (Sydney: The Law Book Company)

Fletcher, G. (1972) 'Fairness and Utility in Tort Theory', *Harvard Law Review* 85: 537

Forell, C. (1992) 'Reasonable Woman Standard of Care', *University of Tasmania Law Review* 11: 1

Fox, A. (1974) *Beyond Contract – Work, Power and Industrial Relations* (London: Faber & Faber)

Friedmann, L. (1972) *A History of American Law* (New York: Simon and Schuster)

Gamble, A. (1988) *The Free Economy and the Strong State* (London: Macmillan)

Gearty, C. (1989) 'The Place of Private Nuisance in a Modern Law of Torts', *Cambridge Law Journal* 48: 214

Gibson, J. (1991) *Living Marxism* (October)

Giles, M. and Szyszczak, E. (1991) 'Negligence and Defective Buildings: Demolishing the Foundations of *Anns*', *Legal Studies* 11: 85

Gilligan, C. (1982) *In a Different Voice* (Cambridge: Harvard University Press)

Gilmore, G. (1977) 'From Tort to Contract: Industrialisation and the Law', *Yale Law Journal* 86: 788

Givelber, D. (1998) 'Cigarette Law', *Indiana Law Journal* 73: 867

Goldberg, R. (1996) 'Vaccine Damage and Causation: Social and Legal Implications', *Journal of Social Security Law* 3: 100.

Gordon, R. (1975) 'J. Willard Hurst and the Common Law Tradition in American Legal Historiography' *Law and Society* 10: 9

Gorz, A. (1989) *Critique of Economic Reason* (London: Verso)

Graycar, R. (1985) 'Compensation for Loss of Capacity to Work in the Home', *Sydney Law Review* 10: 528

Graycar, R. and Morgan, J. (1990) *The Hidden Gender of Law* (Annedale, NSW: The Federation Press)

Green, L. (1958) *Traffic Victims: Tort Law and Insurance* (Chicago: Northwestern University Press)

Gregory, C. (1951) 'Trespass to Negligence to Absolute Liability', *Virginia Law Review* 37: 359

Griffiths, J. A. G. (1997) *The Politics of the Judiciary* 5th edn (London: Fontana)

Grigg-Spall, I. and Ireland, P. (1992) *The Critical Lawyers' Handbook* (London: Pluto Press)

Habermas, J. (1976) *Legitimation Crisis* (London: Heinemann)

Harlow, C. and Rawlings, R. (1984) *Law and Administration* (London: Weidenfeld and Nicolson)

Harris, D. et al. (1984) *Compensation and Support for Illness and Injury* (Oxford: Clarendon Press)

Hayek, F. A. (1982) *Law, Legislation and Liberty*, 3 Vols (London: Routledge and Kegan Paul)

Hepple, B. and Matthews, M. (1991) *Tort: Cases and Materials*, 4th edn (Butterworths)

Heuston, R. F. (1977) *Salmond on the Law of Torts*, 17th edn (London: Sweet & Maxwell)

Heuston, R. F. and Buckley, R. A. (1992) *Salmond and Heuston on Torts*, 20th edn (London: Sweet & Maxwell)

Heuston, R. F. and Buckley, R. A. (1996) *Salmond and Heuston on Torts*, 21st edn (London: Sweet & Maxwell)

Hilliard, F. (1859) *The Law of Torts*, 2 Vols (out of print)

Hilson, C. (1996) 'Cambridge Water Revisited', *Water Law* (May–June) 126

Hindess, B. (1987) *Freedom, Equality and the Market* (London: Tavistock Publications)

Holmes, O. W. (1871) 'Book review', *American Law Review* 5: 340

Holmes, O. W. (1873) 'The Theory of Torts', *American Law Review* 7: 652

Holmes, O. W. (1881) *The Common Law* (Boston: Little, Brown)

Horwitz, M. (1977) *The Transformation of American Law, 1780–1860* (Cambridge, Mass.: Harvard University Press)

Howarth, D. (1995) *Textbook on Tort* (London: Butterworths)

Howarth, W. (1988) *Water Pollution Law* (London: Shaw & Sons)

Howarth, W. (1992) *Wisdom's Law of Watercourses*, 5th edn (London: Shaw & Sons)

Hutchinson, A. C. (1988) *Dwelling on the Threshold: Critical Essays on Modern Legal Thought* (London: Sweet & Maxwell)

IRLIB (1988) *Industrial Relations Legal Information Bulletin* 352: 11

Ison, T. G. (1967) *The Forensic Lottery* (London: Staples Press)

Ison, T. G. (1980) *Accident Compensation: A Commentary on the New Zealand Scheme* (London: Croom Helm)

Jackson, E. (1993) 'Contradictions and Coherence in Feminist Responses to Law', *Journal of Law and Society* 20: 398

Jones, M. (1996) *Textbook on Torts*, 5th edn (London: Blackstone Press)

Kamenka, E. and Tay, A. (1975) 'Beyond Bourgeois Individualism: The Contemporary Crisis in Law and Legal Ideology', in Kamenka, E. and Neale, R. (eds) *Feudalism, Capitalism and Beyond*, p. 127 (Edward Arnold)

Keeton, R. and O'Connell, J. (1965) *Basic Protection of the Traffic Victim: A Blueprint for Reforming Automobile Insurance* (Boston: Little, Brown)

Kerber, L. et al. (1986) 'On "In a Difference Voice": An Interdisciplinary Forum', *Signs: Journal of Women in Culture and Society* 11: 304

Lahey, K. (1991) 'Reasonable Women and the Law', in Fineman, M. and Thomadsen, N. (eds) *At the Boundaries of Law*, pp. 3–21 (London: Routledge)

Landon, P. A. (1941) *Law Quarterly Review* 57: 183

Law Commission No 224 (1994) 'Structured Settlements and Interim and Provisional Damages' (London: HMSO)

Law Commission No 225 (1994) 'Personal Injury Compensation: How Much is Enough?' (London: HMSO)

Law Commission No 140 (1996) 'Damages for Personal Injury: Non-Pecuniary Loss' (London: HMSO)

Law Commission No 147 (1997) 'Damages for Personal Injury: Collateral Benefits' (London: HMSO)

Law Commission No 148 (1997) 'Claims for Wrongful Death' (London: HMSO)

Law Commission No 247 (1997) 'Aggravated, Exemplary and Restitutionary Damages' (London: HMSO)

Law Commission CP No 151 (1998) 'Making the Law on Civil Limitation Periods Simpler and Fairer' (London: HMSO)

Law Commission No 248 (1998) 'Liability for Psychiatric Illness' (London: HMSO)

Law Quarterly Review (1951) 67: 460

Le Grand, J. (1985) *Economics of Social Problems* (London: Macmillan)

Lester, T. (1993) 'The Reasonable Woman Test in Sexual Harassment – Will it Really Make a Difference?', *Indiana Law Review* 26: 227

Lewis, R. (1981) 'No-fault Compensation for Victims of Road Accidents: Can it be Justified?', *Journal of Social Policy* 161

Lewis, R. (1993) *Structured Settlements: The Law and Practice* (London: Sweet & Maxwell)

Lewis, R. (1994) 'Structured Settlements: An Emergent Study', *Civil Justice Quarterly* 13: 18

Lewis, R. (1997) 'Lobbying and the Damages Act 1996: Whispering in Appropriate Ears', *Modern Law Review* 60: 230

Lewis, R. (1998) 'Deducting Collateral Benefits from Damages: Principle and Policy', *Legal Studies* 18: 15

Liebman, L. (1976) 'The Definition of Disability in Social Security and Supplemental Security Income: Drawing the Bounds of Social Welfare Estates', *Harvard Law Review* 89: 833

Lloyd, G. (1984) *The Man of Reason: Male and Female in Western Philosophy* (London: Methuen)

Lord Chancellor's Department (1997) 'Consultation Paper on Proposed New Procedures for Clinical Negligence'

Lord Chancellor's Department (1998) 'Consultation Paper on Access to Justice with Conditional Fees'

McBride, N. J. and Hughes, A. (1995) '*Hedley-Byrne* in the House of Lords: an Interpretation', *Legal Studies* 15: 376

McGillivray, D. and Wightman, J. (1997) 'Private Rights and Environmental Protection', in Ireland, P. and Laleng, P. (eds) *The Critical Lawyers' Handbook 2*, p. 176 (London: Pluto Press)

McGlynn, C. (forthcoming) 'Judging Women Differently: Gender, the Judiciary and Reform', in Millns, S. and Whitly, N. (eds) *Feminist Perspectives on Public Law* (London: Cavendish)

MacKinnon, C. (1979) *Sexual Harassment of Working Women* (New Haven and London: Yale University Press)

MacKinnon, C. (1989) *Towards a Feminist Theory of State* (Cambridge, Mass.: Harvard University Press)

McLaren, J. (1983) 'Nuisance Law and the Industrial Revolution -Some Lessons from Social History', *Oxford Journal of Legal Studies* 3: 155

McLean, S. (1988) 'No-fault Liability and Medical Responsibility', in Freeman, M. D. A. (ed.) *Medicine, Ethics and the Law*, pp. 147–61 (London: Stevens & Sons)

Magruder, C. (1936) 'Mental and Emotional Distress in the Law of Torts', *Harvard Law Review* 49: 1033

Malone, W. (1946) 'The Formative Era of Contributory Negligence', *Illinois Law Review*, 41: 151

Manchester, A. H. (1980) *Modern Legal History* (London: Butterworths)

Mansell, W. (1997) 'Tort and Socio-Legal Studies – The Road to Damascus: Paved with Good Intentions but Few Epiphanies', in Thomas, P. A. (ed.) *Socio-Legal Studies* (Aldershot: Dartmouth)

Markesinis, B. S. and Deakin, S. (1994) *Tort Law*, 3rd edn (Oxford: Clarendon Press)

Marshall, T. H. (1950) *Citizenship and Social Class* (Cambridge: Cambridge University Press)

Martin, J. (1993) *Hanbury & Martin: Modern Equity* (London: Sweet & Maxwell)

Martin, R. (1990) 'The Duty of Care of Professional Advisors: Further Applications of *Caparo*', *Professional Negligence* 6: 176

Martyn, R. (1994) 'A Feminist View of the Reasonable Man: An Alternative Approach to Liability in Negligence for Personal Injury', *Anglo-American Law Review* 25: 334

Mill, J. S. (1974) *On Liberty* (Harmondsworth: Penguin)

Millner, M. A. (1965) 'The Retreat of Trespass', *Current Legal Problems* 18: 20

Millner, M. A. (1967) *Negligence in Modern Law* (London: Butterworths)

Molloy, J. (1942) '*Fletcher* v. *Rylands*; A Re-examination of Juristic Origins', *University of Chicago Law Review* 9: 266

Mullis, A. (1997) 'Compounding the Abuse: The House of Lords, Childhood Sexual Abuse and Limitation Periods', *Medical Law Review* 22

Mullis, A. and Nolan, D. (1997) 'Tort', *All ER Annual Review* 490

Nelken, D. (1982) 'Is There a Crisis in Law and Legal Ideology?', *Journal of Law and Society* 9: 177

Newark, F. H. (1949) 'The Boundaries of Nuisance', *Law Quarterly Review* 64: 480

Nicolson, D. and Sanghvi, R. (1993) 'Battered Women and Provocation: the Implications of *R.* v. *Ahluwalia*', *Criminal Law Review* 145: 728

Nicolson, D. and Sanghvi, R. (1995) 'More Justice for Battered Women', *New Law Journal* 1122

Nolan. V. and Ursin, E. (1987) 'The Revitalization of Hazardous Strict Liability', *North Carolina Law Review* 65: 257

Nolan, V. and Ursin, E. (1995) *Understanding Enterprise Liability: Rethinking Tort Reform for the Twenty-first Century* (Philadelphia: Temple University Press)

Ogus, A. (1994) 'Civil Liability for Environmental Damage: *Cambridge Water Case* v. *Eastern Counties Leather Co Plc*', *Journal of Environmental Law* 6: 137

Ogus, A. and Richardson, G. (1977) 'Economics and the Environment: A Study of Private Nuisance', *Cambridge Law Journal* 36: 284

Oliphant, K. (1996) 'Distant Tremors; What's Happening to Accident Compensation in New Zealand?' (unpublished paper presented at Torts section of SPTL (Society of Public Teachers of Law) Annual Conference, Cardiff, 1995 and Staff–Graduate Seminar Programme, University of Kent, February 1996)

Oliver, M. (1990) *The Politics of Disablement* (London: Macmillan)

Olsen, F. (ed.) (1995) *Feminist Legal Theory 1: Foundations and Outlooks*; *Feminist Legal Theory II: Positioning Feminist Theory Within the Law* (Aldershot: Dartmouth)

Owens, A. (1988) *Medical Economics* 18 April: 88–100

Palmer, G. W. (1979) *Accident Compensation: A Study of Law and Social Change in New Zealand and Australia* (Wellington, New Zealand: Oxford University Press)

Palmer, G. W. (1994) 'New Zealand's Accident Compensation Scheme: Twenty Years On', *University of Toronto Law Journal* 44: 223

Pearce, D., Markandya, A. and Barbier, E. B. (1989) *Blueprint for a Green Economy* (London: Earthscan Publications)

Pearson, H. (1978) 'The Report of the Royal Commission on Civil Liability and Compensation for Personal Injury', Cmnd. 7054, 3 Vols (London: HMSO)

Polinski, A. M. (1989) *An Introduction to Law and Economics*, 2nd edn (Boston: Little, Brown)

Pollock, F. (1887) *The Law of Torts* (London: Stevens)

Pollock, F. (1939) *Pollock on Torts*, 14th edn (London: Stevens)

Posner, R. A. (1972) 'A Theory of Negligence', *Journal of Legal Studies* 1: 29

Posner, R. A. (1973) 'Strict Liability: A Comment', *Journal of Legal Studies* 2: 206

Posner, R. A. (1977) *Economic Analysis of Law*, 2nd edn (Boston and Toronto: Little, Brown)

Pritchard, M. J. (1964) 'Trespass, Case and the Rule in *Williams* v. *Holland*', *Cambridge Law Journal* 234

Prosser, W., Wade, J. and Schwarz, V. (1988) *Cases and Materials on Torts*, 8th edn (New York: Foundation Press)

Rabin, R. (1969) 'Some Thoughts on Tort Law from a Sociopolitical Perspective', *Wisconsin Law Review* 51

Rabin, R. (1977) 'Nuisance Law: Rethinking Fundamental Assumptions', *Virginia Law Review* 63: 1299

Reid, Lord (1972) 'The Judge as Law-Maker', *Journal of the Society of Public Teachers of Law* 12: 22

Rogers, W. (1979) *Winfield & Jolowicz on Tort*, 11th edn (London: Sweet & Maxwell)

Rogers, W. (1989) *Winfield & Jolowicz on Tort*, 13th edn (London: Sweet & Maxwell)

Rogers, W. (1994) *Winfield & Jolowicz on Tort*, 14th edn (London: Sweet & Maxwell)

Rose, F. (1977) 'Liability for an Employee's Assaults', *Modern Law Review* 40: 420

Sagoff, M. (1988) *The Economy of the Earth* (Cambridge: Cambridge University Press)

Salmond, J. (1924) *Law of Torts*, 6th edn (London: Sweet & Maxwell)

Saville, J. (1975) 'The Welfare State: An Historical Approach', in Butterworth, E. and Holman, R. (eds) *Social Welfare in Modern Britain* (London: Fontana)

Schwartz, G. (1981) 'Tort Law and the Economy in Nineteenth-Century America: A Reinterpretation', *Yale Law Journal* 90: 1717

Selznick, P. (1969) *Law, Society and Industrial Justice* (New York: Russell Sage Foundation)

Sheldon, S. (1998) '"A Responsible Body of Medical Men Skilled in that Particular Art...": Rethinking the *Bolam* Test', in Sheldon, S. and Thomson, M. (eds) *Feminist Perspectives on Health Care Law* (London: Cavendish)

Simpson, A. W. B. (1975) 'Innovation in Nineteenth Century Contract Law', *Law Quarterly Review* 91: 247

Simpson, A. W. B. (1979) 'The Horwitz Thesis and the History of Contracts', *University of Chicago Law Review* 46: 533

Smart. C. (1989) *Feminism and the Power of Law* (London: Routledge)

Smith, A. (1910) *The Wealth of Nations* (London: J. M. Dent & Sons)

Smith, J. (1914) 'Sequel to Workmen's Compensation Acts', *Harvard Law Review* 27: 235, 344

Smith, J. C. and Burns, P. (1983) '*Donoghue* v. *Stevenson*: the Not So Golden Anniversary', *Modern Law Review* 46: 147

Smith, R. (1995) 'The Changing Nature of Legal Aid', in Smith R. (ed.) *Shaping the Future: New Directions in Legal Services*, p. 16 (London: Legal Action Group)

Smith, R. (1996) 'The Domestic Context', in Smith, R. (ed.) *Achieving Civil Justice: Appropriate Dispute Resolution for the 1990s*, p. 7 (London: Legal Action Group)

Sprince, A. (1998) 'Negligently Inflicted Psychiatric Damage: A Medical Diagnosis and Prognosis', *Legal Studies* 18: 59

Stanley, L and Wise, S. (1983) *Breaking Out: Feminist Consciousness and Feminist Research* (London: Routledge and Kegan Paul)

Stanton, K. (1994) *The Modern Law of Tort* (London: Sweet & Maxwell)

Stapleton, J. (1986) *Disease and the Compensation Debate* (Oxford: Clarendon Press)

Stapleton, J. (1994) *Product Liability* (London: Butterworths)

Steele, J. (1995) 'Private Law and the Environment: Nuisance Law in Context', *Legal Studies* 15: 236

Stychin, C. (1996) 'Dangerous Liaisons: New Developments in the Law of Defective Premises', *Legal Studies* 16: 387

Sugarman, D. (1986) 'Legal Theory, the Common Law Mind and the Making of the Textbook Tradition', in Twining, W. (ed.) *Legal Theory and the Common Law*, pp. 26–61 (Oxford: Basil Blackwell)

Sugarman, D. (1991) '"A Hatred of Disorder": Legal Science, Liberalism and Imperialism', in Fitzpatrick, P. (ed.) *Dangerous Supplements*, p. 34 (London: Pluto Press)

Taylor, A. J. (1972) *Laissez-faire and State Intervention in Nineteenth-century Britain* (London: Macmillan)

Temkin, J. (1987) *Rape and the Legal Process* (London: Sweet & Maxwell)

Thomson, A. (1987) 'Critical Legal Education in Britain', *Journal of Law and Society* 14: 183

Thomson, A. (1991) 'Taking the Right Seriously: the Case of F. A. Hayek', in Fitzpatrick, P. (ed.) *Dangerous Supplements*, p. 68 (London: Pluto Press)

Thompson, E. P. (1975) *Whigs and Hunters* (Harmondsworth: Penguin)

Thornton, P. (1989) *Decade of Decline: Civil Liberties in the Thatcher Years* (London: National Council for Civil Liberties)

Trindade, F. A. (1980) 'A No-Fault Scheme for Road Accident Victims in the United Kingdom', *Law Quarterly Review* 96: 581

Trindade, F. A. (1982) 'Intentional Torts: Some Thoughts on Assault and Battery', *Oxford Journal of Legal Studies* 2: 211

Trindade, F. A. (1986) 'The Intentional Infliction of Purely Emotional Distress', *Oxford Journal of Legal Studies* 6: 219

Unger, R. M. (1976) *Law in Modern Society* (New York: The Free Press)

Ursin, E. (1981) 'Judicial Creativity and Tort Law', *George Washington Law Review* 49: 229

Veljanovski, C. (1986) 'Legal Theory, Economic Analysis and the Law of Torts', in Twining, W. (ed.) *Legal Theory and the Common Law*, pp. 215–37 (Oxford: Basil Blackwell)

Vennell, M. (1989) 'Medical Misfortune in a No-Fault Society', in Mann, R. D. and Havard, J., *No Fault Compensation in Medicine*, p. 33 (London: Royal Society of Medicine Services)

Watson, G. (1996) 'From an Adversarial to a Managed System of Litigation: a Comparative Critique of Lord Woolf's Interim Report', in Smith, R. (ed.) *Achieving Civil Justice: Appropriate Dispute Resolution for the 1990s*, p. 63 (London: Legal Action Group)

Weinrib, E. (1995) *The Idea of Private Law* (Cambridge, Mass.: Harvard University Press)

Weir, T. (1979) *A Casebook on Tort*, 4th edn (London: Sweet & Maxwell)

Weir, T. (1988) *A Casebook on Tort*, 6th edn (London: Sweet & Maxwell)

Weir, T. (1992) *A Casebook on Tort*, 7th edn (London: Sweet & Maxwell)

Weir, T. (1996) *A Casebook on Tort*, 8th edn (London: Sweet & Maxwell)

White, G. E. (1985) *Tort Law in America – An Intellectual History* (Oxford University Press)

White, G. E. (1988) *The American Judicial Tradition* (Oxford University Press)

Wightman, J. (1996) *Contract: A Critical Commentary* (London: Pluto Press)

Wightman, J. (1998) 'Nuisance – the Environmental Tort? *Hunter* v. *Canary Wharf* in the House of Lords', *Modern Law Review* 61 (forthcoming)

Wilkinson, D. (1994) '*Cambridge Water Co* v. *Eastern Counties Leather plc*: Diluting Liability for Continuing Escapes', *Modern Law Review* 57: 799

Wilkinson, D. (1997) 'An Idiomatic Discussion of Environmental Legislation', in Ireland, P. and Laleng, P. (eds) *The Critical Lawyers' Handbook 2*, p. 161 (London: Pluto Press)

Williams, G. (1951) 'The Aims of the Law of Tort', *Current Legal Problems* 137

Williams, G. and Hepple, B. (1984) *Foundations of the Law of Tort*, 2nd edn (London: Butterworths)

Winfield, P. (1926a) 'The Myth of Absolute Liability', *Law Quarterly Review* 41: 37

Winfield, P. (1926b) 'The History of Negligence in the Law of Torts', *Law Quarterly Review* 42: 184

Winfield. P. (1927) 'The Foundation of Liability in Tort', *Columbia Law Review* 27: 1

Winfield, P. (1931a) *Province of the Law of Tort* (Cambridge: Cambridge University Press)

Winfield, P. (1931b) 'Nuisance as a Tort', *Cambridge Law Journal* 4: 189

Winfield, P. (1934) 'Duty in Tortious Negligence', *Columbia Law Review* 34: 41

Winfield, P. and Goodhart, A. (1933) 'Trespass and Negligence', *Law Quarterly Review* 49: 359

Woodhouse, Sir A. O. (1967) 'Report of the Royal Commission of Inquiry into Compensation for Personal Injury in New Zealand' (New Zealand: Government Printer)

Woolf, Lord (1996) 'Access to Justice: Report to the Lord Chancellor'

World Commission on Environment and Development (1987) *Our Common Future* ('The Brundtland Report') (Oxford: Oxford University Press)

Wright, J. (1998) 'Local Authorities, the Duty of Care and the European Convention on Human Rights', *Oxford Journal of Legal Studies*

Index